DATE DUE

COOKING IN
ANCIENT CIVILIZATIONS

COOKING IN
ANCIENT
CIVILIZATIONS

Cathy K. Kaufman

The Greenwood Press "Daily Life Through History" Series

Cooking Up History
Ken Albala, Series Editor

Greenwood Press
Westport, Connecticut • London

Library of Congress Cataloging-in-Publication Data

Kaufman, Cathy K.
  Cooking in ancient civilizations / Cathy K. Kaufman.
      p.   cm.—(The Greenwood Press "Daily life through
history" series, ISSN 1080–4749, Cooking up history)
  Includes bibliographical references and index.
  ISBN 0–313–33204–5
  1. Food—History.   2. Cookery—History.   3. Civilization, Ancient.
I. Title.   II. Series.
  TX353.K38   2006
  641.309—dc22   2006015692

British Library Cataloguing in Publication Data is available.

Library of Congress Catalog Card Number: 2006015692
ISBN: 0–313–33204–5
ISSN: 1080–4749

First published in 2006

Greenwood Press, 88 Post Road West, Westport, CT 06881
An imprint of Greenwood Publishing Group, Inc.
www.greenwood.com

Printed in the United States of America

The paper used in this book complies with the
Permanent Paper Standard issued by the National
Information Standards Organization (Z39.48–1984).

10   9   8   7   6   5   4   3   2   1

Copyright Acknowledgments

CONTENTS

LIST OF RECIPES

2. ANCIENT EGYPT

3. ANCIENT GREECE

4. ANCIENT ROME

 GLOSSARY

AGORA: The Greek marketplace.

AMARNA: Capital city of the Egyptian pharaoh Akhenaten (ca. 1351–1334 B.C.E.).

AMPHIDROMIA: A Greek feast held to celebrate the birth of a child.

AMPHORA: Greek term for a long, bulbous clay jug used for storing liquids, particularly wines and oils.

AMULUM: A starch used by the Romans to thicken sauces; it was made by soaking emmer wheat in water to dissolve surface starch and then evaporating the water. Cornstarch functions similarly and can be substituted, although it is anachronistic.

ANAEROBIC PRESERVATION: Preserving foods by cutting off oxygen, thereby inhibiting the growth of aerobic bacteria. In the ancient world, anaerobic preservation was accomplished by submerging foods in fats, oils, or syrups.

ANATOLIA: The ancient name for what is now the Asian part of modern Turkey.

ANDRON: Literally, "men's room." The Greek room for dining and entertaining, with couches lining the walls.

ANNONA: State-run system of distributions of grain or bread, wine, and other foodstuffs to Roman citizens. It began during the late Roman republic and expanded under the empire.

APICIUS: The name of several figures associated with gourmandism and gastronomy in the Roman world; authorship of the Roman cookbook *De Re Coquinaria* (On Cookery) has traditionally been attributed to Apicius, although contemporary scholars believe the work is compiled from many different hands.

ARCHESTRATUS OF GELA: Greek author of the late fourth to early third centuries B.C.E. whose *Life of Luxury* contained descriptive recipes and dining advice for travelers in the Greek world.

ARISTON: A late-morning Greek meal; brunch.

ARISTOPHANES: Late-fifth-century B.C.E. Greek playwright; his works contain passing references to food and drink.

ASAFETIDA *(FERULA ASSAFOETIDA)*: A garlicky-flavored resin from a fennel-like plant; use as a substitute for the extinct silphium.

ASSURNASIRPAL: Ninth-century B.C.E. Assyrian king.

ATHENAEUS: Third-century C.E. Greek author who lived in Roman Egypt; his *Deipnosophists*, written in Greek, is a lengthy discourse on food and drink in the Greco-Roman world that takes the form of a discussion among learned men over dinner and a symposium. It preserved many fragments of Greek culinary references that otherwise would have been lost.

BAPPIR: An underbaked barley bread used in making Mesopotamian beer.

BEDOUIN: A nomadic group whose range extended in antiquity through Mesopotamia, the Levant, and Anatolia.

BRAN: The outer layer of cleaned wheat, made largely of cellulose.

BRAZIER: A pan for holding burning coals or charcoal, over which is placed a stewing or frying pan or a grill.

BREAD WHEAT *(TRITICUM AESTIVUM)*: The last species of antique wheat to emerge, probably in northwestern Iran; it is a naked grain and is thought to have resulted from crosses of wild spelt with wild einkorn. Because of its unique gluten structure, bread wheat is best suited of all the wheats for making light, leavened breads. Approximately 90 percent of modern flour is made from bread wheat.

BRINING: Submerging a foodstuff in a concentrated salt solution.

BULGUR: Flakes of steamed, dried, and coarsely ground wheat.

CAROB (*CERATONIA SILIQUA*): The podded fruit of evergreen trees native to the Near East; also known as locust bean and, possibly, St. John's bread. The pulp is quite sweet.

CAROENUM: A Roman term for wine that has been reduced by half; it was a pantry staple in well-stocked Roman kitchens.

CATARACTS: Any of six waterfalls or rapids creating breaks in the flow of the Nile.

CATO THE ELDER: Late-third- to mid-second-century B.C.E. patrician Roman, author of *De Agricultura* (On Farming).

CENA: The main meal of the Roman day; dinner.

CHAPATI FLOUR: A type of flour used nowadays for making chapatis, a type of Indian flatbread that may be similar to certain ancient flatbreads. Modern chapati flour can be made from either very fine durum flour or a blend of whole wheat and malted barley flours. Either would be appropriate to the ancient world.

CHATE MELON (*CUCUMIS MELO VAR. CHATE*): A fruit similar to cucumbers used in ancient Egypt.

CITRON (*CITRUS MEDICA*): A citrus fruit from Asia that is generally believed to be the only citrus to reach the Near East and Mediterranean in antiquity. It is similar to a lemon but has a much thicker rind and relatively little juicy carpel.

CLEMENT OF ALEXANDRIA: Second-century C.E. Christian theologian whose writing *Christ the Educator* included detailed lessons in diet and etiquette reflecting upper-class Roman habits.

CLIBANUS OR KLIBANUS: The Greek term for a clay dome used to form an oven; *see* **testum.**

COLUMELLA: First-century C.E. agricultural writer from Roman Spain, author of *De Re Rustica* (On Agriculture).

CUNEIFORM: A complex writing system invented by the Sumerians around 3100 B.C.E. in which reeds were impressed into wet clay, leaving wedge-shaped script.

DEBEN: An ancient Egyptian measurement equal to approximately three ounces.

DEFRUTUM: Grape must that has been reduced by boiling to one half or less of its original volume; the ancient authors disagree as to precisely how much to reduce the grape must to achieve *defrutum*, but the final texture should be viscous. *Mosto cotto* (*see* **must**) can be substituted.

DEIPNON: The main meal of the Greek day; dinner before the symposium.

DEIPNOSOPHISTS: *See* **Athenaeus.**

DEIR EL-MEDINA: Egyptian village near Thebes that housed workers building the great tombs in the Valley of the Kings and the Valley of the Queens.

DIPHILUS OF SIPHNIS: Fourth-century B.C.E. Greek physician whose writings contain the first culinary recipe using long pepper.

DRY AGRICULTURE: Agriculture dependent on rainfall, not irrigation.

DURUM *(TRITICUM DURUM)*: A naked wheat that is believed to result from crosses of wild einkorn with wild emmer; in the modern world, it is primarily used in pasta making, although leavened bread can successfully be made from durum. It is an essential substitute for emmer in bread and porridge recipes from the ancient world.

EINKORN *(TRITICUM MONOCOCCUM)*: The earliest form of cultivated wheat; it is hulled, requiring laborious processing, and is thought to be an ancestor of most wheats used in the ancient and modern worlds.

EMMER *(TRITICUM DICOCCUM)*: Probably the second form of wheat to be cultivated; it is hulled and contains forms of gluten that allow it to be made into leavened bread through laborious processing. It was an extremely important grain in the ancient world and is thought to be one of the ancestors of durum wheat. It is very difficult to find commercially nowadays, and durum wheat is a good substitute.

ENDOSPERM: The main portion of cereal kernels, comprised of proteins and starches.

ENLIL: A major Babylonian god of wind and sky.

EXTRACTION RATE: The amount of grain remaining after milling and sifting, expressed as a percentage. The higher the percentage, the more of the grain that remains. Whole wheat flours (including germ and bran in addition to endosperm) have higher extraction rates than refined white flour (pure endosperm).

FAIENCE: In ancient Egypt, the term applied to glazed ceramics often made with silica or quartz; beads, statuary, and drinking vessels were made of faience and often brightly colored.

FARRO: A contemporary Italian name for wheat that is grown in the mountainous Garafagnana area of northern Tuscany. True farro is emmer wheat and takes many hours to cook. Italian spelt is sometimes labeled farro, although it cooks much more quickly.

FATBACK: Fat cut from the back of swine, used to make lard.

FERMENTATION: Chemical changes in foodstuffs attributable to either bacteria, molds, or yeast. Most successful fermentation suppresses harmful microbes, acting as a preservative and in certain cases enhancing nutritional value. Grains and fruits can be fermented into beer and wine, porridges fermented into raised bread, or milk fermented into yogurt.

FREEK: Immature wheat grains that are tender enough to be eaten raw when freshly picked. The freek available commercially in the United States is imported from North Africa and is dried and smoked to preserve the grain in transit; it must be cooked.

GALEN: Second-century C.E. physician from Pergamum in Anatolia; a major follower of Hippocrates, Galen authored several medical treatises, including *On the Properties of Foods,* and was physician to the Roman emperor Commodus.

GARUM (LATIN)/GAROS (GREEK): A liquid made by fermenting small fish or fish entrails in salt and exposing them to the sun for at least several weeks and up to three months. The salt inhibited the growth of harmful bacteria, while beneficial ones broke down the fish into a thin, concentrated brine and a thicker, residual paste. The brine is the *garum* and is similar to the modern Asian fish sauces *nuoc mam* or *nam pla. Garum* often was used in place of salt, much like soy sauce or the Asian fish sauces. By the later Roman empire, the term *garum* was applied by gourmets and knowledgeable cooks to a specialized table sauce made from the fishy brine combined with wine and herbs, while the term *liquamen* identified the pure fish sauce and is the term used virtually exclusively in the Apicius manuscript. Use any good-quality fish sauce in recipes calling for *garum.*

GERM: The reproductive structure of cereal kernels; it is the only portion of grain to contain fat and can cause whole wheat flours to go rancid.

GLUTEN: A complex mixture of wheat proteins, primarily glutenin and gliadin, that allow wheat doughs to stretch without tearing. Each species of wheat has a different ratio of glutenin to gliadin, which affects the texture of doughs made from the wheats. Bread wheat has the optimal balance of these proteins for stretching and baking into leavened bread.

GRANO: The wheat kernel that has been lightly pearled, that is, some or all of the bran has been removed. It is a light golden color, paler than the brown wheat berry, which still contains all of its bran.

GUSTATIO: The appetizers at a Roman *cena*.

HALOUMI: A Greek cheese suitable for grilling or frying.

HAMMURABI: Babylonian ruler ca. 1700 B.C.E.; Hammurabi's Code regulated some aspects of food and drink.

HAPI: The Egyptian god of the Nile.

HERODOTUS: Fifth-century B.C.E. Greek traveler, often considered the first historian.

HESIOD: Eighth-century B.C.E. Greek poet whose *Work and Days* is the first known Greek treatise to include food-related advice.

HIPPOCRATES: Fifth-century B.C.E. Greek physician; the early medical works *On Regimen* and *On Regimen in Acute Diseases* are widely attributed to him. His theories of medicine and diet influenced medicine through the Renaissance.

HOMER: Greek poet ca. ninth century B.C.E. whose *Iliad* and *Odyssey* describe early Greek dining habits.

HULLED GRAIN: Grain kernels encased in a thin, papery coat that must be removed for human consumption. Emmer and spelt are both hulled grains.

HYDROMEL: A fermented honey drink.

KAMUT: A variety of wheat introduced to North American markets in the 1970s and thought to be related to ancient forms of emmer; the kamut grown in North America is claimed to have been carried back by a serviceman from Egypt, although the grains are larger than those of emmer.

KASSERI: A firm Greek cheese suitable for grilling or frying.

KHAR: An Egyptian volume measurement equal to approximately 310 liters.

KNEAD: To push and fold bread dough to develop the gluten, and thus create a better texture, before baking.

LASER: An alternative Roman name for *silphium*.

LEAVENER: A fungal or chemical substance that generates carbon dioxide in doughs and causes them to rise.

LEGUME: A plant with double-seamed seed pods; depending on the variety, the seeds may be eaten fresh, with or without the pods, or dried (pulses). Examples include peas, beans, lentils, and lupines.

LEVANT: The Near Eastern area bounding the Mediterranean Sea including modern-day Syria, Lebanon, Israel, and parts of Turkey.

LIFE OF LUXURY: *See* **Archestratus.**

LIQUAMEN: A fermented fish sauce used as an ingredient in the cooking of the Roman empire; see **garum.**

LIVY: Roman historian ca. 59 B.C.E.–17 C.E.

LONG PEPPER *(PIPER LONGUM):* A form of pepper originating in northern India with long spikelets; it is hotter and was generally more expensive in the ancient world than the round black pepper *(Piper nigrum)* from southwestern India.

LOVAGE *(LEVISTICUM OFFICINALE):* An herb rarely seen in grocery stores in the United States, although popular in England, with a celerylike flavor. It is easy to grow in an herb garden and is available at better-stocked nurseries and by mail order. If unavailable, substitute celery leaves or seed.

MALT: Sprouted grains; sprouting converts some of the complex carbohydrates into simple sugars and releases enzymes, often enhancing the nutritional value of the grain.

MARTIAL: First-century C.E. Roman writer; his *Epigrams* encompassed invitations to middle-class Roman dinner parties that listed the foods on the menu.

MASTIC *(PISTACIA LENTISCUS):* The resin obtained from incising the bark of the lentisk tree, a plant growing only on certain Greek islands and in Asiatic Turkey. It adds a distinctive, smoky-musty flavor and was often included in medicinal preparations. There is no adequate substitute, so omit it if it is unavailable. The resin is chewy and is the origin of the verb masticate.

MATZOH: An unleavened, quick-baking flat bread associated particularly with the holiday Passover commemorating the Jews' exodus from Egypt.

MAZA: A type of Greek barley cake; its exact nature is disputed.

MINOAN: Culture centered on the island of Crete from ca. 3000–1000 B.C.E.

MOHLUHKIA *(CORCHORUS OLITORIUS):* A leafy green used in ancient Egypt and the Levant. It is available canned or frozen from markets specializing in Egyptian foods; otherwise substitute kale, beet greens, sorrel, or spinach.

MONSOON: Seasonally shifting wind patterns accompanied by heavy rains.

MORTAR AND PESTLE: A bowl, usually with a rough, abrasive interior, and a blunt, thick pounding implement for grinding foodstuffs against the bowl's interior.

MULSUM: Wine mixed with honey and other flavorings, used as an aperitif in the Roman world.

MUST: The juice of freshly pressed grapes. Must was frequently cooked in the ancient world, as the natural yeasts in the fresh must would have begun to ferment into wine almost immediately. Cooking killed the yeasts, thereby inhibiting fermentation. Press fresh grapes to obtain the juice or use an unsweetened grape juice, preferably made from grapes other than the extremely sweet American Concord variety. Italians manufacture a cooked must product, *mosto cotto*, available at specialty markets, which can be used, although it is expensive.

MYCENAEAN: Culture centered in the Greek mainland and the Peloponnese ca. 2000–1100 B.C.E.

NAKED GRAIN: Grain lacking a hull and that can thus can be processed without labor-intensive parching or pounding. Durum and bread wheat are examples.

NIGELLA *[NIGELLA SATIVA]:* A small, triangular-shaped black seed originating in the Mediterranean and Near East with an oniony taste; onion seed can be substituted.

NINKASI: Sumerian goddess of brewing.

OENOGARUM: A Roman pantry sauce made from wine and *garum.*

OPSON: The side dishes, especially fish, that enhanced the *sitos* of the Greek meal.

ORIBASIUS: Fourth-century C.E. physician from Pergamum, author of *Medical Compilations*, which contains detailed dietary information and recipes.

OVID: Roman poet (43 B.C.E.–18 C.E.), author of *Metamorphoses.*

OXYGARUM: A Roman pantry sauce made from vinegar and *garum.*

PASSUM: A sweet, raisiny wine for cooking, probably like a modern passito or Spanish muscatel, made from the pressing of late harvest grapes that have started to dry on the vine.

PATINA: A category of Roman dishes often including eggs; also, a cooking vessel that may resemble a modern soufflé dish.

PELOPONNESE: The large Greek peninsula that was home to the Spartans and Corinthians and was linked to the mainland by the Isthmus of Corinth.

PETRONIUS: First-century C.E. Roman writer and taste maker to the emperor Nero; his fictional *Satyricon* contained an extended description of Trimalchio's Feast, one of the most notorious, excessive dinner parties in all of literature.

PHILOXENUS: Fourth-century B.C.E. Greek poet, known for the poem *Banquet*.

PLATO: Greek philosopher of the late fifth and early fourth centuries B.C.E. whose extensive writings touched upon social and ethical aspects of diet, especially in his dialogues *Republic* and *Gorgias*.

PLINY THE ELDER: First-century C.E. Roman writer, author of *Natural History*.

POMEGRANATE MOLASSES: A thick sweet-and-tart syrup made from boiled pomegranate juice.

POPINA: A tavern in ancient Rome where one could get a quick, informal meal.

POTAGER STOVE: A stove, usually made of clay in antiquity, with large openings in the top in which pans were placed, with a fire below; the term *potager* was coined later, but it aptly describes the type of stove.

POTTAGE: A generic category of dishes cooked with liquid, ranging in texture from soups to stews to porridges.

PREDYNASTIC EGYPT: Period in Egyptian history (ca. 4000–3150 B.C.E.) prior to the unification of Upper and Lower Egypt.

PRIMA MENSA: The "first table" of main dishes at a Roman *cena*.

PROPOMATA: Appetizers in a Greek meal.

Psw: A variable unit of measure in Egypt to describe the number of loaves of bread that could be baked from a set measure of grain; the higher the *psw*, the greater number of (smaller) loaves.

PULSE: The dried, edible seed of podded plants (legumes), such as beans, lentils, lupines, and peas.

RENNET: An enzyme used to curdle milk as a step in cheese making; rennet is found in certain plants and in the stomachs of very young calves, kids, and lambs.

RETSINA: Wines flavored with pine resin, originating from the practice of coating the inside of amphorae with pine pitch to make the vessels airtight.

RUE *(RUTA GRAVEOLENS):* An herb generally unavailable as a culinary product in the United States, although available in Europe and North Africa. Like lovage, it can easily be grown in an herb garden and is available from well-stocked nurseries. Rue has a bitter, musty taste; rosemary is a decent substitute.

SAJ: A convex metal dome, similar to an inverted wok, that forms a cooking surface for flat breads.

SALT PORK: Salt-cured fatty pork from the hog's sides or belly.

SAPA: A Roman term for a wine that has been reduced by about two thirds; it was a pantry item in well-stocked Roman kitchens.

SAQIYA: An animal-powered waterwheel originating in Mesopotamia.

SARGON: The Akkadian leader who conquered Sumer ca. 2350 B.C.E. and temporarily united the states of Sumer and Akkad into the Akkadian empire.

SATURNALIA: Roman holiday celebrated in December and lasting several days; slaves and masters exchanged roles and the government and well-to-do private citizens were expected to host feasts and entertainments for their dependents.

SECONDA MENSA: The "second table" at a Roman *cena*, comparable to the *tragemata* of a Greek *deipnon*.

SEMOLINA: A yellowish flour made from the endosperm of durum wheat; it is milled to different degrees of fineness, each with slightly different culinary uses.

SHADUF: A counterweighted device for lifting water to irrigate crops, originating in Mesopotamia.

SILPHIUM: Described by Pliny the Elder in the first century C.E., but thought to be going extinct at that time, silphium was the root of a wild fennel plant that grew in Cyrenia and Armenia. Silphium was very rare and costly in the first century C.E.; some of the earliest recipes that eventually were compiled in the Apicius collection described how to stretch the spice by storing it in a jar with pine nuts and then using the infused pine nuts to flavor dishes, much like the contemporary practice of storing vanilla beans in sugar to flavor the sugar. Asafetida, a garlicky-smelling dried rhizome of another fennel plant, was used as a substitute even in the Roman world.

SIQQU: A briny condiment used in Mesopotamia, made either from fish or locusts; it was probably similar to *garum* or *liquamen*.

SITOS: The staple grains that formed the core of the Greek meal, in porridge, pilaf, or especially bread form.

SMEN: The Mesopotamian term for pure butterfat, also known as clarified butter, that is, melted butter with milk proteins and water removed. Removing the milk proteins extended the storage life of the butter.

SOCRATES: Fifth-century B.C.E. Greek philosopher; he advocated a vegetarian diet.

SOLON: Sixth-century B.C.E. Athenian lawmaker who regulated various aspects of food production and distribution.

SPELT *(TRITICUM SPELTA):* A hulled wheat used for groats, porridges, and dense breads; it was widely distributed throughout the ancient world, except in Egypt.

STARTER: A porridgelike mass containing yeast that can be mixed with flour and liquid to make leavened bread.

STATIUS: First-century C.E. Roman poet whose *Silvae* contains a description of Saturnalian celebrations.

SUD: A wife of the Mesopotamian god Enlil.

SUMAC *(RHUS CORIARIA):* A red spice berry, native to the Levant, with a tart taste.

SYMPOSIUM: The drinking party that followed a Greek dinner; it might have entertainment and be rowdy, or it could be a restrained, intellectual affair.

TAHINI: A thick, oily purée made from crushed sesame seeds.

TANNUR: A tapering, cylindrical clay oven with a large opening at the top by which the cook would slap flat breads against the hot walls for baking. The fire in the bottom was fed through a small hole.

TESTUM: The Roman term for the clay dome used to form small ovens; *see* **clibanus.**

THEOPHRASTUS: Fourth-century B.C.E. Greek philosopher who wrote the influential treatises *Study of Plants* and *Plant Physiology;* his works contained the earliest reports in the European Mediterranean of Asian foods such as the citron.

TIGER NUT *(CYPERUS ESCULENTUS):* A rhizome that was used in ancient Egypt; it has a sweet, nutty taste and is also known as chufa or earth almond.

TRAGEMATA: The dishes that appeared at the "second table" of a Greek dinner, including fruits and sweets as well as small savory items such as little birds. *Tragemata* also could accompany the wine at a symposium.

TRICLINIA: Literally, "room of the three couches." A Roman dining room was arrayed with three couches in a U-shape, each typically accommodating three diners, around a central table from which all diners took their foods from shared platters.

TRIMALCHIO: The wealthy but gauche host of Trimalchio's Feast, part of Petronius's fictional *Satyricon*.

TROTTERS: Hooves of sheep, pigs, or calves.

VARRO: First-century B.C.E. Roman writer whose works included *De Re Rustica* (On Agriculture).

VIZIER: Except for the king (eventually known as the pharaoh), the highest-ranking Egyptian administrator.

WHEAT BERRIES: Unmilled kernels of wheat.

WHOLE WHEAT FLOUR: Flour, made from any species of wheat, retaining at least part of the bran and germ after milling; *see* **extraction rate.**

YALE BABYLONIAN COLLECTION: A series of cuneiform tablets located at Yale University including three tablets of culinary recipes.

YEAST: A single-celled organism that consumes carbohydrates and expels carbon dioxide, creating leavened doughs for bread and cakes.

ZAGROS: A mountain chain in western Iran; its melting snows drained into the alluvial plains of Mesopotamia.

✑ SERIES FOREWORD

The beasts have memory, judgment and all the faculties and passions of our mind, in a certain degree; but no beast is a cook.

This quip by the eighteenth-century Scottish biographer James Boswell defines the essence of humanity in a way his contemporaries would have found humorous but also thought provoking. It is neither an immortal soul, reason, nor powers of abstraction that separate us from animals but the simple ability to use fire to transform our daily fare into something more palatable and nutritious. We are nothing more than cooking animals. Archaeological evidence bears this out; it is our distant Neanderthal relatives, whose sites offer the earliest incontrovertible evidence of cooking. From those distant times down to the present, the food we eat and how it is prepared has become the decisive factor in the survival of both individuals and whole civilizations, so what better way to approach the subject of history than through the bubbling cauldron?

Growing and preparing food has also been the occupation of the vast majority of men and women who ever lived. To understand ourselves, we should naturally begin with the food that constitutes the fabric of our existence. Yet every culture arrives at different solutions, uses different crops and cooking methods, and invents what amount to unique cuisines. These are to some extent predetermined by geography, technology, and a certain amount of luck. Nonetheless every cuisine is a practical and artistic expression of the culture that created it. It embodies the values and aspirations of each society, its world outlook as well as its history.

This series examines cooking as an integral part of important epochs in history, both as a way to examine daily life for women and men who cooked, and as a way to explore the experiences of people who ate what was served. Cookbooks are thus treated here as primary source documents that students can interpret just as they might a legal text, literary or artistic work, or any other historical evidence. Through them we are afforded a glimpse, sometimes of what transpired in the great halls of the powerful, but also of what took place in more modest households. Unlike most forms of material culture, we can also recreate these dishes today to get an immediate and firsthand experience of the food that people in the past relished. I heartily encourage you to taste the past in these recipes, keeping in mind good taste is not universal and some things are simply impossible to make today. But a good number of dishes, I assure you, will both surprise and delight.

We begin the series with six volumes stretching from ancient times to the twentieth century, including European and American regions, written by experts in culinary history who have done a superb job of interpreting the historical texts while remaining faithful to their integrity. Each volume is designed to appeal to the novice cook, with technical and historical terms amply defined, and timely advice proffered for the adventurous time traveler in the kitchen. I hope your foray into the foods of the past is nothing less than an absolute delight.

Ken Albala
University of the Pacific

ACKNOWLEDGMENTS

Few books are written without considerable help from friends and colleagues, and this one is no exception. Trying to construct a cookbook of ancient recipes required drawing on the work of many distant scholars, but no book could have been more fun to discuss, as we debated and speculated what the foods prepared 3,000 or 4,000 years ago might have been like.

I owe a deep debt of gratitude to Joan Alcock, Andrew Dalby, Nawal Nasrallah, Gerri Sarnartaro and Susan Weingarten, who reviewed or discussed different aspects of the manuscript and helped resolve knotty issues where the historical record was vague or nonexistent. I owe an incalculable debt to Sally Grainger and Chris Grocock, who offered many practical and scholarly insights, and who generously invited me to their home to cook Roman food in a recreated Roman field kitchen; Roman food never tasted so good as when reclining in their outdoor *triclinia* after an afternoon of pounding, stewing, and baking. William Rubel provided firsthand knowledge of emmer wheat.

I could never have written this book without the support and amused toleration of Rick Smilow and Richard Simpson of the Institute of Culinary Education, who have allowed me to conduct classes in historical cookery for modern kitchens for the past eight years; the hundreds of students who have prepared and tasted these recipes have helped refine my approach. Also thanks to Renée Marton, Ken Ovitz, Meryl Rosofsky, Daniel Stone, and Carolyn Vaughn, members of Culinary Historians of New York, who cheerfully experimented with some of the recipes presented here.

Acknowledgments

    Ken Albala, as the Series Editor, was enthusiastic, encouraging, and joyous beyond the call of duty. Wendi Schnaufer at Greenwood was always receptive to the more unusual recipes that emerged as this book took shape.

    Andrew F. Smith, teacher, mentor, colleague, and friend, has provided more help than he will ever know, even if we disagree about the interchangeability of *garum* and *nuoc mam*. My husband, Tom Pippert, with his impressive knowledge of the ancient world, has listened to my theories with good humor and has eaten more than his fair share of ancient foods over the years; I can never repay him for his unwavering support of my culinary adventures.

✛ INTRODUCTION

Man is the cooking animal. No other creature subjects its food to heat to change its flavor before eating it. No other creature has developed such a sophisticated array of strategies and customs for acquiring, processing, distributing, and consuming foodstuffs.

Early human foodways were simple: Paleolithic men and women got their food by hunting the vast animal herds that covered the ancient Near East and Mediterranean and by gathering whatever wild fruits, vegetables, and grains they encountered along the way to augment the meat-based diet. Very little is known about how these earliest nomads prepared their foods, but at some point between 1 million and 500,000 years ago, early man learned how to use fire to transform the raw into the cooked. Anthropologists hypothesize that the original form of cookery was roasting over open fires, quickly supplemented by baking on hot stones placed near the fire or in the ashes from the fire. Boiling is technologically more complex: it required some way of heating liquids in watertight containers and is thought to have been accomplished by plunging hot stones from fires into stone-lined earthen pits. As this primordial cooking emerged, so too did people's tendency to select among the many wild foods available to sate hunger.

About twelve thousand years ago, the Pleistocene Ice Age ended, altering the environment of the northern hemisphere and changing the plant and animal life that could be supported in the late prehistoric Near East and Mediterranean. Exactly how and why agriculture—the deliberate cultivation of crops and domestication of animals—emerged is unclear, as the evidence varies from site to site. One theory is that wild game became less plentiful, making hunter-gatherers depend more on grains for sustenance. They favored certain of the wild grains, for either their reliability, ease of processing, or flavor. These nomads spread those preferred grains while following the wanderings of the diminishing herds, supplementing the hunting lifestyle with cultivated crops. By about 9000 B.C.E., there is evidence of harvests being stored for future consumption. These storehouses needed to be protected against animal and human thievery. Villages formed around them, turning nomads into settled farmers.

One drawback of agriculture is that it is very time-consuming. Using contemporary primitive societies as a model, anthropologists speculate that hunter-gatherer societies spent only about three hours a day obtaining food, while agriculture was much more labor-intensive. One benefit of agriculture, however, is that a good harvest creates food surpluses and frees some members of the community from the need to obtain food. When the food supplies are successfully controlled and organized, some individuals can engage in other specialized endeavors, allowing villages to grow into towns, cities, and eventually into civilizations. One such activity is preparing the food for others. Most successful societies develop a cadre of skilled workers who can prepare food in complex, culturally specific ways that become the civilization's haute cuisine. Other styles of food preparation within the society are simpler, although they too become part of that society's cuisine.

This cookbook illuminates ancient Mesopotamia, Egypt, Greece, and Rome through recipes that illustrate what the highest rulers to the lowest peasants or slaves may have eaten thousands of years ago. The recipes are interesting in themselves as culinary curiosities, but, more importantly, they help reveal each civilization's environment, technology, economy, trade practices, religious and philosophical beliefs, and social and political organization.

Consider bread made from wheat, something nowadays taken for granted as available virtually anywhere and affordable by nearly everyone. In the ancient world, wheat bread was a bit of a luxury; early varieties of wheat did not grow well in all climates, and wheat flour often was more expensive than flours made from other grains. By the second century C.E., when Roman soldiers were stationed at Hadrian's Wall near England's border with Scotland, they insisted on wheat to satisfy their demand for the types of bread familiar to them from Italy. Local grains such as oats could have filled hungry legionnaires' stomachs. Yet wheat was shipped to the ends of the known world to feed the soldiers, who gladly paid for the expensive grain out of their generous salaries, as ancient Romans considered wheat bread essential to their cultural identity.

Many of the foods found in the various chapters are similar because the climates in the Mediterranean and Near East supported many similar agricultural practices, flora, and fauna. Moreover, from early times, these areas traded foodstuffs, so that plants, animals, and the methods of raising and processing them spread from their points of origin to new environments. Yet each civilization also had unique issues arising from variations in their ecosystems, technologies, trading habits, religions, and philosophies. These variations are expressed in the slightly different foodways found in each civilization.

How This Book Is Organized

This introduction introduces the foods and dining customs of the ancient world; provides the tools needed to think about the recipes in their cultural and historical context; examines the ancient world's staple foods, barley and wheat, especially the chemistry and technology of ancient bread making; and describes ancient cooking and food preservation techniques, offering practical advice for preparing the recipes in modern kitchens. Each of the chapters on Mesopotamia, Egypt, Greece, and Rome opens with a summary of the most important environmental and technological challenges facing each civilization's food supply. Each society's basic socioeconomic structure is reviewed, along with any cultural or religious factors influencing food choices. The sources for the ancient recipes are discussed, followed by annotated recipes. Whenever possible, the ancient texts on which the adapted recipes are based are quoted or described; when no texts are available, the evidence supporting the recipe is provided. The recipes are grouped by categories: breads and grains; dairy; meats, poultry, and fish; vegetables; condiments and sauces; pastries and sweets; and beverages, with some suggestions for assembling a meal. Although written for modern kitchens, cooking techniques and equipment are suggested to imitate ancient methods whenever practical. Appendixes provide a glossary, including suggested substitutions for unavailable ingredients as well as mail-order sources for unusual ingredients.

The Ancient World's Food Habits in a Nutshell

- Barley and wheat-based foods (breads, cakes, and porridges) were the most important foods, consumed by nearly everyone in the ancient world. Grain-based foods were considered a sign of civilization; "uncivilized" nomads and barbarians were identified by diets heavily dependent on milk and meat.

- Legumes supplemented grains and provided essential protein, minimizing the dietary need for meat for much of the ancient world.
- Land ownership generated wealth and influenced diet. Meat, especially from large domesticated animals, was expensive and eaten more often by those who could afford to raise the animals on their farms and estates. Public festivals sponsored by the government or wealthy patrons were rare opportunities for poor urbanites to eat farmed meat. Animal fat was regularly used in cooking by those with access to animal products.
- The poor foraged for foods in the wild out of necessity, gathering fruits, herbs, and vegetables and hunting for fish, birds, and small game; the well-to-do might hunt for sport and enjoyed certain wild foods for their gourmet value. However, most wild foods were disdained because of their association with the poor or with uncivilized peoples.
- All Mesopotamians and Egyptians drank beer daily, although the wealthy also drank wine; Greeks and most Romans shunned beer in favor of wine, with the exception of poorer Romans living in areas of the Roman empire where climate did not support viniculture.
- Milk was a seasonal food available when animals were nursing their young; it spoiled quickly in hot climates and was preserved by processing into butter or cheese, which removed excess water, or fermenting into yogurt.
- Most people ate locally produced foods. The wealthy enjoyed more diverse diets enhanced by imported luxury foods. The Greeks and Romans imported significant amounts of wheat to supplement local agriculture.
- Everyone's diet reflected what was "in season." Drying, salting, smoking, fermenting, and pickling preserved foods for the winter months. These processes greatly affected the flavors of ancient cuisine. Mesopotamians, Greeks, and Romans flavored foods with a salty, fermented fish brine, virtually identical to the modern Southeast Asian fish sauces *nuoc mam* and *nam pla*. It was often used in place of salt, much like soy sauce in Chinese and Japanese cookery.
- Spices from Southeast Asia, such as cinnamon, nutmeg, and cloves, were generally too expensive for cooking but were imported in small quantities for perfumes and medicines. One exception is black pepper, which was used in small quantities by the Greeks and in great quantities by the Romans, who opened substantial trade routes to India and beyond. Local herbs and spices, such as onions, garlic, cumin, dill, fenugreek, fennel, and coriander, flavored ancient cuisines.

- Sesame and linseed oil were the primary vegetable fats in Mesopotamia and Egypt, as these areas had difficulty cultivating olive trees in early times; olive trees fared better in the Mediterranean climate. Olive oil was exported to Mesopotamia and Egypt from archaic Greece as a luxury item; it was widely used in Greco-Roman areas.

- Honey, figs, dates, and concentrated grape syrups sweetened food; sugar was unknown in the West before the fourth century B.C.E. and then was used only as a medicine.

- Food was perceived as a tool to preserve health and to treat illness and disease.

- Different table manners required foods to be prepared differently. The ancients typically took food with their fingers from communal serving platters, sometimes without placing it on individual plates. Most foods were either cut into small pieces before serving or were tender enough to tear or cut apart at the table. Formal meals were often eaten while reclining rather than sitting up. Depending on the culture, women, children, and social inferiors might be excluded from formal meals.

- Modern ingredients differ from their ancient equivalents. Modern fruits and vegetables have been bred for sweetness, size, and sturdiness for shipping; ancient forms of familiar vegetables, such as celery or lettuce, were tougher, bitterer, and smaller. Domesticated animals were often smaller than their modern counterparts. Different feeds and grazing patterns change the meat's texture and taste.

- Foods such as tomatoes, potatoes, chocolate, chili peppers, and vanilla were unknown in the ancient world.

> *The man with whom I do not dine is a barbarian to me.*
>
> *Graffito scrawled on a wall at Pompeii, Italy, before the eruption of Mount Vesuvius buried the town in 79 C.E.*

Romans had a cliché, *de gustibus non disputandum*, "there's no arguing about taste." There are no absolutes that govern what tastes "good" or "bad"; taste is individual and is shaped by a lifetime of experiences. Although some ancient foods may seem unappealing to modern palates, ancient diners enjoyed their foods for the same reasons we enjoy eating today: the foods sated hunger and matched the diner's expectations of "good food." If you expect all ancient food to taste like modern food, you will be disappointed; if you try the recipes and are open to different flavor combinations and ingredients, you may find some tasty, but unusual, novelties.

In addition to different flavors, ancient dining habits differed from modern ones in several key aspects. The number of daily meals taken varied; while virtually everyone ate the main meal in the late afternoon or evening, lunch was seldom eaten, except in ancient Rome. Morning meals were common, but they did not resemble modern American breakfasts with special foods eaten just for the day's first meal. Ancient breakfasts were leftovers from yesterday's dinner; or, for those rushing out of the house, a dish of olives, a slug of beer or wine, and a crust of bread equaled the modern commuter's muffin and orange juice. When lunch was eaten, it was always light: people snacked on portable foods, such as breads and fruits; nibbled more leftovers; or grabbed a quick dish from food stands and taverns found in towns and cities so they could return to work, maximizing daylight for productive labor. Dinner usually started shortly before sunset. Most people followed the sun closely, retiring soon after sunset, as lamp oils for artificial illumination were expensive. The wealthy, however, entertained with nocturnal dinner parties; torches burning brightly were a form of conspicuous consumption. Guests at fancy dinners were amused by musicians, poets, dancers, and acrobats, and drink flowed freely.

The ancients used every part of the animal. Foods infrequently seen on contemporary tables, such as lungs, stomach, kidneys, thymus glands (known as sweetbreads), liver, and udders, are all described in ancient culinary literature. Some were used from economy, while others, such as the sow's womb of a famous Roman recipe, were gourmet treats. Meats, especially tough, less desirable cuts, often were minced for soft-textured patties and sausages.

The ancients depended on locally produced, seasonal foods for much of their diet. The slowness of ancient transportation limited long-distance trade in food primarily to grains, oils, wines, spices, and preserved items that could survive weeks or months of shipping. Except for grains, salted fish, and a few basic condiments, most imports went to wealthy tables. Unlike the ability of modern supermarkets to ignore the seasons, making culinary anachronisms such as fresh grapes in February available to virtually every American through rapid transport, out-of-season foods were a rare luxury affordable only by the affluent. Perishable foods were grown in greenhouses or stored in cool underground pits. Most Romans who wanted grapes in February had to choose among grapes in a processed form: fermented into wine or vinegar, dried into raisins, concentrated into syrups, or preserved in honey or boiled juices.

Etiquette books schooled people in proper table manners. Tables might have been dressed with richly worked gold, silver, and bronze vessels; exquisite glassware; and handsome ceramics. Lesser tables might have had cruder earthenware or woodenware or might have dispensed with serving and dinner plates altogether. Everyone ate with their fingers, even at the most formal meals; no one in the ancient world thought forks necessary to dine elegantly or hygienically. Public hand washing preceded the meal, using basins and ewers found in all but destitute households. Breads or balls of ground grains could be used to scoop up foods and soak up liquids, keeping the diner's fingers relatively clean. Forks, knives, and spoons all existed as cooking equipment, and diners might have used personal knives to cut cheeses or other items at table, but the fork never reached the dinner table with one exception: tiny one- and two-prong forks have been found in some Roman sites. These may have extracted recalcitrant snails from their shells at formal dinners or pierced eggshells so that the soft-cooked contents could be sucked out. They may also have been used at *popinae*, Rome's equivalent of fast-food, greasy-spoon joints popular for quick lunches or cheap dinners. These gobble-and-go places dispensed with proper hand washing, so Romans may have thought the fork necessary to substitute for unwashed fingers.

How one sat at table varied. Mesopotamians and Egyptians preferred small, portable tables that might serve only one or two diners, although many tables could be brought into an area for a banquet. The Greeks ate in many different styles, from individual tables to the boardinghouse-style dinners for which Sparta was famous. Rome boasted formal dining rooms, called *triclinia*, in which three couches were aligned in a U-shape. Each couch traditionally accommodated three diners, who took foods from a central table. Formal dining posture changed during the ancient period. In archaic times, polite society sat upright to dine; by about the seventh century B.C.E. the well-to-do started reclining on couches for formal meals, a custom attributed to the Persians. Upright posture remained the rule for informal meals among all classes and civilizations. Women were usually excluded from dinner parties in Greece; they might attend Roman parties, but many times they sat, rather than reclined, on couches. In the Greco-Roman world sitting up to dine signaled social inferiority.

SOURCES FOR ANCIENT RECIPES

Cookbooks are the single best source for understanding the culinary habits of a society, for recipes are practical instruction manuals that allow people to replicate dishes. Few ancient cookbooks have survived the ages; there are only scattered recipe fragments from Mesopotamia and none from Egypt. Extant Greek works refer to general cookery books and specialty treatises on baking bread, preserving meats, and preparing vegetables, but again, only fragments survive. The first detailed, reasonably complete cookbook, with nearly 500 recipes, comes from Rome and is called "Apicius."

Low literacy rates partially account for the small number of ancient cookbooks. Mesopotamian cuneiform is extremely complicated and was understood by small numbers of educated elites. Egyptian hieroglyphics were not suited for recording subtle instructions. Most cooks in those civilizations, either professional chefs or housewives, learned by example rather than by reading. Greek and Latin alphabets are easier to read, and literacy penetrated deeper into those societies. In major Greek cities such as Athens, estimates are that over half of the adult male citizenry could read and write, and the numbers are even higher for Rome.[1] This suggests that practical manuals could have been widely used. Experts on Apicius believe that, based on its inelegant Latin, it was written by and for working cooks.[2] Cooking schools existed in the Classical world, again suggesting the need for culinary manuscripts.

Even if more ancient cookbooks survived, they might not tell the whole story of ancient foodways. Cookbooks usually include only those dishes deemed important, complex, or unusual enough to merit writing down, and not every culinary preparation meets that standard. Few modern cookbooks have recipes for making coffee or tea; they are too ubiquitous to need many recipes. Yet the lack of recipes could mislead one into concluding that the drinks were seldom consumed, when precisely the opposite is true. Likewise, relatively few ancient bread recipes survive, but this hardly means that bread was unimportant. Commercial or government-run bakeries supplied many townspeople with their daily bread; others baked at home. Daughters learned the process from their mothers (grinding grain and making bread at home was a daily chore for females or slaves) and passed the art down through the generations. These "silent" recipes need to be reconstructed from other evidence to gain an accurate picture of ancient cuisine.

Electron microscopic analysis of food residues from pottery shards has unlocked some of the mysteries of ancient foods. Statistical analysis of midden heaps identifies the amount and type of animals eaten at archaeological excavations. Governmental ration lists record food payments to soldiers, bureaucrats, and slaves. Models of granaries, bakeries, and breweries buried in elite Egyptian tombs to ensure plentiful foods in the afterlife demonstrate successive steps in processing grains into bread and beer. Literature describes the pleasures and gluttonous perils of the table, while medical books offer dietary advice. These all contribute to understanding the ancient world's culinary habits.

A NOTE ON AUTHENTICITY

How authentic are the recipes in this volume? The answer depends on the particular recipe.

Because so few recipes have survived, many of the recipes in this book have been inferred from all the available evidence to fill in the glaring gaps in the cookbook record. These "silent" recipes are of two types: reconstructed recipes, based on scientific data about ancient ingredients and the immutable chemistry of cookery, and invented recipes, based on artistic representations. Most of the bread recipes are reconstructions, using the best modern equivalents of ancient flours. While not identical to ancient breads, they are fair approximations. Many of the meat, fish, and vegetable dishes, especially in the Egyptian chapter, are inventions. We know of many foods that the Egyptians ate and the cooking techniques used, but we have no descriptions of seasonings or any of the subtle choices a good cook makes in preparing foods. Adding flavorings to these dishes has been educated guesswork. The Mesopotamian and Greek recipes are a bit more certain, as those recipes have been based on literary descriptions and recipe fragments, although gaps in seasonings or technique are still filled in with educated assumptions. Only with the Roman chapter do we have complete, explicit recipes that can be directly adapted for modern kitchens.

Barley and Wheat, the Staples of the Ancient World

- Wheat is more difficult to grow than barley but was always desirable because it can be used in more ways, including for leavened bread.

The "grain-giving land" was the poet Homer's epithet for Greece, but the phrase could have been applied to any of the ancient civilizations. Grain-based foods—porridges, breads, and cakes—were daily fare in virtually every ancient diet. Beer, usually made from fermented barley, although wheat might also be used, was essential in Mesopotamia and Egypt. Most people—excluding the very rich—took in substantial calories from grains; therefore, understanding these staples is essential to understanding the ancient world.

Barley and several species of wheat were the most popular, desirable, and widespread grains. Millet, sorghum, oats, bitter vetch, and rye were used in areas where the climate and soil did not support barley and wheat. Scholars used to claim that the Greeks preferred barley while the Romans preferred wheat, because the Greeks ate relatively more barley. This claim of different cultural "taste" put the cart before the horse: cultural taste was often determined by practicality. Differences in climate, soil, and irrigation technology dictated the relative success of the two grains and thus influenced how each culture devoted its resources. Barley grows more easily than wheat, thriving in a range of ecosystems from hot, arid areas to cold ones, and can tolerate saline or poor-quality soil. Wheat needs a moister, more temperate environment and more nutrients in the soil. Barley also is less susceptible to disease. It thus would seem a superior grain from the cultivator's perspective, and one might imagine that it was the most popular grain in the ancient world.

Yet, even with these advantages, ancient cultures tried to cultivate wheat in place of barley, at least as an upscale item. The reason is simple: wheat is uniquely suited for leavened bread, and leavened bread has been one traditional measure of wealth and technological advancement in premodern societies. Once the Mesopotamians and Egyptians were able to control their rivers for irrigation, they were able to cultivate wheat in addition to barley, although the harsh Mesopotamian environment still made barley more important. The Attic Greeks lacked rich, alluvial soils and were especially dependent on barley—one famous writer praised high-quality barley from the island of Lesbos as worthy of the gods' finely milled porridges.[3] They nonetheless preferred wheat bread to barley cakes whenever available and imported wheat from the Ukraine and Egypt to feed Greek elites.[4]

The Egyptians and the Romans used barley but made comparatively greater use of wheat. The Nile's regular overflowing provided ideal circumstances for growing wheat, and some parts of the Italian peninsula supported wheat, although it was often beyond the purse of poor Romans when sold on the open market. This eventually led to state subsidies of wheat and an elaborate import and distribution system to make wheat available to the Roman citizenry throughout the farthest reaches of the empire.

VARIETIES AND CHARACTERISTICS OF ANCIENT GRAINS

The ancients used four important types of wheat, in addition to barley, to make porridges, breads, and cakes that were the ancient world's daily fare. Ancient sources discuss many varieties of cakes, breads, and pastries, but they use these terms in ways that confuse modern readers. Ancient cakes and pastries bear scant resemblance to the confections found in modern bakeries. They were simply foods made from grains ground into flour or smaller groats and baked or fried.

Pastries were usually sweetened, while cakes could be sweet or savory and were most often shaped into individual portions, although large cakes might be made for religious offerings. Breads covered the gamut from crackerlike flat breads through soft rolls to intricately shaped loaves. Any of these products could be combined with honey, cheese, oil, herbs, spices, nuts, fresh or dried fruits, juices, wine, or other ingredients. Breads made from certain species of wheat, however, were noteworthy because they could be successfully raised with yeast, resulting in a light texture. Ancient literature praises these light-textured breads as gourmet treats, and although no one knows exactly how leavened breads originally developed, once people became familiar with them, they were frequently preferred to all other grain products. The choice of grain used to make breads versus cakes and pastries is key: barley cannot be leavened because barley lacks certain key proteins that allow dough to stretch. Only certain forms of wheat have the essential proteins that will bake into fluffy breads. The many bread and cake recipes that follow require a detour into ancient grains and the chemistry of baking.

> Each recipe will specify the best flours to use; depending on the recipe, it might be semolina, spelt, stone-ground all-purpose white or whole wheat flour, or a blend of these. If these are not available, you can use regular all-purpose flour, but the textures and flavors will be different from what might have been eaten in antiquity. You may also have to adjust the amount of liquid in the recipes; start by adding slightly less than the original recipe calls for, and slowly add liquid in small amounts until the dough becomes workable.

Barley (genus *Hordeum*) is thought to originate in the Zagros Mountains of Western Iran. It spread in prehistoric times to Mesopotamia, Egypt, the Mediterranean, and then into Europe. There were two main species in the ancient world, but both had similar culinary properties, making them interchangeable from the cook's perspective. Most barley is hulled, that is, the grains are encapsulated in a thin shell that attaches them to the plant and must be removed to reach the nourishing grains. The most efficient means is to parch the husks, which then can be loosened by threshing. Final cleaning takes place by winnowing out remaining bits of chaff, dirt, and other impurities. Pounding unparched grains to loosen the husks is another alternative, although harder work. Barley can be fermented into beer, boiled or cooked whole, or ground into flour for making porridges, dense cakes, or flat breads.

Wheat (genus *Triticum*) is more complicated, as there were six important species of wheat in the ancient world, five of which are still used. Each species had slightly different amounts and proportions of key proteins, making some better for chewy breads and others for tender cakes. Wheats can be hulled (like most barleys) or naked (the grains lack the encapsulating shell). These differences affected the storage, transportation, and processing of the grains.

The hulled wheats are the earliest species and include einkorn *(Triticum monococcum)*, emmer *(T. dicoccum)*, and spelt *(T. spelta)*. Like barley, all needed to be parched or vigorously pounded before threshing and winnowing to release the grains from the hulls. Einkorn, the earliest of all the wheats, was a low-yielding crop that was supplanted by the better-yielding emmer and spelt once farming, with its ability to select crops for planting, became the ancient world's way of life. The naked wheats are bread *(T. aestivum)*, durum *(T. durum)*, and club *(T. compactum)*. All could be threshed without the intermediate parching or pounding, saving considerable labor. Significantly, *T. aestivum* got its colloquial name "bread" wheat from anthropologists, who noted its primary use in the ancient world.

There were good reasons for the ancients to value both hulled and naked wheats. Hulls protected grains from insects. For civilizations that grew most of their own grain or were exporters of grain, such as Mesopotamia and Egypt, the hulls helped ensure the crop while in storage or transit. Slave or poor laborers could perform the unskilled task of parching or pounding the grains. Naked wheats, although more vulnerable to infestation, were more compact and cheaper to process and ship, important to societies importing large amounts of grain, such as Greece and Rome. Even so, the Romans continued to cultivate larges amounts of hulled emmer on the Italian peninsula to be processed by slaves.

Emmer and spelt reached Europe and parts of the Mediterranean from their places of origin in prehistoric times. Emmer was gathered for food in the Levant no later than 12,000 B.C.E. and was domesticated there by about 9000 B.C.E. It spread to Mesopotamia by the sixth millennium B.C.E. and to Egypt and the western Mediterranean in the fifth and fourth millennia B.C.E., respectively. Emmer was the dominant wheat of pharaonic Egypt. Spelt probably originated in modern Pakistan's Indus Valley. It traveled northward through Central Asia, reaching northern and central Europe before filtering down to the European Mediterranean and eventually to the Levant and Mesopotamia. Spelt did not reach Egypt.

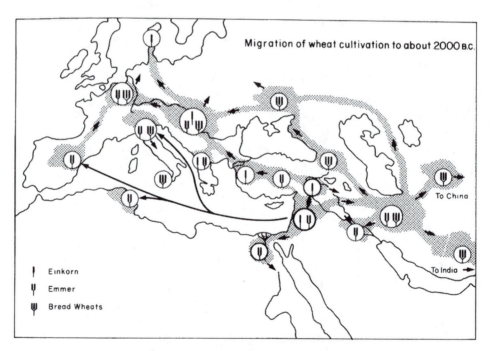

Distribution of cultivation einkorn, emmer, and bread wheats in the ancient world as of 2000 B.C.E. The wheats spread from the Near East to Europe, Africa and Asia. From John Storck and Walter Teague, Flour for Man's Bread: A History of Milling, *illustrated by Harold Rydell (University of Minnesota Press). Copyright 1952 by the University of Minnesota, renewed 1980.*

Durum and bread wheat, the most important of the naked wheats, are a bit of a scientific mystery. Their exact origins have not been definitively established, but current theories hypothesize that they result from naturally occurring crosses of wild emmer and wild spelt, respectively, with wild einkorn. Recent research suggests that durum arose in Mesopotamia or the Levant and spread to the Mediterranean in late prehistoric times.[5] Bread wheat probably followed a more circuitous path, similar to spelt, eventually becoming the dominant grain because of its exceptional baking qualities and ease of processing. By the Classical era, bread and durum wheats had thoroughly penetrated the Mediterranean and Egypt, where they shared center stage with emmer and, to a much lesser extent, spelt.

Barley and wheat are primarily carbohydrates but also contain proteins and trace amounts of fats. The amount and specific type of protein varies among the different species of grains. Breads and cakes react differently in baking depending on the grain used. Wheat, especially bread wheat, has much more of certain critical proteins than does barley, allowing wheat to stretch, a requisite for leavened bread.

There are three basic components of a grain of wheat: the germ, the endosperm, and the bran. The germ, also known as the embryo, is the reproductive structure from which new plants sprout. It contains oil, vitamins, minerals, and proteins and contributes much of the flavor of wheat. The endosperm is the bulk of the grain, made up primarily of starches held in a protein web. The bran is the thin covering surrounding the endosperm; it is distinct from the hull. All grains, both hulled and naked, have bran. The fiber-rich bran is laxative, a trait noticed by the second-century C.E. physician Galen.[6]

After grains are ground, the impurities (which can be specks of dirt, the bran, or the germ, depending on the type of flour desired) can be sifted out. Through repeated grindings and siftings, it is possible to create a flour that is pure endosperm, called white or refined flour, although no one in the ancient world had this type of highly refined flour. Millers, both ancient and modern, have been concerned with extraction rates, that is, how much of the grain, usually from the germ and bran, is lost in the grinding and sifting process. The higher the extraction rate, the less is lost and the more "whole" the flour is. The major downside to whole flours is the shorter shelf life: the oils in the germ can become rancid, spoiling the flour within a few months of milling. Modern white flour has an extraction rate of about 72 percent; modern whole wheat flour, which incorporates the ground germ and bran, has an extraction rate of about 90 percent. As a useful comparison, the extraction rate for the finest, whitest flour in the ancient world was around 80 percent. Thus, antiquity's best "white" flour was a bit darker than modern white flour, with flecks of germ and bran tinting the blend, although it remained whiter than modern whole wheat. Some of the recipes will blend white and whole wheat flours to approximate the ancient extraction rates.

Many times the ancient miller or the home grinder looked for the highest extraction rate to stretch grain as far as possible. In times of shortage, many adulterated wheat with ground acorns and other filler. Several of the recipes will incorporate a range of flours and pulses to illustrate the different ingredients the ancients used to make their daily bread. Even without the need to augment flour, tiny bits of grit from grinding stones often remained in flour, judging from the severe wear on the teeth of some ancient skeletal remains.

Most modern flours are made from bread wheat. Unfortunately for the history student (but helpful to the fledgling baker), bread flour is packaged under several confusing names. Supermarkets may carry flours labeled "bread," "all-purpose," or "cake," and may also have the additional words "red," "white," "winter," "spring," "hard," or "soft" on the label. These latter terms convey helpful information about specific strains of wheat to experienced bakers but are irrelevant for our purposes. Most ancient breads should be made with a blend of all-purpose white and whole wheat flours. Stone-ground all-purpose flours, available by mail or in well-stocked grocery stores, come closest to ancient milling technologies and, thus, to capturing the texture of ancient flours. They are ideal for the recipes. If stone-ground flours are unavailable, try the all-purpose flours from brands such as Hecker's, King Arthur, Pillsbury, or Gold Medal. Specialty "bread" flours should be avoided, as they have too much protein, while brands such as White Lily, Downey's, or Swan's are too low in the specific proteins needed.

Durum flour is essential for approximating ancient breads made from emmer. Emmer is impossible to find commercially in America, but the specific proteins found in emmer are believed most similar to those found in durum wheat. Indeed, efforts in the United Kingdom to grow emmer have shown some striking similarities with durum: both yield pale yellow flours that make sturdy doughs. Durum (sometimes called semolina, macaroni, or chapati) flour is available in ethnic markets or by mail order and is the only substitute for emmer.

BREAD-BAKING CHEMISTRY AND TECHNIQUES: ADVICE FOR MODERN COOKS

When wheat flour is moistened into a dough and kneaded, the liquid interacts with the proteins to form gluten, a stretchy mat. If the dough contains yeasts, single-cell living organisms, and it is left in a warm place, the yeasts greedily eat the carbohydrates in the flour. Then, in a case of microscopic indigestion, the yeasts belch carbon dioxide gases, which are trapped in the gluten mat and are visible in the weblike structure of the raw dough. If there is insufficient gluten in a dough, the carbon dioxide will escape, leaving a flat loaf.

 KITCHEN DEMONSTRATION: MAKING GLUTEN

Make a doughy paste with 1/3–1/2 cup of water and 1 cup of all-purpose flour. Stir vigorously with a wooden spoon. At first the paste is lifeless, but as you continue to stir it for a few minutes, the paste will develop extensibility (the ability to stretch) and elasticity (the ability to spring back to its original shape.) You have made gluten. The protein gliadin accounts for the dough's extensibility, and glutenin accounts for its elasticity. Try the same experiment with barley flour and other wheat flours to compare their gluten-forming capabilities.

Two basic styles of bread were popular in the ancient world and remain so nowadays: flat breads and formed breads. As the name suggests, flat breads are thin, usually no more than a half inch thick when raw, and cook quickly on a very hot surface. They may contain yeast to lighten the texture, but just as often, steam from moisture evaporating in the dough provides the texture. Pita, pizza, pancakes, and tortillas are all flat breads. Although flat breads are sometimes cooked in ovens, they can be successfully baked with the simplest equipment, such as a hot stone, or even in the ashes around an open fire. Hunter-gatherers made flat breads from coarsely ground wild grains. Although there is no conclusive evidence establishing when they were first made, some archaeologists speculate that they date back more than 20,000 years. Over time, clever equipment evolved for baking flat breads. The most important are the *saj*, a convex metal dome similar to an upside-down wok, and the *tannur*, a tapering cylindrical clay oven with a large opening at the top; both are still widely used from the Levant through Central Asia and India.

Saji are heated over a fire. Flat breads are cooked on its curved surface. There is no enclosure to trap hot air, so the breads must be flipped halfway through to cook both sides. The *tannur* cooks both sides simultaneously. After building a fire in the bottom to heat the oven, the baker adroitly slaps flat breads on the blazingly hot walls. The moist dough sticks to the wall, where the bottom bakes quickly and crisply from the intense direct heat, while the top bakes to a softer doneness from the hot air reflected off the oven walls. The baker watches carefully through the top opening for signs that the bread is about to slip, which signals doneness. The baker retrieves the bread, usually with a hook or spear, before it dries completely and falls into the fire at the *tannur*'s bottom.

Formed breads, which are most of the loaves found in supermarkets and bakeries and coming out of bread machines, are later developments. They must be baked in an oven, which can be as simple as a small clay mold into which a dough is placed and then covered with embers to bake; a *clibanus* or *testum,* a portable domed clay oven favored by the Greeks and Romans; or a larger, stationary brick or clay beehive oven that bakes multiple, free-standing loaves simultaneously. These last ovens are still in use by artisanal bread makers and are appreciated for the even heat that the beehive shape provides.

All ovens worked by burning fuel (wood, charcoal, or dung) in the oven chamber. The ashes were swept out, then the breads were placed in the heated molds or on the oven floor, and the chamber was quickly sealed. Embers were piled around the smaller molds and *testum* to maintain baking temperatures, while the greater size of the stationary ovens allowed the bricks or clay to absorb more heat, so that bread baked thoroughly in the radiant heat of the slowly cooling chamber. Formed breads are often raised with yeast and can be thicker than flat breads because they are cooked by gentler heat that allows the center of the raw dough to cook without incinerating the outside.

The simplest breads are unyeasted, such as Whole Wheat Flat Bread (Recipe 1). Flour and liquid are combined and kneaded thoroughly. Kneading is the process of pushing and folding dough to create gluten, which allows the bread to be stretched and shaped and improves the texture of the finished bread. Once these doughs are kneaded, they must rest to relax the gluten before shaping, because otherwise the doughs will not roll out easily; the resting period can be any time from 30 minutes to overnight. After resting,

Greek clibanus, *or portable cooking bell, used as an oven for breads and other items. Romans called a similar apparatus a* testum. *Courtesy of the American School of Classical Studies at Athens.*

the doughs are shaped by rolling a small piece to the desired dimensions and cooked on a preheated surface. Unyeasted breads tend to be dense or even crackerlike.

Yeasted breads are slightly more complicated. The trick to successful yeasted doughs is to keep the temperature of the liquid added to the dough no more than 105°F, barely warm to the touch. Anything hotter risks killing the yeast before it has leavened the dough.

 ## HOW TO KNEAD: PUSH, FOLD, AND FLIP

Once you have combined the liquid and dry ingredients and made a dough, it must be kneaded. Gather the dough into a ball and place on a smooth, lightly floured surface. Place the heels of your palms in the center of the dough and forcefully push the dough away from you. Fold the edge of the dough farthest away from you back over the dough and turn the ball 90°. Repeat the process, adding a thin dusting of flour to the work surface if the dough starts to stick. You will find that you will use one hand to fold the dough back on itself and the other to flip the dough between each push. Once you become comfortable with the process, each push-fold-flip will take less than 1 second. Continue kneading until the dough is very elastic, that is, if you pull a bit of dough, it will return to its original shape and feel smooth and silky. It often takes 7 to 10 minutes of vigorous kneading to fully develop the gluten in the dough, so be patient and keep kneading.

Two types of yeast were used in the ancient world, although exactly how the ancients learned to harness their leavening power remains a mystery. Wild yeasts, *Saccharomyces exiguus,* are everywhere; they are visible and concentrated as the white bloom on ripening fruits, particularly grapes and plums. Given enough time, any starch-based batter can trap wild yeasts from the air and begin to ferment, making what modern bakers call sourdough. A plausible scenario, probably repeated innumerable times in different locations, is that some ancient cook was interrupted (perhaps by wild beasts or the neighboring marauding tribe) while mixing up a porridge with ground grains and water; she abandoned it uncooked, only to return later to a bubbly mix with a tangy odor. Undeterred by the strange mass, or perhaps just very hungry, the intrepid gourmand baked the mush on a hot stone and devoured the spongy-textured product greedily. Whether she initially liked the tangy flavor is unknown, but the lighter texture probably was easier to chew. Eventually enough people repeated the process, developed a preference for leavened bread, and learned that a bit of raw dough saved from each day's baking could leaven the next batch without waiting for wild yeasts to collect.

The second yeast was a by-product of making beer. *Saccharomyces cerevisiae* is found in the foamy layer that rises to the top of the containers holding the fermenting grains. It was a popular leavener through the nineteenth century until dried commercial yeasts were developed. Again, the origins of beer and beer-yeasted bread are unknown, but one can imagine a bit of beer accidentally mixing with a flat bread dough, the magical rising taking place, and brave souls who ventured to bake and taste the result. Given its vast granary-brewery-bakery complexes, Egypt is thought to be the source of bread leavened by *S. cerevisiae.*

Modern bakers use *S. cerevisiae,* now known as baker's yeast, which has been cultivated on molasses and dried. It is sweeter than wild yeasts. The easiest, most reliable, and least expensive baker's yeast to work with is instant yeast, which can be mixed directly with the dry ingredients in a recipe without the initial step of rehydrating the yeast in liquid. There are several brands of instant yeast; the SAF brand is available nationwide or by mail order and comes in small bulk packages that allow measurement of the exact amount needed for a recipe. Do not confuse instant yeast with "rapid rise" yeast; they are different products, and rapid rise is not very reliable. The recipes are written for instant yeast because of its ease and economy, but traditional dry envelope yeast, which is premeasured into the amounts typically used in a single recipe, can be substituted. It is a fine, but expensive, product and must be rehydrated in lukewarm (no more than 105°F) liquid to make sure the yeast is alive before proceeding with the recipes. To rehydrate the yeast, sprinkle it on about 1/4 cup of lukewarm liquid and a pinch of flour from the recipe and wait a few minutes for bubbles to collect on the surface. Add the hydrated yeast to the rest of the liquid and continue with the recipe.

Yeasted doughs can be made in two basic ways: either as a straight dough or in two stages, with a starter. Straight doughs are mixed in one step. Flour, yeast, liquid, and any other ingredients are kneaded together, allowed to ferment (rise), and then the dough is shaped, allowed to ferment once more, and baked. Starter doughs require two steps to mix the dough. The first step is to make a soupy porridge of yeast, some flour, and liquid. The porridge, often called a starter, ferments until bubbly, at least 30 minutes but possibly overnight. In the second step, more flour and other ingredients are added to the starter to make the dough. It is kneaded, allowed to rise, then shaped, allowed to rise once more, and then baked. The additional fermentation given to starter doughs results in more flavorful breads.

The ancient-world technique of cooking on a *saj,* in a *tannur,* or on a hot stone can be approximated in modern kitchens by using an inverted wok over a gas cooktop, a clay baking stone in the oven, or a heavy iron griddle, heated either on a cooktop or in the oven. The *testum* can be closely imi-

---

 BEER AND BREAD: ANCIENT HEALTH FOODS?

The proteins in barley and wheat are not in forms that are easily absorbed by the body. Both are low in the essential amino acid lysine, which limits the body's ability to use the other proteins. Fermenting these grains with yeast raises the lysine levels and thus makes more protein usable. Fermentation also augments the amount of B vitamins in these grains and increases the body's ability to absorb the calcium needed for strong bones and other minerals. There are, however, limits to improving the nutrition of barley and wheat by turning it into beer or bread. The heat needed to bake bread kills the yeast. Alcohol, a by-product of fermentation, also inhibits yeast. Even so, these fermented foods are more nutritious than either raw or cooked grain and were an important contribution to the health of ancient folks.

---

tated with a baker's cloche, an earthenware dome designed for baking bread at home and available through kitchen equipment stores.

OTHER COOKING TECHNIQUES

Ancient cooks prepared and preserved foods by techniques that have changed little in 5,000 years. In addition to baking, which could also be used for foods other than bread, the basic cooking techniques were roasting, boiling and stewing, grilling, and frying. Some foods, of course, were eaten raw or in preserved form.

Roasting required only a fire and an open environment. Roasting evaporates surface moisture. The heat creates a reaction between meats' amino acids and carbohydrates to form a crispy, flavorful crust. Although modern cooks roast by cranking up the oven to a high heat, the texture and flavor of oven-roasted meats differs from spit-roasted meats. Oven-roasting is often a necessary compromise, but the difference is evident each time the oven door is opened and steam escapes: the meat has been steeping in the steam that would dissipate in open-air spit-roasting. Ancient roasting can be duplicated with an outdoor fire and a spit to secure the meat in front of (not directly over) the flames.

Grilling, in its most primitive form, could take place on heated stones. Once metalworking developed in the fourth millennium B.C.E., bronze and iron grills facilitated cooking smaller items over small fires, a fuel-efficient technique. Modern iron grill pans used on stove tops closely simulate the ancient technique, or outdoor grills can be used.

Boiling and stewing require impermeable cooking vessels that can withstand fire. The earliest cook pots were animal stomachs. Clay pots, if heated gently, could withstand the heat of a fire but are prone to thermal shock and breakage. Pots could be nestled in the ashes of fires or in the opening of *tannur* ovens to create a potager stove to simmer stews and porridges. Metal pots tolerated high heat better. The technique is easily duplicated in modern kitchens with metal pans set on gas or electric stoves.

Frying, submerging items in hot fat, was used in the ancient world but was a relatively late and luxurious technique. Frying requires a container, usually metal, that can withstand high heat and a profligate use of cooking fat or oil. Shallow-frying or sautéing, in which food is browned in a pan lubricated with a thin layer of fat to facilitate heat transfer and prevent sticking, was more efficient and more common. Frying pans are frequent archaeological artifacts, including the Greek *tegamo* and the Roman *patella.*

One important preparatory technique for many different foodstuffs was grinding. In a world before food processors and other labor-saving devices, grinding was a tedious necessity to turn grains into flour; purée fruits, vegetables, and herbs; pulverize nuts; and otherwise break down foods. Mortars, often with very rough interiors that abraded foods, and pestles were ubiquitous, with examples found in many archaeological sites. The Mexican *molcajete* (mortar) and *tejolote* (pestle), tools dating back thousands of years but still in use in Mexican cookery, are available in well-equipped kitchen supply stores. They are good modern equivalents that will make grinding herbs, spices, and nuts much easier and will be true to the ancient techniques. Grains were usually ground into flour on saddle querns.

FOOD PRESERVATION

Once plants are harvested or animals slaughtered, the foods begin to deteriorate. The major cause of food spoilage comes from unwanted microbial action that can make foods unappetizing or even toxic. Many microbes can be killed or controlled by heating or chilling; by introducing chemical preservatives, such as through wood smoke; by dehydrating foods through salting, brining, or air-drying; by removing oxygen, an element necessary for most microbes to survive and reproduce, by storing foods in oil; by altering the pH of foods by adding acids such as vinegar, wine, grape must, or honey; or by fermenting.

The modern world relies heavily on cold (refrigeration and freezing) and lack of oxygen (anaerobic canning or vacuum-packing) to inhibit microbial activity for long periods. These processes have comparatively little effect on the flavor of foods: blueberries frozen in August and baked into muffins the following January will taste much like the fresh product, even if the texture suffers a bit. The ancient world's preservation techniques were not as subtle. Salting, drying, smoking, and pickling, all of which are still used to create some luscious foods, were especially important to create stockpiles of foods for the winter and early spring, when few fresh plant foods could be harvested and only the wealthiest regularly could afford freshly slaughtered meat. Although there is some evidence of ice pits, these seem not to have been used for preservation of foods. Instead, stored snow and ice cooled beverages for the elites in the hot summer.

Salting (coating with a generous layer of dry salt) and brining (soaking in a concentrated salt solution) inhibit bacterial growth by drawing water from foods through osmosis. The cell walls of plants and animals are semipermeable, and the cells typically contain small amounts of salt. By introducing a greater concentration of salt around the food, moisture from inside the cells crosses over to the greater concentration to attempt to equalize the concentrations on both sides of the membranes. The resulting cured meats, fishes, and even vegetables were widely used in the ancient world. One significant difference between ancient and modern salted foods is that most of the ancient products were saltier and drier. Nitrites, used in most modern curing blends, reduce the amount of salt needed to inhibit bacterial action. Most modern hams can be eaten without the initial soaking to remove the excess salt, a typical step in ancient times. Salt cod and salted anchovies are still made in much the same way as ancient cooks preserved fish: dry-salting followed by air-drying. Today, dried fish are soaked in water or milk to desalinate and rehydrate before cooking, a practice that began in the ancient world.

Smoking preserves foods by introducing certain chemicals, primarily antioxidant phenols found in wood smoke, to foods. The wood smoke coats foods with tars that both kill bacteria and seal out air, preventing rancidity. Smoke could not eliminate all microbial action and usually was preceded by salting or drying. Smoking required little equipment and could take place at home over an open flame, in a chimney, or in a specially constructed smokehouse, although some smoked foods were commercial products. Many smoked fishes, meats, and cheeses were considered gourmet items by Classical times. Contemporary cooks can use home smokers, including stove-top lidded boxes, to imitate the ancient technique.

The hot, arid environments of parts of the ancient world made air-drying an efficient preservation technique, one that is still practiced in rural areas relatively free of airborne contaminants. The only tools required were knives to cut the foodstuffs into relatively thin pieces that could dehydrate before spoilage set in, strings or mats for suspending or laying out the drying items, and perhaps a light covering or whisk to shoo away insects. Commercial dehydrators or an oven that can maintain very low temperatures (under 200°F) can simulate air-drying if your environment is not suitable.

Ancient anaerobic preservation, submerging foodstuffs in fats and oils, depended on cutting off the supply of oxygen that most bacteria need to reproduce. This technique might be combined with a preliminary salting to remove some moisture, especially from meats. Tomb finds in Egypt and northern Europe include meats stored in fats.

Pickling submerges foods in acid, primarily vinegars, to increase the foods' acidities, rendering them inhospitable to bacteria. Salt is often added to pickling liquids for its osmotic effect, as well as spices for flavor. The ancients pickled meats, fish, vegetables, and fruits. A variation on the traditional pickling technique is storing foods in honey, which is both acidic and mildly antiseptic, or reduced fruit juices, especially must made from grape juice.

Fermentation is a broad term for beneficial chemical changes brought about by yeasts, molds, and bacteria. Most fermentations change foods from highly perishable to more stable states, such as turning fruit juices into wines or milk into yogurt or cheese. One important exception was fermenting grains into beer, which shortened the shelf life of the grain because ancient beers lacked hops, an essential preservative, and the addition of water encouraged bacteria. In this case, the fermentation was appreciated for the pleasing flavor of and potential intoxication from the low-alcohol ancient beers.

WHAT'S MISSING FROM THE ANCIENT PANTRY?

Imagine Italian food without tomatoes and peppers or Greek food without lemons. Many now-popular Mediterranean fruits had not yet spread from their places of origin to the Near East and the Mediterranean during the period covered in this book. Lemons, limes, and oranges all originated in Southeast Asia and became a part of Mediterranean cuisine only after the Arab expansion through North Africa, Spain, Sicily, and southern Italy in the eighth century C.E. In the ancient world, sour tastes were provided by wines and vinegars (based on grapes or other fruits) or sumac, a lemony-tasting spice berry. Only relatively late in the ancient world (first century C.E.) did the citron, the first citrus fruit to reach the Levant and Europe, become part of the culinary repertory. The New World's tomatoes and chilies were not introduced to Europe and the Near East until the early sixteenth century.

Other vegetables conspicuously absent from the ancient pantry are all forms of potatoes, most squashes, and pumpkins. The very Italian-sounding zucchini is indigenous to the New World. Ancient-world beans were all from the flat *Vicia* genus; string, snap, and kidney beans, the most common varieties nowadays, are members of the *Phaseolus* genus and are New World plants. With the important exception of the fava, most dried beans were missing from the ancient pantry; their place was taken by various peas, lupines, and lentils .

Ancient vegetables were different. Lettuces were all of the loose cos variety that includes romaine and chicory and had an intense and somewhat bitter flavor; the sweeter, round head lettuces result from modern breeding. Carrots were not the familiar orange color, which was a result of hybridization by the Dutch in the seventeenth century, but were a rainbow of colors ranging from purple to red to yellow to white. Ancient versions of celery, fennel, artichokes, cabbages, and turnips were thinner and leafier. Cucumbers and melons were seedier and less fleshy; some may have resembled the Chinese bitter melon, *Momordica charantia,* more than the sweet hothouse varieties prevalent in modern American markets. Most ancient vegetables are thought to have been bitterer than their modern counterparts, which may partially explain why vegetables often were served in pungent sauces or as part of complicated stews.

Two popular grains are also absent from or latecomers to the ancient world. Maize is another New World product that reached Europe in the early modern period. Rice was imported into the Mediterranean in the Hellenistic period but was used as a thickener, for porridge, or as medicine; elegant pilafs did not become a significant part of Mediterranean foodways until the Arab conquest of the Mediterranean in the post-Roman world.

The most significant culinary animal missing during the pre-Classical period is the chicken. Originating in the Indus Valley, the chicken reached Mesopotamia probably in the early first millennium B.C.E., shortly before Mesopotamia fell to the Persians, and reached the Mediterranean by about 500 B.C.E. The Greeks nicknamed chickens "Persian awakeners," referring to the foreign cocks' sunrise crowing. Ducks, geese, quail, pigeon, and guinea fowl were the prime poultry of the Mesopotamians, Egyptians, and early Greeks; as time progressed, the Greeks and the Romans would use chicken freely, even starting the tradition of chicken soup to nurse invalids. Turkey, another New World food, was unknown.

The spice shelf has glaring holes. The popular Southeast Asian spices, cinnamon, ginger, cloves, nutmeg, and cardamom, are missing from culinary uses until very late in antiquity. Very limited quantities of such spices had been traded through Arab and Indian intermediaries, perhaps as early as the mid-second millennium, for medicines, perfumes, and embalming. One exception is black pepper, which was known to the Greeks by about the fourth century B.C.E. and was a common spice for the Romans. The Greeks initiated a small amount of direct trade with sources in northern India for long pepper (*Piper longum*) during the classical period, but it remained too expensive for regular culinary use for most Greeks. The Romans dramatically increased trade, and by the first century, pepper (both *P. longum* and the much more familiar round pepper, *P. nigrum*) became merely minor luxuries. To the extent sugar was known, it was as medicine. Coffee, tea, chocolate, and vanilla had yet to be introduced from their diverse points of origin. Distilled spirits, a medieval invention, were centuries in the future.

WHAT'S ADDED TO THE ANCIENT PANTRY?

Ancient cookbooks and culinary literature mention certain ingredients that no longer exist in Western kitchens. *Silphium* was a type of wild umbellifer found in a small area of North Africa that went extinct around the first century C.E., sometimes known in the Roman literature by its alternate name, *laser*. *Silphium* was esteemed and rare in the Greco-Roman world. When soldiers in Alexander the Great's campaigns in Iran and Afghanistan came across asafetida, also an umbellifer with a similar flavor, it quickly became part of Greek and Roman cookery. Asafetida fell out of use in Europe after the fall of the Roman empire, although it remains an important ingredient in modern Indian food. It is available in ethnic markets.

A key ingredient in most ancient cuisine is fermented fish brine made from salting fish for weeks or months and allowing natural bacterial action to degrade the flesh. Known primarily under the names *garos* (Greek) and *garum* or *liquamen* (Latin), the product is virtually identical to the Asian fish sauces *nuoc mam* and *nam pla*. Whether the Egyptians used fish brine is open to debate: Egyptians salted fish and thus could have had the brine as a by-product, but there is no archaeological or written evidence for its manufacture or use in pre-Classical Egypt. The Mesopotamians used a condiment called *siqqu*, which was a fermented brine made from either fish or locusts.

There is some confusion because Romans used two terms, *garum* and *liquamen*, to denote fish sauce. *Garum* is the older term, used in works dating from the Roman republic; *liquamen* appears in later works dating from the Roman empire, including Apicius. A British food historian has recently proposed an explanation for this change in language (see the text preceding Recipe 141). For the present, the term *garum* means simply fish sauce, and any good-quality Asian fish sauce makes a perfect substitute. *Garum* often took the place of salt in Roman cookery, much like soy sauce in Asian cookery. Although still made in minute quantities in Italy, *garum* is seldom seen in mainstream Italian cookery. Modern Italians, however, often flavor dishes with salted anchovies slowly dissolved in warm olive oil, a vestige of the Greco-Roman *garum*.

One other important category of ancient ingredients is fruit wines and syrups, usually made from grapes, but also made from carobs, figs, pomegranates, and dates. These fruits could be juiced and then the juices boiled down into syrups, used either as seasonings or as preservatives. Sometimes the juices would be fermented into wine before concentrating. Near Eastern cookery still makes use of syrups such as pomegranate molasses and dibs (syrups from carobs or dates), which are available in ethnic markets. The Italians still make *vin cotto* (a sweet and tart reduced wine) as a gourmet item.

Steps for Organizing Your Cooking and Kitchen Safety

1. Read each recipe thoroughly before starting to cook. Make sure you have all the ingredients and equipment needed, from knives, measuring spoons, and cooking pots to potholders for handling hot pans.
2. Many of the recipes call for beer or wine. De-alcoholized beer or wine may be used successfully in the recipes, but do not substitute "cooking wine" from the supermarket; it is expensive and of poor quality.
3. Wash your hands with soap and water before starting to cook; after handling any raw meats, fish, or poultry; or any time they seem dirty.
4. Place a damp paper towel underneath cutting boards to prevent them from slipping while you are cutting or chopping.
5. Immediately wash with hot water and soap knives, cutting boards, and any other surfaces that have come in contact with raw meats, fish, or poultry to prevent accidental bacterial cross-contamination.
6. Keep meats, fish, poultry, and any other perishable items refrigerated at all times, except when working with them.
7. Observe the recommended cooking temperatures for meats and poultry; they are specified to kill any bacteria that might be in the meat through thorough cooking. Instant-read thermometers confirm internal meat temperatures more accurately than estimated cooking times, which may vary depending on individual ovens.
8. Use only dry potholders to handle hot pans; damp ones create steam and can cause painful burns.
9. When you remove an item from the oven or stove top, make sure you have a landing space for the hot pan. Flag hot pans by placing

      a towel on the edge or through the handle; this is the professional kitchen warning for "hot pan, do not touch with bare hands."

10. When walking with a knife in the kitchen, keep the blade by your side with the tip pointing down; never run in the kitchen.

11. If oil spills on the floor, after mopping up the excess, sprinkle salt over any remaining slippery areas to provide secure footing.

The recipes are only suggested ways of putting together ancient foods. Have fun experimenting with different herbs and spices that might have been found in ancient pantries to create your own ancient-world recipes.

1

⚱ MESOPOTAMIA

Mesopotamia is a word invented by ancient Greek historians that means the land between two rivers. The rivers were the Tigris and the Euphrates, and Mesopotamia occupied the area roughly equivalent to modern-day Iraq, although Mesopotamia's fluctuating boundaries extended at various times to parts of modern-day Turkey, Iran, and the Levant. During the 7,000 years stretching from the time of the area's earliest agriculture to Mesopotamia's fall to the Persians in 539 B.C.E., Mesopotamia expanded and contracted as different peoples entered and exited the region. Mesopotamia was mostly a patchwork of smaller states, with Sumerians, Akkadians, Assyrians, and Babylonians dominating at different times. Groups such as the Elamites and the Hittites invaded from Iran and Anatolia and temporarily took up residence. Mesopotamia was attractive because its two great rivers provided irrigation and ready transportation for trade.

FOODSTUFFS AND AGRICULTURE

- Barley and emmer were the most important early grains; bread wheat, durum, and spelt appeared later in the period. Millet was used when these were unavailable. The grains were fermented into beer for universal consumption.
- Dates were the single most important fruit, especially in Lower Mesopotamia, and were an important source of calories. Apples, figs, grapes, and pomegranates were widely used where climate permitted, or were imported in dried or preserved form; other fruits

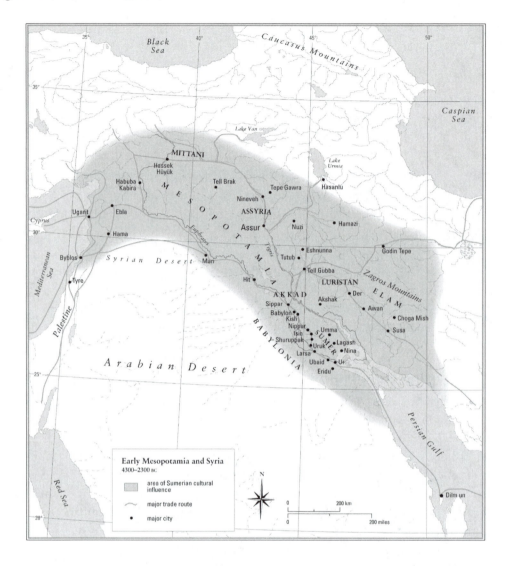

Early Mesopotamia and Syria
4300–2300 BC

area of Sumerian cultural influence

major trade route

• major city

used in smaller quantities were apricots, cherries, melons, mulberries, pears, plums, and quinces.

- The most widely consumed vegetables were onions, garlic, and leeks. Other vegetables included ancient forms of lettuces, cabbage, cucumbers, carrots, radishes, beets, turnips, lentils, chickpeas, broad beans, and peas.
- Sheep and goats were widely used for meat and dairy products, although milk was generally thought a lower-class beverage. Cattle, water buffalo, and pigs were raised where pasturage and water supply permitted. Game birds and gazelle were hunted, while ducks, geese, and quail were domesticated. More than 50 varieties of fish were eaten in fresh, salted, brined, pickled, dried, or smoked form. Locusts were considered a delicacy.

- Cooking fats primarily came from animals in the form of lard, suet, butter, and fish oils; scholars disagree about whether plant oils (sesame, linseed, and olive) were used for cooking in early times, although they were used as perfume bases, in medicine, for lighting, and for other technical applications. Plant oils probably became a regular part of the culinary pantry relatively late, in the second or first millennium B.C.E.
- Lower Mesopotamia was too hot to grow olives and grapes, but improvements in irrigation allowed cultivation in carefully tended gardens in Upper Mesopotamia. The ninth-century B.C.E. king Assurnasirpal claimed credit for introducing these plants as spoils from his war in the eastern Mediterranean. Before that, olive oil and wine were imported from the Levant, and additional wine came from vineyards in the Zagros. Wines were often flavored with honey, fruit syrups, or wood resins or diluted with brine.
- Seasonings included coriander, cress, cumin, dill, fennel, fenugreek, marjoram, mint, mustard, rue, and thyme. *Siqqu* was a briny condiment. Made from either salted fish or locusts, it may have been similar to Greco-Roman *garum*. Lexicons list many other seasonings that have not yet been identified.
- Beekeeping and honey came to Mesopotamia only in the first millennium B.C.E., although elites imported honey. Date syrup was a common sweetener.

Mesopotamia's geography and ancient climate ranged from pastoral wooded foothills and arable plains to steppe, desert, and low-lying marshes. It was divided into upper and lower regions, with different agricultural potential.

Upper Mesopotamia started in the areas around the foothills of the Taurus and Zagros mountains, forming the border with Anatolia and Iran. This northernmost fringe had good rainfall and moderate summers that supported wild cereals, fruit orchards, vegetables, vineyards, nuts, and grazing pasture. Although it offered the greatest natural agricultural diversity and a gateway to a range of crops, arable land was limited. Heading farther south, the lands became steppe, inhabited by nomads and small farming villages, with the earliest known agricultural settlements dating to about 7,000 B.C.E. In most years there was adequate rainfall to support agriculture, but the gravelly soil could not support extensive grain cultivation. Nonetheless, Upper Mesopotamia was defined by the area in which dry (that is, rainfall-dependent) agriculture usually could be practiced. This area reached down to the ancient city of Hit, north of modern Baghdad.

Lower Mesopotamia, the flatlands stretching south to the Persian Gulf, had a less hospitable climate and topography. These challenges required large-scale cooperation to make farming successful and, ironically, made inhospitable Lower Mesopotamia home to the earliest civilizations. By the fourth millennium B.C.E., Lower Mesopotamia had extremely hot summers and inadequate rainfall for dry agriculture. The soil, however, was fertile, owing to the wet silt deposited by the annual springtime overflowing of the twin rivers as they carried the melting winter snows from the Taurus and Zagros mountains to the Persian Gulf. Lower Mesopotamia's immense potential was tapped through irrigation. Canals and reservoirs for channeling and controlling the floods were dug, reaping huge agricultural surpluses with easy access to the gulf for trade. Cereal farming and maintaining the irrigation infrastructure were very labor intensive, but in good years the Sumerians reaped greater harvests than at any time in the area's history, with the possible exception of the medieval Abbasid caliphate. Cereal cultivation was not without risk: because the southern Mesopotamian climate was too hot to grow cereals in the summer, planting was delayed until the autumn for springtime harvest. The grains lay dormant through the winter (just like the winter wheat crops grown in America) and sprouted in the early spring, about the time when the Tigris and Euphrates flooded. In years with particularly high floodwaters in Lower Mesopotamia, the fields of ripening grains could be ruined. Storing grain against such disasters was a principal concern of early government.

To supplement the cereals, Sumerians developed shade gardens in which sun-tolerant towering date palms shielded the more delicate fruit trees and vegetables planted beneath. Cattle were expensive to raise because of lack of good pasture; sheep and goats, however, survived on the stubble after the grain harvests, and pigs thrived as scavengers in urban settings. Salt and freshwater fish lived in the canals and reservoirs, adding more diversity to the Mesopotamian diet. The wealth generated by collaborative action explains why Near Eastern civilization began at Sumer in the southernmost cities of Ur and Uruk in the late fourth millennium B.C.E., even though Upper Mesopotamia had earlier small settlements. The Akkadians succeeded the Sumerians under the leadership of Sargon, ca. 2350 B.C.E., who temporarily united most of Mesopotamia into an Akkadian empire. By the end of the third millennium B.C.E., the Babylonians emerged as the dominant culture within Lower and parts of Upper Mesopotamia; among the Babylonians' achievements were the Hanging Gardens, famous as one of the seven wonders of the ancient world.

This agricultural paradise did not last. Lower Mesopotamia suffered from poor drainage, and salts accumulated in the soil. By the second millennium, wheat yields had decreased, leading Lower Mesopotamians to rely more heavily on two saline-tolerant plants: barley became the staple grain, and date palms became a key source of calories (from the fruit sugars) and the nutrient iron. With the fertility of the land compromised (but not eliminated), the powerful centers of Mesopotamian civilization shifted northward, to the Upper Mesopotamian cities of Mari, Kalhu, and Nineveh, the last being the showplace of the Assyrians.

> *Some believe that the biblical Garden of Eden was in Mesopotamia.*

RECIPE SOURCES

Although Mesopotamia was a hodgepodge of ethnic groups, the written evidence indicates that the different peoples shared many food habits. The Sumerians invented cuneiform writing around 3100 B.C.E. The writing system spread to Mesopotamia's other groups to record their languages, and by about 1900 B.C.E., the Babylonians compiled a concordance with more than 800 food and drink terms in Sumerian and Akkadian (the language spoken by the Babylonians) using the common cuneiform script. One of the largest categories was for foods cooked in liquid. These are simply names without gastronomic detail, but the large number of culinary terms suggests that sophisticated cooking had spread throughout Mesopotamia's different groups.

Cooking equipment also evolved to allow more sophisticated cookery. The Sumerians in their prehistory developed stone ovens capable of baking loaves of bread. Fired brick ovens followed by about 2,500 B.C.E., some designed with flat areas that could hold stewing or frying pans, made from either clay or bronze, allowing the efficient use of fuel. Cooking was considered an art; Akkadians honored the person in charge of a kitchen with the title *mubannu,* or embellisher.

Very few recipes survive from Mesopotamia. The exceptions are 35 recipes incised on three clay tablets that form part of the Yale Babylonian Collection, now held at Yale University. These tablets, created ca. 1650 B.C.E., form the earliest known recipe collection, plus a few additional recipes written much later. Cuneiform is complex and requires years of study. Only selected government bureaucrats, priests, and merchants could read, and it is unlikely that Mesopotamian cooks could read. If cooks were illiterate, why were these recipes written? One theory ties these recipes to religion. Caring for the gods was an important government obligation, and food was offered daily by priestly bureaucrats acting on behalf of the king. The Yale recipes may document the formal "culinary liturgy" of these government-sponsored religious offerings, memorialized to ensure that the offerings were prepared in accordance with religious dictates.[1] Whether literate priests did the cooking for the gods or merely supervised the cooks, the written instructions standardized the process. This practice has parallels in Judaism, in which rabbis ritually slaughter animals or supervise others preparing kosher products.

The Yale tablets are damaged and contain words that scholars have been unable to translate. They are difficult guides because so many parts are missing. Nonetheless, they are the single best evidence of how dishes dating back more than 3,600 years might have been prepared, and several of the fragments have been adapted into modern recipes. These reconstructions are highly speculative, and most of the recipes presented in this chapter are invented or reconstructed from other literary and archaeological evidence. The present state of research tells little about the sauces, seasonings, and condiments used in Mesopotamian cookery.

CUISINE AND SOCIAL CLASS

- Urban elites ate four times daily: two main meals, one in the morning and one at twilight, with two smaller snacks; laborers, especially farmers out in the fields, tended to have only two meals.
- Kings hosted banquets at night, made more luxurious because of expensive torches and oil lamps illuminating the feast. Formal dinners opened and closed with hand washing. Guests were anointed with perfumed oil and incense was burned.
- Guests at formal banquets observed strict hierarchy and sat at specified places according to profession, ethnicity, and status at the court. It was an insult to accuse a guest of eating and drinking with the servants or to refuse to share food. Women sometimes attended banquets and sat on stools or in chairs; by the first millennium, wealthy men reclined.
- Elegant dishes, beakers, and cups were made from gold, silver, semiprecious stones, ostrich eggs, and other valuable materials for the elites; inexpensive but attractive clay vessels served everyone else.
- People used bread to scoop up many foods and probably ate directly with their fingers, although it is possible that wooden picks, which may have vanished without a trace in the archaeological record, were used to spear bits at table. Meats were carved into serving pieces before presentation. Knives and spoons, presumably made from metal, are listed in household inventories; given the small numbers, they were most likely kitchen tools or shared as dining utensils.
- Taverns where wine, beer, and food could be enjoyed existed throughout Mesopotamia's cities; women frequently were tavern keepers and responsible for brewing beer. Women also were responsible for cooking at home. According to a Sumerian proverb, "Since my wife is at the outdoor shrine and my mother is at the river, I shall die of hunger."[2]
- Palace and temple elites had access to meat from large animals more regularly than did urban workers and farmers; most Mesopotamians would have enjoyed beef at holidays and public celebrations when large numbers of cattle were slaughtered to feed large groups

Mesopotamian literature seldom describes mortal feasts. The gods' meals, however, were a popular literary theme, and Mesopotamians believed that the gods' needs paralleled human wants. Thus the gods' meals may be a model for elite mortal dining. The gods enjoyed four daily meals, large and small ones in the morning, and large and small ones again in the afternoon and evening. To meet this need, the palaces and temples collected taxes in the form of grain, animals, and other foodstuffs. Priests and priestesses offered the gods basins for washing and then presented the foods in richly decorated plates, bowls, and goblets set on movable trays. The priests withdrew, letting the gods eat behind linen curtains, a practice emulated by Babylonian kings. After an appropriate interval, the priests

Grain tributes offered to a Babylonian king, seated at right, ca. 2,000 B.C.E. Plaque of Ur-Nina.

removed the gods' meal and served the "leftovers" to members of the royal household. Unlike the gods of Egypt, Greece, and Rome, who "consumed" offerings through the smoke of burnt sacrifices, the Mesopotamian gods "ate" by looking at the offerings. The volume of religious offerings required was so large that foods were available for distribution among the many residents of the palace and temple complexes, and possibly to townspeople as alms.[3] The system was efficient and limited the need for private kitchens, with the risk of fire, in compact urban settings.

The gods' meal opened with beverages, porridges, and breads. Beer, wine, and water were offered at all meals; milk was offered only in the morning, to coincide with the traditional milking of the dairy animals. Roasted and braised meats (the latter often served with cereals), eggs, and possibly fish followed. Artistically presented fruits concluded the meal. Third- and second-millennium palace inventories list pork and fish deliveries, but mention of these foodstuffs drops off by about the twelfth century. This may reflect a shifting hierarchy in the Mesopotamian mind of foods worthy of the gods and their servants, as pork became associated with the lower classes, and fish became taboo for priests. Beef, sheep, and goats were preferred for the elites. The lack of vegetables in later inventories is a common problem in culinary history; rather than assume that vegetables were not eaten, this lack of evidence may simply indicate that vegetables were grown in kitchen gardens rather than purchased or acquired through levy.

A GARGANTUAN BANQUET

The Assyrian king Assurnasirpal held a banquet in 879 B.C.E. to commemorate the renovation of the ruined city of Kalhu into his new military capital. He hosted a 10-day eating and drinking festival; the foods consumed were recorded on a stela, an inscribed stone pillar, found during archaeological excavations in 1951. According to the inscription, Assurnasirpal fed and housed an astonishing 69,574 people. Some 47,074 were laborers who rebuilt the city; most were prisoners of war captured during Assurnasirpal's initial campaigns. Another 5,000 of the guests were dignitaries from the conquered territories; their presence contributed to his power and prestige. Sixteen thousand attendees were local inhabitants, and the remaining 1,500 were palace bureaucrats. If anyone doubted Assurnasirpal's dominance, the stela exalts Assurnasirpal as "the king who has made to submit those who were not subject to him, who has conquered all mankind."

Among the foods served were

- 1,000 barley-fed oxen;
- 200 oxen and 1,000 young cattle;
- 1,000 young sheep;
- 14,000 "common" sheep;
- 1,000 fattened sheep;
- 1,000 lambs;
- 500 each deer and gazelles;
- an impressive array of geese, fowls, pigeons, doves, small birds, and several varieties undecipherable from the original cuneiform;
- 10,000 eggs;
- 10,000 fish (no variety specified); and
- 10,000 locusts (served on skewers).[4]

BREADS AND GRAINS

Flat and leavened breads and porridges were a significant part of the diet; sweet and savory elements, such as dried fruits or onions, were often added. Sumerian and Akkadian glossaries distinguished different breads, cakes, flours, and grains, with more than 300 different varieties of breads documented in writings or evidenced through molds and pans for baking intricately shaped and decorated loaves. Bread could be baked at home, in neighborhood bakeries, or in palace and temple complexes to supply hundreds or thousands of loaves daily. Some texts suggest that the average urban dweller preferred homemade bread to purchased loaves. This is quite understandable in the case of unleavened flatbreads, which are most tender when eaten fresh from the oven or baking stone but quickly become tough.

All of the breads are denser than modern loaves, due to the relative lack of gluten in the barley and spelt flours. Also, the bran retained in whole-wheat flour interferes with gluten formation, resulting in heavier bread.

𒉿 1. WHOLE WHEAT FLAT BREAD 𒉿

The best city bread cannot match the pancake baked under the ashes.

From Poem of Erra[5]

Simple flat breads were baked on hot stones buried among the ashes of open fires, a practice that continues in nomadic and primitive cultures. The *Poem of Erra* exalts soldiers enduring the privations of battle; unleavened breads were especially important to soldiers on the move or to the poor, who might not have ovens. Cylinder seals show flat breads topped with grilled or roasted meat or fish, possible forerunners of shish kebabs and souvlaki sandwiches, and suggest the popularity of breads such as this.

You can approximate some of the feel of ash-baked breads by coating the breads in bran before baking them, although the bread will lack the smoky taste imparted by the ashes. You can brush off the "ashes" after baking. This recipe uses bread flour, but versions were undoubtedly made from emmer, spelt, or a combination of grains.

1 cup whole wheat flour
1 cup all-purpose flour
1 teaspoon salt
3/4 cup water, more or less
3/4 cup wheat bran

1. Combine the flours and salt in a bowl. Slowly stir in as much water as needed to moisten all the flour and make a dough. Turn the dough onto a work surface and knead until smooth and elastic, about 7–8 minutes. If the dough gets sticky, lightly dust the surface with additional flour and continue kneading.
2. Cover the dough with plastic wrap or a towel and set aside for at least 30 minutes, or as long as overnight, to relax the gluten.
3. Place a baking stone or iron griddle on the lowest rack of the oven. Preheat the oven to 450°F.
4. Divide the dough into six equal pieces and pat into disks. Sprinkle the work surface with the bran and lightly roll each disk with a rolling pin into 4-inch rounds on the bran. Some of the bran should stick to the dough.

5. Place two or three breads on the baking stone and close the oven. Bake for 4 minutes. Turn the dough with tongs and bake an additional 3 minutes. Hold the loaves in a warm spot wrapped in a towel or foil while you bake the remaining loaves. Serve immediately.

𐎜 2. SPELT BREAD 𐎜

They will take 486 liters of barley flour and 162 liters of spelt flour, from the mixture of which the cooks will prepare and bake 243 epu.
From third-century B.C.E. tablet from the temple at Uruk[6]

An *epu* was a round loaf used in religious offerings and as part of the gods' meals. This dough is baked in a cake pan to imitate some of the many bread molds found in temples and palaces. The proportion of barley to spelt flour is 3:1 and results in a dense, cakelike loaf because of the low protein content of the grains. Each loaf would have had 2 liters (approximately 8 cups) barley flour and 2/3 liter (approximately 2 and 2/3 cups) spelt flour. The following recipe has been divided in half to make the quantities easier to work with, as the dough is quite tough.

Uruk is in Lower Mesopotamia: hence the preponderance of barley at this late date. Even though foreigners dominated Mesopotamia when this recipe was written, it likely represents traditional practice because it was used as a religious offering.

4 cups barley flour
1 1/3 cup spelt flour, plus more as needed
1 tablespoon instant yeast
2 teaspoons salt
2 1/4 cups water, more or less
1 tablespoon vegetable oil

1. Combine the barley and spelt flours, the yeast, and the salt in a large bowl. Slowly pour in as much water as needed, stirring with a wooden spoon, to moisten the flours. Turn the dough out onto a clean board and knead for 10 minutes. This dough will not be very smooth or elastic.
2. Oil the inside of an 8-inch round cake pan and dust lightly with spelt flour. Shape the dough into a ball and place in the cake pan (it will not fill the pan completely). Cover loosely with plastic and let rise at room temperature for 45 minutes to an hour, or leave overnight in the refrigerator.
3. Preheat the oven to 400°F. If refrigerated, let dough come to room temperature. Gently slash an X 1/4 inch deep into the top of the dough with a paring knife. Bake for 45–50 minutes or until the bread sounds hollow when tapped on the bottom. Cool on a rack.

ᛦ 3. SCALLION BREAD ᛦ

Fine flour is appropriate for women and the palace.

Sumerian proverb[7]

Fine flour would have had a low extraction rate; the generous proportion of modern white flour to whole wheat in this recipe approximates this. Although yeasted, this dough will be baked as flattened loaves, a common practice throughout the Near East. A baking stone or griddle in the oven will approximate a tannur, a heat-retaining cylindrical clay oven.

2 tablespoons butter
3/4 cup thinly sliced scallions, white and light green parts only
1 teaspoon salt
2 1/2 cups all-purpose flour
1/2 cup whole wheat flour, plus more for baking
1/2 tablespoon instant yeast
1 1/4 cup lukewarm water, more or less
Vegetable oil as needed
Stone-ground flour for dusting the baking stone

1. Melt the butter in a small sauté pan over medium heat and add the scallions. Cook gently until soft, and season with the salt.
2. Mix the flours and yeast in a large bowl. Stir in the scallions. Slowly add as much water as needed to moisten the flours, stirring with a spoon.
3. Remove the dough from the bowl and knead until smooth and elastic, about 7–8 minutes. Lightly oil a clean bowl, place the dough in it, and cover with plastic wrap. Let rise until doubled, about 1 hour.
4. Meanwhile, place a griddle or a baking stone on the bottom rack of an oven and preheat to 425°F.
5. Deflate the dough and divide it into 4 pieces. Flour the work surface and roll each piece into oblongs about 10 inches long and 5 inches wide. Cover with a towel and let rise until doubled, about 30 minutes.
6. Scatter some stone-ground flour on the hot baking stone to prevent the bread from sticking. Working in batches if necessary, transfer the loaves to the stone using a broad-bladed spatula. Bake for 10 minutes, or until golden brown on the bottom. The top should remain soft.

The Akkadian word for a clay oven is tinuru; *other languages have borrowed the root so that today tannurs and tandoori ovens are found throughout the Near East, Central Asia, and India.*

⚜ *4. EZEKIEL'S MULTIGRAIN FLAT BREAD* ⚜

And you take wheat and barley, beans and lentils, millet and spelt, and put them into a single vessel, and make bread of them.

Ezekiel 4:9

This mixture of grains makes a coarse bread. According to the Old Testament's Book of Ezekiel, the disobedient Israelites were punished by having only one meal a day comprised of water and a small measure of this bread, baked on stones over dung fuel. Foods of this sort would have been common in times of famine, when the superior grains of wheat and barley were in short supply and needed to be stretched with less desirable pulses and grains. Ezekiel lived in the sixth century, shortly before the Persians conquered Babylonia. War-torn Babylonians probably subsisted on a similar bread that could cook quickly.

1 cup whole wheat flour
1/2 cup barley flour
1/2 cup chickpea flour
1/4 cup millet, soaked in 1 cup water overnight and drained
1/4 cup lentil flour
1/2 cup spelt flour
1/4 cup vegetable oil or melted butter
1 tablespoon salt
1 cup water, or more as needed
4 teaspoons vegetable oil

1. Combine all of the ingredients except the 4 teaspoons vegetable oil in a large bowl and stir thoroughly with a wooden spoon to make a dough. Knead the dough on a clean surface for 10 minutes, or until it holds together as a smooth mass. Divide the dough into 8 pieces and shape into balls. Cover with a clean towel and let rest for 30 minutes.
2. Pat each ball into a disk about 5 inches in diameter. Heat a griddle or frying pan on top of the stove until hot. Rub each disk with 1/2 teaspoon oil and cook about 3 minutes on the first side, reducing the heat if the disks start to scorch. Turn with broad spatula and continue cooking about 2 minutes. Serve hot.

⚜ 5. PAPPASU *(BARLEY GROATS)* ⚜

This very simple preparation could have been a staple food for those low on the socioeconomic scale, but it was not limited to the poor. Early second millennium records from the palace at Mari show rich Mesopotamians enjoying barley groats as a side dish with stews to absorb the flavorful sauces, much like rice or pasta, or eating them on their own with cream and date syrup. The poor, who could not afford the embellishments, might add flavor with raw onions, wild herbs and vegetables, or *smen* (Recipe 10), which is clarified butter. This type of dish remained popular in Mesopotamia for centuries after its surrender to foreign forces. Palestinian Jews mocked Babylonian Jews for eating "bread with bread," that is, for dipping bread into porridges such as this.

1 cup barley groats
2 quart waters
Seasonings as desired, such as *Smen* (Recipe 10), Cress Pesto (Recipe 25), *Za'tar* (Recipe 29), Applesauce (Recipe 30), or Elamite Pottage (Recipe 14, if serving the well-to-do).

1. Rinse the barley thoroughly under cold running water for 2 minutes to remove the excess starch. Place the barley in a 3-quart saucepan and cover with the water. Bring to a boil and cook for 45 minutes, or until tender and the grains begin to burst. Drain.
2. Season the groats with salt and any of the suggested flavorings according to whether you are making a dish for rich or poor people.

𒀭 6. MUN-DU *(EMMER GROATS)* 𒀭

Early second millennium texts from Girsu in Lower Mesopotamia describe emmer groats as a breakfast offering to the gods. Presumably mortals also would have breakfasted on this, flavoring the *mun-du* much like *pappasu*.

Whole-grain emmer can occasionally be found in markets specializing in Italian foods under the name *farro*, but much of what is imported into the United States as *farro* is actually spelt berries. If you find true *farro*, it will take several hours to cook, whereas spelt will cook in about 30–45 minutes. Wheat berries, the whole grain of bread wheat, can be substituted and will cook like spelt.

1 cup *farro* or wheat berries
1 quart water
1 teaspoon salt

Place the grain in a mortar and pound with a pestle to break it up into coarse groats. Place in a saucepan with the water and salt and bring to a boil. Cook until tender; cooking time will depend on the grain used. Drain. Season according to economic class. Follow the seasoning suggestions for *pappasu*.

⚚ 7. SASQU *(PORRIDGE WITH DATES)* ⚚

Sasqu is a creamy porridge described in the palace records at Mari. It could be made from ground emmer or barley cooked to a soupy consistency with milk, oil, or water. Dates were added on ritual occasions for elite tables. It is a smoother version of *pappasu* (Recipe 5) and *mun-du* (Recipe 6), showing the diversity among basic grain preparations.

2 cups milk or water
3/4 cup barley flour
Salt and date syrup to taste
3/4 cup chopped dates

1. Place the barley flour in a saucepan. Slowly whisk in the milk, stirring constantly. Bring to a boil, reduce the heat, and cook for 5 minutes.
2. Season with salt and date syrup. Turn into serving cups and scatter with the chopped dates.

Biscuits

A liturgical text from the temple at Uruk tells of an offering of "1,200 biscuits fried in oil," along with cakes of dates.

The term *biscuit* has conflicting culinary meanings: biscuits might mean tender, not too sweet little cakes or a twice-cooked dough. Two versions of cakes fried in oil are offered to illustrate these different meanings. The first (Recipe 8) is for pan-fried cakes made tender with milk. The second (Recipe 9) cooks the dough twice, first by boiling and then by deep-frying. The Yale recipes show multiple cooking processes in a single recipe, so perhaps biscuit should be interpreted in this double-cooking sense. Mesopotamians had copper and bronze kettles and clay pans that all could have withstood the heat of frying, although clay was more vulnerable to high heat.

Serve either version with Date Cakes (Recipe 32). *Smen* (Recipe 10) was often called oil in texts, so it could have been the frying medium. Buttermilk has a tangy flavor and thicker texture that may approximate ancient fermented milk products.

⚚ 8. TENDER CAKE BISCUITS ⚚

1/2 cup whole wheat flour, plus additional for shaping the biscuits
1 1/2 cups all-purpose flour
6 tablespoons butter, cut in 1/2-inch cubes
10 tablespoons milk or buttermilk, or more if needed
3/4 cup vegetable oil or *smen*, as need, for pan-frying the biscuits

1. Place the flours and butter in a bowl, and with your fingers, pinch the butter to break it up into bits with flour. The mixture should have the texture of coarse meal. Stir in the milk. Turn the dough out and knead briefly three or four times, just until the dough holds together.
2. Turn the dough out onto a lightly floured surface and pat into a square about 1/2 inch thick. Cut the square into 3 strips. Cut each strip in half crosswise and then cut each half on the diagonal to form 4 triangular shapes.
3. Heat half of the fat in a frying pan over medium heat. Add the biscuits, reduce the heat to medium-low, and cook the biscuits slowly, until they are golden brown, about 4–5 minutes. Turn the biscuits with a broad spatula and continue cooking another 3–4 minutes, adding more fat to the pan as needed. Serve warm.

⚜ 9. TWICE-COOKED FRIED BISCUITS ⚜

1 cup milk
4 tablespoons butter
1 cup all-purpose flour
1/2 teaspoon ground coriander
Generous pinch salt
3 eggs
2 cups melted lard or vegetable oil for frying

1. Place the milk and butter in a saucepan and bring to a boil. Remove from the heat and stir in the flour, coriander, and salt. Return to the heat and cook over low heat, stirring constantly, for 1 minute. Remove from the heat and cool to lukewarm.
2. Beat the eggs together and slowly stir into the cooled dough. The dough will separate at first but will come together with vigorous stirring.
3. Using a deep-fat or candy thermometer, heat the oil to 350°F in a deep saucepan. The oil should come no more than halfway up the sides of the pan to avoid bubbling over when you add the dough. Scoop generous tablespoons of batter into the oil and cook until golden brown, about 2–3 minutes, turning to cook all sides. Remove and drain on absorbent toweling.

Dairy

Sheep, goats, and cows all were used as dairy and meat-giving animals. Sheep's and goats' milk products were more common (and continue to be so today) because the Near Eastern climate favored these animals, although the first written evidence of sheep's cheeses comes late, after the Persians controlled Mesopotamia.

⚕ 10. SMEN *(CLARIFIED BUTTER)* ⚕

Smen is usually made from sheep's milk butter. When the butter is melted, the milk proteins fall to the bottom, leaving a layer of pure butterfat. Removing the milk proteins made the fat less perishable in hot climates and was another way of preserving milk and cream, albeit in an altered form. Clarifying butter is simple but results in a loss of about 20 percent of the volume of the butter. Accounts from Ur list the amount of butter that could be made from a given measure of cream; the yields make it clear that the final product was *smen*.

2 sticks (16 tablespoons) butter

Melt the butter in a small saucepan. It will separate into three layers: froth on the top, a thick layer of yellow butterfat (*smen*), and some whitish milk solids that will fall to the bottom. Carefully spoon off the froth and discard. Simmer gently until the milk solids turn nutty brown; this will given the *smen* made from cow's milk a richer flavor. Spoon out the *smen* and reserve, leaving the milk solids in the pan. Use to season groats, enrich breads, or drizzle over fish, meat, or vegetables. The *smen* can be stored at room temperature for several weeks.

⚕ 11. YOGURT ⚕

In the warm Near Eastern climate, fresh milk sours within hours. It could be preserved for several days by adding a controlled amount of the bacteria *bulgaris*, which thickened the milk into yogurt. The yogurt should last, refrigerated, one week and can be used to start a fresh batch.

1 quart milk (sheep's or goat's is preferred, but cow's milk will do)
2 tablespoons fresh, plain yogurt with live cultures (the container will indicate)

1. Bring the milk to a simmer in a large saucepan and cook gently for 2 minutes. Remove from the heat and allow the milk to cool to lukewarm. (**Important:** An instant-read thermometer should register between 105°F and 110°F.)
2. While the milk is cooling, put the yogurt in a large bowl and beat it with a whisk or fork to liquefy. Add the warm milk slowly, beating thoroughly to mix. Cover the bowl tightly with plastic wrap and wrap in cloth towels. Leave undisturbed in a warm spot for 12 hours or overnight; the milk should thicken and have a

delicate tang. The longer the milk is cultured, the sourer it will become. Transfer to a clean container and refrigerate.

⚚ 12. MUSTARD CHEESE ⚚

A Sumerian myth listing the foods served at the marriage feast of the goddess Sud to the god Enlil included "mustard-flavored cheeses."[8] There is some debate as to whether the word mustard referred to the seeds or to the green leaves from mustard plants, which you could purée in a mortar and pestle with a bit of oil to flavor the cheese instead.

Rennet is an enzyme found in calves' stomachs that helps them digest milk. Rennet coagulates milk into curds and whey, a first step in cheese making. Ancient nomads are thought to have invented cheese by carrying milk in pouches made of animal stomachs, selected because they were watertight. Most rennet available today is processed from vegetables, but it works just as well. You will need an instant-read thermometer to check the temperature of the milk.

1 gallon whole milk
4 tablespoons yogurt, preferably homemade (Recipe 11)
1 tablet rennet
1/2 cup water
2 tablespoons coarse salt
2 tablespoons prepared mustard (Recipe 28) or mustard powder

1. Combine the milk and yogurt and let sit overnight at cool room temperature.
2. Dissolve the rennet in the 1/2 cup water. Place the milk in a high-sided container in a saucepan of water to form a water bath. The water should come halfway up the side of the milk container. Heat the water bath until the milk reaches 86°F–90°F. Stir in the dissolved rennet and hold at that temperature for 5 minutes. Remove the milk from the water bath, cover, and let sit for 1 hour.
3. Break up the curd with a whisk. Add half of the salt and all of the mustard. Return the container to the water bath and heat to 102°F; hold at that temperature for 30 minutes, stirring periodically. Remove and cover for 1 hour.
4. Line a colander with four layers of moistened cheesecloth and rest over a bowl to catch the whey. Pour the curds and whey into the colander. Gather up the cheesecloth to cover the curds and press with a weight overnight to force out moisture.

5. Cut the curd into chunks and place into containers that have been rinsed with boiling water and allowed to air-dry. Dissolve the remaining salt in the whey and pour over cheese. The cheese can be refrigerated for several months to age or can be eaten immediately.

⚱ 13. YOGURT SOUP ⚱

Traditional Near Eastern cookery preserves surplus milk by air-drying milk or yogurt mixed with grain or legumes into small pellets that can easily be reconstituted into a portable and nourishing soup. Bulgur, produced from steamed, dried, and coarsely ground wheat berries, is often used, although ground chickpeas can also be used. Scholars have been unable to translate all of the terms found in the Mesopotamian culinary lists, but some speculate that hidden in the untranslated terms is the name for yogurt soup, as the technique is ancient.

1 cup yogurt
1 1/4 cups fine bulgur
2 tablespoons *smen* or butter
1 onion, chopped
4 cloves garlic, chopped
4 cups beef broth or water
1/2 teaspoon ground cumin, or more to taste
1 cup cooked chickpeas
Salt to taste

1. Preheat the oven to 200°F. Combine the yogurt and bulgur to moisten the grain thoroughly. Spread in a thin layer on a baking pan and place in the oven to dehydrate, about 90 minutes. When cool enough to handle, crumble the dried mixture and set aside.
2. Melt the butter, add the onion, and gently cook to soften, about 2–3 minutes. Add the garlic and cook another minute. Stir in the beef broth or water, cumin, and chickpeas. Bring to a boil and add the crumbled bulgur mix. Simmer until lightly thickened and season with salt.

MEAT, POULTRY, AND FISH

Sheep and goats, called small cattle, were more accessible to the middle classes and were sold in urban markets. Meat from beef, called large cattle, tended to be found in the temples and palaces, often as tribute from wealthy landowners or as products of the government's extensive landholdings outside city walls. Pigs were found in urban environments, as they needed water and could subsist on refuse. They became increasingly associated with the middle and poorer classes.

Fatty meats were considered appropriate for the elites, whereas leaner meats were considered inferior. The fat referred to in many of the recipes may be the fat from a special broad-tailed sheep that remained popular in the Near East until recent times. A Sumerian proverb stated: "Meat with fat is too good! Meat with suet is too good! What shall we give to the slave-girl to eat? Let her eat the ham of the pig!"[9]

⚚ 14. ELAMITE POTTAGE ⚚

Meat is used. Prepare water; add fat; dill; suhutinnu; coriander; leek and garlic, bound with blood; a corresponding amount of kisimmu; and more garlic. The original name of this dish is zukanda.[10]

This recipe is from the Yale Babylonian Collection. The title shows that Babylonians identified this dish originally with a distinct ethnic group but that it was assimilated into Mesopotamian cuisine.

A pottage is a dish cooked with liquid that forms part of the final dish; the consistency can range from thick porridges to medium-bodied stews to thin broths. This cookbook uses the generic term pottage to name recipes from the Yale tablets that cook with liquid, but scholars offer competing translations for these recipes, naming them broths, stews, or sauces. All that is known for certain is that the dishes involve liquid, and a definitive translation would help determine how to prepare the dish. If a broth, the ingredients would be strained out after cooking; the flavorful liquid would be part of the liquid first course served to the elites, with the cooked solids either forming part of the second course (the meat course) or perhaps given to the kitchen staff. If a stew, everything would be served together. If a sauce, the flavoring ingredients could be cooked together, with or without the meat, and then used to garnish the meat. This recipe is given as a braise that is then reduced to a sauce, but the final thickness of the liquid is by no means certain. You could strain out the ingredients to make a broth or cut the meat into chunks to make a stew.

Suhutinnu and *kisimmu* have yet to be translated, so other seasonings have been substituted. The fat called for may have been from the fat-tailed sheep, a popular fat in the Near East. Butter is substituted. The recipe adopts the two-step cooking of the meat often found in the Yale recipes.

  2 tablespoons butter
  1 pound beef or lamb shoulder, in one piece
  4 tablespoons butter
  2 sprigs dill
  1 tablespoon ground coriander

1/2 teaspoon ground fenugreek
1/2 teaspoon dried thyme
2 leeks, cleaned and white and green parts cut into 1-inch rings
6 cloves of garlic, crushed
1 tablespoon coarse salt

1. Melt 2 tablespoons of butter over medium heat in a frying pan and brown the meat on all sides.
2. Place the meat and the rest of the ingredients in a large saucepan and cover with cold water by 1 inch. Bring to a boil; reduce the heat to a simmer and cook gently for 2 hours.
3. Remove the meat from the pan and set aside. Remove the leeks and garlic. Mash the garlic to a paste in a mortar and pestle. Return the leeks and garlic paste to the saucepan and boil to reduce the liquid by half.
4. Slice the meat into bite-sized pieces and pour the sauce over it.

♈ 15. ROASTED LAMB OR KID ♈

Let the gods eat roasted meat, roasted meat, roasted meat. . . . After preparing a serving platter made of gold, place on it pieces of roasted meat.[11]

Roasted meats could take many forms, from whole carcasses affixed to massive spits to more manageable legs or shoulders, to small bits of boneless meat skewered and held over a flame. The large joints would be carved into small serving pieces before they were presented to the diners. Absent a large outdoor space to rig up a spit over an open fire, it is difficult to duplicate the smoky roasts of antiquity.

How to season the meat is another question; the texts are silent about what should be added, although well-seasoned meat was preferred. A Sumerian proverb laments the plight of a poor, dead man: "When he had meat, he did not have seasoning, and when he had seasoning, he did not have meat."[12]

1 butt-end leg of lamb, about 3 pounds, or 1 leg of kid
4 cloves of garlic, finely chopped
2 scallions, dark green tops removed, finely chopped
1 tablespoon ground cumin
2 tablespoons ground coriander
1 tablespoon ground fennel
1 teaspoon salt
2 tablespoons vegetable oil

1. Preheat the oven to 450°F, or use an outdoor rotisserie. With a paring knife, make 40 small slits in the lamb, about 1/2 inch deep and 1 inch long.

2. Combine the garlic, scallions, spices, and salt. Stuff a bit of this seasoning mix in each of the slits. Rub the outside of the lamb with the oil.

3. Place the lamb on a rack or attach it to a spit. Roast the lamb for about 1 hour (for medium-rare meat the internal temperature should register 135°F on a meat or instant-read thermometer), or until the lamb is cooked to the preferred doneness. Let rest 15 minutes before carving into small pieces that can be eaten with the fingers.

𝄐 16. BRAISED AND ROASTED DUCK WITH LEEKS, MINT, AND VINEGAR 𝄐

This reconstructed recipe merges two recipes from the Yale tablets, neither of which is complete enough on its own to be cookable. The language quoted below is from one of the recipe fragments and gives a sense of the complexity of Mesopotamian cooking. The overall gist seems to be a stew, with pastry-wrapped turnovers. The special instruction that the broth can be served separately from the meat shows that broths could be used independently in Mesopotamian cookery. The recipe's grammar alternates between first and second person; perhaps it records a formal ritual, with two cooks having assigned roles. Scholars have been unable to translate the ingredients *amursanu, samidu, andahsu, kisimmu,* and *baru.*

To prepare amursanu-pigeon in broth, after slaughtering the pigeon, you heat some water and pluck the bird. Once plucked, you wash it with cold water. I skin its neck and you cut out the ribs, I open its underbelly and remove the gizzards and pluck [the lungs, heart, and esophagus]; I wash the body and you soak it in cold water. Then I slit and peel the membrane from the gizzard; I

Banquet scene, based on an 8th century B.C.E. Assyrian relief. The men are drinking from rhyta, cups terminating in animal or human portraits. Illustration © The Israel Museum, by Pnina Arad based on G. Lerer-Jacobson and Z. Simon, *Bameh haym shatu (What did they drink from?).* An Exhibition of Drinking Vessels from the Ancient World. *Haaretz Museum, Tel Aviv, 1983, fig. 20.*

slit and chop the intestines.

When I am ready to prepare the broth, you place the gizzard and pluck into a kettle, with the intestine, and the head, as well as a piece of mutton (and you place everything on the fire). After removing the meat from the fire, you wash it well in cold water, and I wipe off the skin. I sprinkle the meat with salt and I assemble all ingredients in the pot.

I prepare water; I add a piece of fat after removing the gristle. I pour in vinegar to taste. You mash together samidu, leek, and garlic with onion; you also add water if necessary. When these are cooked, mash together some leek, garlic, andahsu, and kisimmu; if there is no kisimmu, you mash baru and add it.

After removing the amursanu-pigeon from the pot . . . roast the legs at high heat; I wrap them in dough, and I place the amursanu-pigeon filets on the dish. When it is all cooked, I remove the pot from the fire, and before the broth cools, you rub the meat with garlic, add greens and vinegar. The broth may be eaten at a later time. It is ready to serve.[13]

For the stew:

2 tablespoons butter
1 leek, dark green leaves removed, cut in half, rinsed, and cut crosswise
    into 1/4-inch half moons
6 cloves garlic, minced
1 teaspoon ground coriander
1/2 teaspoon ground fennel
1 duck cut as follows: 2 drumsticks, 2 thighs, 2 wings (last joint
    removed), skin removed from the breast, the breast cut in half,
    and each half cut into thirds
Salt to taste
1 quart veal, beef, or chicken broth
1/4 cup wine vinegar
2 tablespoons raisins
1 sprig mint
1 clove garlic, cut in half

For the turnover dough:

1 cup barley flour
1 cup stone-ground whole wheat flour
6 tablespoons cold butter, cut into small cubes
5/8 cup beer, or more as needed

For the final garnish:

2 bunches arugula, cleaned, dried, and coarsely chopped

1. Melt the 2 tablespoons butter in stewing pan over low heat. Cook the leeks until soft and translucent, about 3 minutes; add the minced garlic and cook for 1 minute. Add the spices and cook for 1 minute. Season the duck with salt and add to the pan. Pour in the broth, vinegar, raisins, and mint. Bring to a boil, cover, reduce the heat, and let simmer gently until tender, about 1 1/2 hours.

2. Meanwhile, make the turnover dough: Toss the flours with the butter in a bowl. Pinch the mixture until it resembles a fine meal. Stir in just enough beer to make a firm but malleable dough. Transfer to a bowl and cover with a clean towel or plastic wrap and let rest while the bird braises.

3. When the duck is tender, remove the meat from the pot. Raise the heat and boil the liquid rapidly for 10 minutes to reduce slightly.

4. Meanwhile, preheat the oven to 400°F. Pat the legs, thighs, and wings dry. Divide the dough into 6 pieces and roll each piece out about twice as long and wide as each leg, thigh, and wing. Wrap legs, thighs, and wings in the dough, pinching the edges together to form turnovers. Bake the turnovers for 20 minutes, or until lightly browned.

5. While the turnovers are baking, rub the breast meat with the cut garlic. Return all of the duck pieces to the pot and simmer gently to warm through. Remove the mint sprig from the broth and stir in the arugula to wilt. Adjust the seasonings, adding more vinegar or salt as needed. Serve one turnover and one piece of breast with broth.

⚚ 17. LAMB TARTAR (KIBBEH NAYÉ) ⚚

Modern Syrians and Lebanese consider *kibbeh nayé* a national treasure. Raw meats were eaten in ancient times but were considered uncivilized by the Sumerians, who mocked Bedouin nomads, claiming that the Bedouin ate only raw food.

Properly butchered, flesh from a healthy animal is sterile; contamination occurs only when butchering has been poorly done or is performed on a sick animal. Large meat-processing plants may accidentally nick the intestines during butchering, unknowingly introducing *e. coli* and other bacteria. The problem is compounded in plants producing ground meats, where grinding equipment may not be thoroughly cleaned between batches. The best way to enjoy this tasty dish is to buy whole chunks of meat from a good butcher and grind or finely chop the meat yourself.

1 cup bulgur, medium grain preferred
1 cup finely minced onion
1 pound lamb meat, surface fat removed, thoroughly chilled

Salt to taste
2 tablespoons vegetable oil
3 tablespoons chopped mint
Lettuce leaves for serving

1. Bring 1 cup of water to a boil. Place the bulgur in a mixing bowl and add just enough boiling water to cover the wheat. Let sit for 10 minutes to absorb the liquid. Drain off any excess liquid and fluff the wheat with a fork. Stir in the minced onion.
2. Grind the meat in a meat grinder or mince finely with a knife. The meat will be easier to chop if it is very cold.
3. Combine the meat with the bulgur mixture. Season with salt, oil, and chopped mint. Mound on lettuce leaves and serve immediately. Leftovers can be cooked into meatballs the following day.

⑆ 18. GRILLED FRESH FISH ⑆

Fish played an important role in the Near Eastern diet. A Sumerian natural history dating to ca. 2000 B.C.E. catalogues many different species of freshwater and saltwater fish. Saltwater fish could be caught in the Persian Gulf, while freshwater fish were caught in rivers or were cultivated in reservoirs that fed the canals used for transportation and irrigation. The palace archives at Mari, ca. 1700 B.C.E., record: "Received: 180 small *kamaru* fish for the meal of the king and his people."[14] After the twelfth century B.C.E., the mention of fish drops off in the texts, and it is unclear whether fish's popularity declined or simply whether the focus of record keeping changed.

> *A Sumerian proverb describing an indulged wife concludes: "Let my mate remove the bones from the fish for me."*[15]

1 small whole fish, such as sea bream or bass, about 1 pound, gutted and cleaned
1 tablespoon vegetable oil
Salt to taste

1. Preheat a grill pan to smoking hot.
2. Rub the outside of the fish with the oil and season with salt. Place the fish on the grill and cook for 6–8 minutes. Turn with a large spatula and finish cooking, another 5–6 minutes. Serve with any of the condiments.

VEGETABLES

There are few ancient descriptions of how vegetables were prepared. The Yale tablets document stewed vegetables, usually as part of a meat dish, but vegetables, especially those in the onion family, were also eaten raw. Raw foods saved fuel, a boon for the poor, but also were associated with uncivilized people.[16]

𐎛 19. ROASTED ONIONS 𐎛

Onions might have been cooked in the ashes of a fire, along with flat breads.

2 large onions, peeled and cut into eight wedges
1 1/2 tablespoons vegetable oil
1/2 teaspoon salt
1/2 teaspoon coriander
1/2 teaspoon cumin

Preheat the oven to 350°F. Toss all the ingredients together in a bowl, coating the onions evenly. Transfer to a roasting pan and bake for 30 minutes, or until onions are tender.

𐎛 20. GARDEN TURNIPS POTTAGE 𐎛

Meat is not used. Prepare liquid; add fat; [ ]; onion, arugula; coriander, and cake crumbs (?), bound with blood.[17]

This recipe is from the Yale Babylonian Collection. The recipe omits turnips from its procedures, but the use of turnips should be inferred from the title. The ancients would likely have used both the turnip greens and the turnip bulbs, as the bulbs would have been much smaller and thinner than contemporary turnips.

Blood is a traditional thickener for sauces and stews and is still used to make sausages in many places. When gently heated, the proteins in the blood coagulate into a thick, rich sauce. Fresh blood can be difficult to obtain, although there is sometimes a bit of blood in packages of frozen meats or chicken livers. The basic recipe omits the blood, but if you want to try using blood to thicken the broth, you can follow the variation below. Fatback is solid fat that runs along the backbone of pigs; it is very white and easy to find in large supermarkets.

1 1/2 pounds turnips, with greens, if available
2 cups water
1/4 cup fatback, diced, or 1/4 cup (1/2 stick) butter
1 onion, chopped
1 bunch arugula, cleaned and chopped
1/4 cup chopped fresh coriander
2 tablespoons bread crumbs

Salt to taste

1. Peel and coarsely grate the turnip bulbs. Wash the turnip greens and coarsely chop.
2. Place the water and fat in a saucepan and bring to a boil. Add the turnips, turnip greens, and onion and cook until tender, about 10 minutes.
3. Add the remaining ingredients and stir to incorporate.

Variation: 1/4 cup animal blood, any type, plus 1 cup beef stock

This variation can be done once the recipe is completed through step 2. To prevent the blood from curdling when added to the hot liquid, you need to warm it gently beforehand, a process called tempering. Place the blood in a bowl. Bring the beef broth to a boil and slowly stir the broth into the blood, constantly whisking the mixture rapidly. The mixture will thicken noticeably. Add the warmed blood-broth mixture back to the turnip mixture and stir in the arugula, coriander, and breadcrumbs. Serve.

⚓ 21. PEA SOUP ⚓

Dried peas, along with other pulses, could be stored for the lean season when there were no fresh crops. This recipe incorporates *siqqu*, Mesopotamia's approximate equivalent of *garum*, to flavor the thick soup. Given that the exact nature of *siqqu* is unknown, you can use an Asian fish sauce or substitute soy sauce. Mesopotamians salted meat to preserve it.[18] Bits of salt meat have been added for flavor, much like a Western split pea soup, on the assumption that Mesopotamians also wanted to jazz up bland pulses.

Pea soup is mentioned in a text on the interpretation of dreams; the text is damaged, so we do not know what dreaming of pea soup meant.[19]

    1 onion, chopped
    1 1/2 tablespoons vegetable oil
    1 tablespoon *siqqu* (fish sauce), or more to taste
    1 1/2 cups dried split peas
    2 quarts water
    1/2 pound ham, cut in small dice (optional)

Sweat the onion in the vegetable oil in a saucepan until soft. Add the *siqqu*, peas, and water. Bring to a boil. Cook for 30 minutes, periodically skimming the foam that rises to the top. Add the ham, if desired, and continue cooking until the peas break down and create a thick soup.

⚓ 22. EGGPLANT PURÉE ⚓

"Ten homers of eggplant" was listed on the stela of Assurnasirpal, the ceremonial pillar describing the feast in his honor. A homer equaled approximately 100 gallons, but we have no clue as to how this vegetable was prepared.

A popular Middle Eastern way of preparing eggplants is to roast them whole in the fire's embers (or in an oven) until quite soft. The pulp is then scraped out and seasoned with tahini, a sesame paste. Modern versions flavor the purée with olive oil and lemon, ingredients that are anachronistic to early Mesopotamia, in addition to the sesame paste.

2 large eggplants, at least 1 pound each
3 cloves garlic, finely minced
1/4 cup tahini, diluted with 1–2 tablespoons water
1 teaspoon salt, or to taste
2 tablespoons vegetable oil
1 1/2 teaspoons ground sumac

1. Preheat the oven to 350°F. Prick each eggplant with a fork about a dozen times to allow steam to escape when roasting. Place the eggplants in a baking dish and roast, turning every 15 minutes, until the eggplants collapse and are thoroughly cooked. Depending on size, this may take 45 minutes to an hour.
2. Remove the eggplants from the oven. When they are cool enough to handle, cut them in half lengthwise and scrape the flesh into a bowl, mashing it with a fork. Add the minced garlic and tahini and stir thoroughly to combine. Season with salt.
3. Transfer to a serving bowl and garnish with the oil and sumac.

𒀭 23. CUCUMBER SALAD 𒀭

Although cucumbers show up in the lexicons, there is little other mention of them in the written record. They do not appear in the recipes from the Yale Babylonian Collection; perhaps they were considered a lower-status food, or perhaps the record is simply incomplete.

2 cups chopped cucumber
2 tablespoons salt
1 cup yogurt
1/2 cup chopped onion

Sprinkle the cucumber with the salt and let it drain in a colander for 20 minutes to release moisture. Pat dry, wiping off the excess salt, and combine with the yogurt and raw onions.

𒀭 24. BEET SALAD 𒀭

Beets are one of the vegetables included in complex dishes in the Yale Babylonian Collection; this invented recipe assumes that beets also were served simply. As with turnips, there is some debate over whether the beet greens or beet bulbs were used, given that in early forms of beets and turnips, the bulbs were smaller than in their modern counterparts.

4 beets
1 tablespoon vegetable oil
2 teaspoons *siqqu* (fish sauce)
1/4 teaspoon ground aniseed
2 scallions, sliced

1. Preheat the oven to 400°F. Wrap each beet in foil and roast until tender, about 1 hour.
2. When cool enough to handle, slip the beets out of their skins and slice thinly. Toss with the oil, *siqqu*, aniseed, and scallions.

CONDIMENTS AND SAUCES

Very little is known about the seasonings that Mesopotamian cooks presumably had. Serve any of the following with meats, fish, breads, or grains.

ψ 25. CRESS PESTO ψ

The dowry of a middle-class Babylonian bride listed one mortar for cress seeds among her kitchen paraphernalia. Watercress is closely related to mustard, and seeds from watercress can be difficult to find. This invented recipe combines mustard seeds with some cress leaves.

1 clove garlic
1 teaspoon mustard seeds
1/4 cup tightly packed watercress leaves
2 teaspoons *siqqu* (fish sauce)
2 tablespoons vegetable oil

Place the garlic and mustard seeds in a mortar and pestle and pound to pulverize. Add the cress leaves in bunches and the siggu and oil, pounding to purée.

ψ 26. FLAVORED YOGURT ψ

Flavored yogurt can accompany any of the dishes in this chapter. To thicken homemade yogurt further, let it drain overnight in the refrigerator in a cheesecloth-lined sieve placed over a bowl to catch the whey.

To 1 cup Yogurt (Recipe 11), add:
1–2 cloves finely chopped garlic plus 1 teaspoon ground cumin; or
2 tablespoons each sesame oil and sesame seeds; or

1/4 cup date syrup or pomegranate molasses, or
1/2 cup chopped herbs.

ϟ 27. HOT YOGURT SAUCE ϟ

Goat's milk has more fat than cow's milk, which prevents the yogurt from curdling when it is heated. If goat's milk yogurt is not available, you can stabilize cow's milk yogurt by adding cornstarch so it will not separate in heating.

1/2 cucumber, coarsely grated
1/2 teaspoon kosher salt
1 cup goat's milk yogurt (if using cow's milk yogurt, dissolve 1 table-
    spoon cornstarch in 1 tablespoon water and add to the yogurt)
2 cloves garlic, finely minced
1 tablespoon chopped mint
2 teaspoons sesame seeds

1. Combine the grated cucumber and salt in a bowl. Let sit for 20 minutes, then squeeze out the excess water with your hands and pat dry.
2. Heat the yogurt and add the drained cucumber, garlic, and mint.
   Garnish with the sesame seeds. Serve with Grilled Fresh Fish (Recipe 18).

ϟ 28. MUSTARD ϟ

Mustard is widely reported in various texts, but no details are given for pre-paring it. Modern mustards are made by an ancient technique: mustard seeds are ground and mixed with vinegar, water, beer, and other flavorings. It is tempting to think that the Mesopotamians used the same process. Flavor the mustard, if desired, with chopped herbs, garlic, or date syrup. This recipe makes a very piquant mustard; if the mustard is too hot, add a bit of cooking oil.

2 tablespoons mustard seeds
1–1 1/2 tablespoons vinegar, water, or flat beer
Salt to taste
Flavorings as desired

Pound the mustard seeds finely in a mortar and pestle. Transfer to a small bowl and slowly stir in the liquid. Season with salt and optional flavorings to taste.

ϟ 29. ZA'TAR (SPICE BLEND) ϟ

Za'tar is a traditional spice mix found throughout the Near East that is added to foods at the table. There is no clear reference to these mixtures in the written record, but perhaps spice blends are some of the unidentified terms found in the Yale recipes.

1 tablespoon dried thyme
1 teaspoon dried marjoram
1 tablespoon sesame seeds
2 tablespoons ground almonds
2 teaspoons minced garlic
1 tablespoon salt

Combine and use at the table to season foods such as roasted meats or porridges. You may also dip breads in *za'tar*.

⊉ 30. APPLESAUCE ⊉

The Hittites were at the geographical fringes of Mesopotamian society. Located in what is now Turkey and northern Syria, they penetrated into Assyria. Archaeological finds indicate many similar foodways with Mesopotamia, and the Hittites absorbed Mesopotamian culture.

Hittite law stipulated fines for cutting down or burning apple trees; the Hittites also celebrated the onion harvest with a religious festival. This savory applesauce is an invented recipe that combines those two plants.

3 tablespoons butter
1 yellow onion, peeled and diced into 1/2-inch pieces
3 apples, preferably a tart variety such as Granny Smith, cored and coarsely chopped (you may leave the peel on or remove it)
1 teaspoon chopped fresh marjoram or *za'tar* (Recipe 29).
Salt to taste

1. Melt the butter over medium heat in the saucepan and add the diced onion. Cook, stirring regularly, until the onion softens, about 3 minutes.
2. Add the apples. Cover the pan with a tight-fitting lid and continue to cook gently, stirring every few minutes, until the apples soften, about 20 minutes. Add a bit of water if the apples seem in danger of burning. Season with salt and the marjoram or *za'tar* and serve at room temperature.

SWEETS AND PASTRIES

It is unclear whether the Mesopotamians considered pastries part of their dessert course. They clearly ate fresh and dried fruits and nuts at the conclusion of meals, and the large number of pastry-related words and artifacts shows that pastries were an important part of the Mesopotamian diet. The meal descriptions, however, do not list pastries as part of either the initial grain course or the concluding fruit course. Pastries were made from dried fruits and grains, so logically they could fit within either. Because the terms for pastry makers were separate from those for bread bakers, perhaps pastries were considered distinct by the Mesopotamians. For that reason, the pastry recipes have been grouped with the fruits as part of dessert foods rather than with the breads and grains.

𒅗 31. MERSU *(DATE AND PISTACHIO PASTRY)* 𒅗

Mersu was a widely known pastry. Different inventories list different ingredients for *mersu*, so there were many recipes. *Mersu* always seemed to contain first-quality dates and butter; beyond that, different records list pistachios, garlic, onion seed, and other seemingly incongruous ingredients. Bakers who specialized in this treat were known as the *episat mersi*, so *mersu*-making was probably an involved and respected process. This recipe is complicated and requires some patience but yields an interesting and very tasty pastry. If the dough is sticky, chill it before proceeding further.

1 1/2 cups dried dates, coarsely chopped
1 cup beer
1 cup water
1/2 cup date syrup
3/4 cup shelled pistachios
2 tablespoons nigella seeds
1 tablespoon ground coriander
1 teaspoon ground cumin
1 clove garlic, finely minced
2 cups all-purpose flour, plus more for rolling out the dough
1/2 cup whole wheat flour
8 tablespoons (1 stick) butter, softened at room temperature
1 egg, lightly beaten with 1 teaspoon water

1. Combine the dates, beer, water, and date syrup in a saucepan. Bring to a boil and poach until the dates are tender, about 15 minutes. Drain, reserving the liquid for making the dough. Chop the dates coarsely and combine with the pistachios, nigella, coriander, cumin, and garlic. Reserve.

2. Combine the flours in a bowl and stir in about 2/3 cup of the reserved poaching liquid to make a dough. You may need to add a bit more liquid. Roll the dough on a floured surface into a 8- by 14-inch rectangle and smear with the butter. Lift a narrow end of

the dough and roll up like a jelly roll. Coil the roll into a spiral and chill for 30 minutes.

3. Preheat the oven to 400°F.

4. Dust a clean work surface and a rolling pin lightly with flour. Roll the coil into a rectangle about 8 by 14 inches, with the narrow edges at the top and bottom. Fold the top third down and the bottom third up, like a business letter. Flour the work surface again and roll this into a circle about 12 inches in diameter.

5. Transfer the dough to a baking sheet and mound the date filling in the center of the dough, leaving about a 3-inch boundary on all edges. Brush the edges of the dough with the lightly beaten egg and pull the edges up to enclose the filling, pinching the dough together to seal the seams. Brush the top of the *mersu* with the egg, place in the oven, and bake for 40 minutes or until golden brown.

ᛈ 32. DATE CAKES ᛈ

The date cakes may be similar to the dried fig cakes still made in Spain and Italy, where they are served with cheese and crackers after dinner.

1 cup dried dates, pits removed
2 cups boiling water
3 tablespoons pine nuts
Flour as necessary

Place the dates in a bowl and pour the water over them. Let sit for 30 minutes to soften. Drain the dates and chop finely with a knife. Knead in the pine nuts. The purée will be sticky, so you may wish to dust your hands lightly with flour to work with the mass. Shape the mixture into a log and wrap in several layers of cheesecloth and chill in the refrigerator for 30 minutes or longer before cutting. Cut 1/2-inch-thick slices from the log and serve.

ᛈ 33. PALACE CAKE ᛈ

Records from Ur identify cakes "for the palace" as containing 1 *sila* of butter, 1/3 *sila* of white cheese, 3 *sila* of first-quality dates, and 1/3 *sila* of raisins.[20] A *sila* equaled a little more than 3 cups. This recipe has been scaled back by one-third to make the quantities more manageable, but it is extremely rich due to the large proportion of butter. Presumably there would be flour and other ingredients that a competent baker would infer to assemble this cake. The dried fruits will stick to the bottom of the pan; if you want to unmold the cake after it cools (rather than serve it from the pan), line the bottom of the pan with baker's parchment, or, to be more authentic, grape leaves. Invert the cake onto a plate and peel off the leaves.

> *A Sumerian proverb claimed that if one gave a Bedouin ingredients for a cake, she would not know what to do with them.[21]*

3 cups dates, finely chopped
1/3 cup raisins
2 teaspoons ground fennel or aniseed
1/3 cup cottage cheese
1 cup (2 sticks) butter, melted and at room temperature
2 eggs, beaten together, at room temperature
2/3 cup milk, at room temperature
1 1/2 cups all-purpose flour

1. Preheat the oven to 325°F. Combine the dates, raisins, and spice and scatter in a 10-inch cake pan.
2. Press the cottage cheese through a strainer to break up the curds. Combine the cheese with the melted butter, eggs, and milk and slowly stir into the flour, moistening thoroughly. Pour the batter over the dried fruits and bake for 45–55 minutes, or until a toothpick inserted into the centers comes out clean.

℣ 34. DRIED APPLES ℣

Tomb excavations at the Sumerian city of Ur showed a funeral meal offering of lamb or goat, dried dates and apple rings, and a flat bread. Apples were cultivated in shade gardens and could be sun dried for long storage. A dehydrator works best, but apple rings can be carefully dried in a cool oven.

2 apples, stemmed, cored, and cut crosswise into 1/4-inch slices, unpeeled

Preheat the oven to 225°F. Spread the apples on a baking sheet and place in the oven. Bake for 2 hours, then turn the heat off and allow the apples to remain in the oven until it is cool.

℣ 35. DRIED FRUIT COMPOTE ℣

Dates, figs, and grapes and something called candy were offered every day to the gods of Uruk.[22] Softening dried fruits would make them easier to chew, an advantage in an era of primitive dentistry.

1/2 cup dried figs, quartered
1/2 cup dried sour cherries
3/4 cup dried apricots, sliced

2 tablespoons pomegranate molasses
2 tablespoons date syrup
Water, as needed, to cover the dried fruits

Combine all of the ingredients in a saucepan and bring to a boil. Simmer until tender, about 10 minutes. Remove the fruit with a slotted spoon and reserve. Reduce the cooking liquid by boiling to a light syrup. Combine with the poached fruits.

⚚ 36. FRUIT AND NUT PLATTER ⚚

Part of the menu for the marriage feast of Sud and Enlil included a cornucopia of fruits and nuts. No separate recipe is needed to assemble a dessert platter based on the literary description that included dates, figs, pomegranates, cherries, plums, pistachios, acorns, and "big clusters of early grapes . . . fruits from the orchard."[23]

BEVERAGES

By modern standards, Mesopotamians had a limited range of beverages: water, beer, date-palm and grape wines, possibly some fruit juices, and milk. Milk had an ambiguous status. Sumerian literature treats fresh milk as a lower-class beverage, perhaps because it was often consumed directly from the animal by shepherds tending flocks and others residing outside urban walls. Yet milk was also offered to the gods in alabaster libation vessels for breakfast at the Sumerian temple at Uruk; presumably milk lost its lower-class associations when offered to the gods and, by extension, to palace and temple inhabitants. The reason for this is unknown; perhaps the milk came from specially anointed temple animals.

Mesopotamians pressed fruits to extract the liquids; the Sumerian *hashur. e.a* means "that which comes forth from the apple."[24] Whether the pressings were drunk as juices or used as ingredients in other recipes is unknown.

⚚ 37. YOGURT COOLER ⚚

Scholars believe that, aside from temple libations, most of the milk drunk by urbanites was fermented; it may have been similar to the diluted yogurt drinks popular throughout the Near East. Snow and ice were brought down from the mountains and stored in underground ice cellars to chill wines for the elites, but there is no evidence that yogurt received the same favored treatment; perhaps cool spring or well water put a slight chill on the drink.

1/2 cup yogurt

1/2 cup cool water

1 teaspoon fresh chopped mint or dill

Combine ingredients thoroughly.

⚕ 38. SUMERIAN BEER ⚕

A Sumerian proverb stated, "Pleasure—it is beer!"[25] Beer was extremely popular and widespread: the thirst for beer may have been a key factor in the domestication of barley in the southern Levant. According to this theory, prehistoric hunter-gatherers stored wild barley in porous containers. If the grain got wet, it sprouted, a process known as malting. Malting converts some of the grains' complex carbohydrates into simple sugars, and naturally occurring yeasts fermented the sugar into a primitive beer that was lightly intoxicating and superior nutritionally. Paleolithic humans probably were not aware of that

Beer Jug, used for straining floating grain out of beer. Collection Israel Museum, Jerusalem. Photo © The Israel Museum, Jerusalem, by Avraham Hay.

side benefit and simply enjoyed the mild buzz. According to this theory, once the process was appreciated, Levantines began to domesticate the wild plant to ensure a steady supply of the raw ingredients, foregoing the nomadic hunter-gatherer lifestyle for that of the settled agrarian, and the Neolithic (food-producing) period was born.[26]

Mesopotamian men and women of all social classes enjoyed beer as a staple, and its role cannot be underestimated: up to 40% of the barley harvest was fermented into beer. Hammurabi's Code (ca. 1700 B.C.E.) regulated beer halls where the working public congregated, sometimes with draconian severity. Brewers who overcharged their customers might be killed by drowning; should a high priestess venture into a tavern, and thus lose her ritual purity for the temples, she would be burned to death.[27] Brewers advertised beers of different strengths, giving trade names to their brews.

Others were identified by added flavorings: pomegranate beer was called *alappanu*. People drank beer through tubes that looked like gigantic straws in huge cups. The straws may have been necessary to pierce through the layer of grain hulls that remained in unfiltered beers or may have been a very sociable way of allowing several people to share the beverage simultaneously, rather like the quaint images of 1950s American teenagers sharing an ice cream soda.

The *Hymn to Ninkasi* (ca.1800 B.C.E.) honored the Sumerian goddess as the great protectress of the art of brewing. The hymn gave directions for making beer, which modern brewers have been able to follow to create a low-alcohol beverage that might resemble the ancient brew. The basic steps include baking a barley bread, called a *bappir*; mixing it with malted grains; adding water, honey, and sometimes other flavorings; and allowing it to ferment. The entire process takes about a week; you should start malting the wheat berries on day 1, then make the *bappir* on day 2, and finally assemble the beer on day 5, to ferment for several days. The resulting brew will have about 2% alcohol, less than half the alcohol content of modern beers. The low alcohol content helps explain how Mesopotamians could drink beer as a staple.

To malt the grain:

1 cup wheat berries

1. Soak the wheat berries overnight in water at room temperature. Drain. Place the wheat berries in a large jar, cover the opening with a double layer of cheesecloth, and secure it with a rubber band. Invert the jar over a bowl so that air can circulate. Lightly mist the wheat berries with water twice a day, so they stay moist but are not submerged in water. Hold at room temperature for 3 days or until little tails emerge from the wheat berries.
2. Once the grains sprout, place the wheat berries on a baking sheet in a 200°F oven for 30 minutes, or until dry. Reserve.

To make the *bappir*:

3 cups barley flour
1 tablespoon yeast
1 cup water

Mix the *bappir* ingredients to form a firm dough and knead for 5 minutes. Shape into a round loaf, cover with a clean towel, and set aside for 2 days.

Preheat the oven to 300°F. Bake the loaf for 15 minutes; the outside should be just dry, but the inside should still be raw (to ensure that the yeast is still alive).

To assemble the beer:

Reserved wheat berries, ground coarsely in a grain mill or food
  processor
Baked *bappir* loaf, torn into bite-sized pieces
4 quarts water
1 tablespoon yeast
1/4 cup date syrup (optional, for flavor)

Combine all of the ingredients in large pot and cover with cheesecloth. Let
sit for 2 days at room temperature to ferment. Strain out the solids.

2
⚱ ANCIENT EGYPT

This chapter spans 3,000 years of Egyptian history, from predynastic times in the late fourth millennium until 525 B.C.E., when the Persians installed the first of several foreign pharaohs on the Egyptian throne. Thereafter Egypt would be dominated by foreigners: after the Persians came the Greeks and Romans, who viewed Egypt's fertile Nile Delta as their breadbasket. All left their mark on Egyptian foodways.

From prehistoric times Egyptian food had been influenced by the outside world: Egypt's staple grains, barley and emmer, originated in the Near East. Many of the recipes found in the Mesopotamian chapter, except those for spelt, might have been equally at home in Egyptian kitchens. Nevertheless, Egyptian dining habits were distinct from those of Mesopotamia, particularly in the Egyptians' emphasis on beef and their use of honey and certain unique fruits and vegetables. The Greeks changed Egyptian foodways by insisting on the widespread cultivation of bread wheat and by introducing new irrigation technologies, shifting Egyptian food habits toward those of the Hellenistic world.

The recipes try to evoke Egyptian foodways before the advent of the Persians, Greeks, and Romans. Much of the evidence for Egyptian foodways comes from the periods known as the Old Kingdom (ca. 2675–2130 B.C.E.), the Middle Kingdom (ca. 1980–1630 B.C.E.), and the New Kingdom (ca. 1539–1075 B.C.E.), times when the government was strong, centralized, and wealthy. Egypt's remarkable architectural achievements, the Great Pyramids and the Valleys of the Kings and Queens, were built during the Old

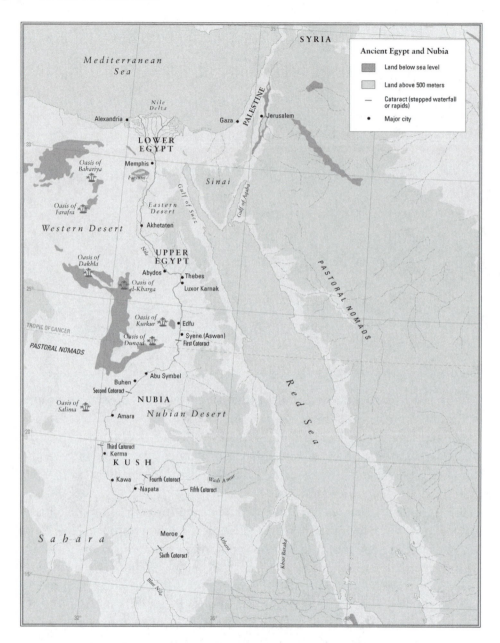

and New Kingdoms, respectively. Extensive bureaucratic records identify payments to workers, always in foodstuffs, on these and other projects. The kingdoms were interrupted by the First, Second, and Third Intermediate Periods, times of weak government and changing social structures often initiated or exacerbated by repeated poor harvests.

FOODSTUFFS AND AGRICULTURE

- Emmer and barley were the two staple grains of Egypt; bread wheat was not important until the Greco-Roman period. Bread and beer made from emmer and barley formed significant parts of everyone's diet.

- Cattle, pigs, sheep, goats, and donkeys were domesticated food animals, along with ducks, pigeons, and geese; wild game, such as deer and antelope, and migratory birds were hunted or trapped. Chicken and hen eggs became important only in the Greco-Roman period.
- Many different freshwater fish were caught in the Nile and in the reservoirs created by the inundation; shellfish and saltwater fish were unimportant.
- Vegetables included onions, garlic, and leeks; melons and several members of the squash (*cucurbitaceae*) family; cos lettuces; celery; and several aquatic plants of the *cyperus* genus: papyrus, lotus, and tiger nuts. Radishes, turnips, and mustard greens may have been available as vegetables in pharaonic times.
- Legumes included lentils, chickpeas, favas, lupines, and peas.
- Many cooking fats came from animals; sesame and olive oils were originally imported from the Levant and cultivated in Egypt only comparatively late, in New Kingdom times, when safflower oil was also introduced. Plant oils used in earlier times came from linseed, radishes, lettuce, and the moringa tree.
- Fruits included dates (both palm and sycamore), grapes, pomegranates, and figs. Other fruits included carobs, *nabk* berries (similar to wild cherry), and *persea* (similar to plums).
- Honey and date syrup sweetened foods; honey was expensive and limited to elites. Culinary herbs and spices probably included aniseed, asafetida, basil, chervil, coriander, cumin, dill, juniper, marjoram, mint, rue, and thyme, all indigenous or acclimated to Egypt. Black pepper and cinnamon were expensive imports, used medicinally and in mummification.
- Wine was more expensive than beer and was made from grapes, dates, figs, and pomegranates. Milk was drunk or processed into cheese.

Paleolithic Egyptians clustered around the lakes that punctuated Egypt's great deserts. Renewed by modest rains, these oases supported wild vegetation and attracted fauna, which in turn attracted hunter-gatherers. The amount of rain fluctuated, effectively limiting the population that could sustain itself around these lakes. To grow into a civilization, the Egyptians would have to increase their food supply, and this required controlling the Nile. Unlike the unpredictable rains of the desert oases, the Nile's floods were triggered by the distant and generally reliable monsoons in the Ethiopian highlands.

Egyptians believed that the world was created when the Nile god Hapi raised an island from the Nile's primordial waters. Hapi was a hermaphrodite who both fertilized and nourished the land. Each June, when the Nile was at its lowest point and the star Sirius appeared in the eastern sky, Egyptians prayed to Hapi, who answered by causing the Nile to rise and deposit rich alluvium over the floodplains abutting the Nile's banks. Egypt's agricultural fields hugged the Nile, and her towns lay just beyond the predicted floodplains. The pattern continues in contemporary Egypt, where much of the population lives on narrow strips running down either side of the Nile and in the Nile Delta, amounting to only about 3 percent of the country's landmass.

The Egyptian year had three seasons. Inundation (the annual flooding) lasted roughly from July through September or October. The season called Emergence followed, lasting roughly through January; planting took place as the waters receded. During the season of Drought, from February through June, grains ripened and were harvested, often with a second, quick-growing crop of pulses planted after the grain harvest.

Egyptian agriculture probably started around the sixth millennium B.C.E. and was easier than in Mesopotamia. The Nile flooded before the planting season rather than during the growing season, and the waters were less torrential than those of the Tigris and Euphrates. Moreover, the Nile's banks are slightly higher than the surrounding floodplain and had better drainage. Simply by cutting breeches in its banks, early Egyptians could inundate specific lower-lying areas. The waters pooled into natural reservoirs, leaving soggy mud. The Egyptians spread grain on the mud, and then either plowed it under or sent in herds of sheep or pigs to trample in the seed. The grain ripened, nourished by occasional rainfall or, eventually, by irrigation canals linked to the reservoirs, which also offered habitat to game and fish.

Egypt's land was fertile. Estimates of the caloric value that a given plot of land could produce suggest that one Egyptian could produce enough grain to feed 20 adults,[1] allowing a large part of the labor force to be devoted to other wealth-producing activities. Nonetheless, Egypt's food security depended on the Nile's proper flooding. Too little, and agricultural yields fell short; too much, and the land was overly saturated, and orchards, gardens, and the dike system were destroyed. The Old Testament story of Joseph predicting seven lean years to Pharaoh reflected anxiety over the Nile's flooding and the need for centralized action to protect the food supply. Scholars disagree as to when the centralized government took control of canal building. Local efforts undoubtedly were made in prehistoric times; Egyptian legend attributes the first breaching of the Nile's banks to a mysterious King Scorpion, who may have lived in the late fourth millennium B.C.E., but only in the Middle Kingdom does clear evidence emerge of the central government organizing canal digging and maintenance. As in Mesopotamia, the canal system served the dual purposes of transportation and irrigation: large canals accommodated barges laden with stones that built pyramids, tombs, and temples.

Although the inundations suited the fields of barley and emmer along the Nile, orchards, vineyards, and shade and vegetable gardens did poorly in soggy lands and thus were planted beyond the floodplain. The single greatest technological challenge to Egyptian agriculture was how to lift water into those gardens. For thousands of years, laborers carried water in two buckets hanging from a bar balanced over the shoulders, making large gardens truly luxurious. In early New Kingdom times, as a result of pharaoh Thutmose III's successful wars in the Near East, the *shaduf*, a counterweighted device for lifting water, was introduced from Mesopotamia, where it had been used for more than 1,000 years. This eased the irrigation burden somewhat for orchards and gardens but remained the only mechanical device for lifting water in pharaonic Egypt. Only when veterans of Greece's wars with Persia settled in Egypt early in the Greco-Roman period was the *saqiya*, an animal-driven waterwheel, introduced from technologically advanced Mesopotamia. The Greeks also introduced the Archimedes Screw, a flattened corkscrew fitted within a barrel that lifted greater amounts of water than the *shaduf*. These machines made commercial agriculture feasible and turned Egypt into an exporter of foods to Greece and Rome.

CUISINE AND SOCIAL CLASS

- Elite Egyptians ate three daily meals: morning, evening, and night. Laborers probably ate twice daily. The wealthy enjoyed a more diverse diet through imported foods.
- Social superiors might include lower-status diners at banquets, with different foods offered to each guest depending on his or her rank. Tablewares varied from magnificent gold, alabaster, and glass for the elites to earthenware and base metals for workers. Spoons and knives appeared at the table.
- High-status banquets were often segregated by gender; those below the elite tended to eat (or drink) in the same room, although men and women might be seated separately. The genders mixed at family meals, regardless of status.
- Egyptians buried food with their dead to ensure a comfortable afterlife.

Diversity in diet was a mark of wealth, and Egyptians became wealthy by owning land or the produce that the land yielded. In the Old, First Intermediate, and Middle Kingdoms, the pharaoh owned all land although he gave important administrators and temples the prerogative to use certain land, effectively creating a small elite class. Money did not exist in Egypt until the Greco-Roman period; the traditional Egyptian economy was redistributive, meaning that all agricultural products (grain, livestock, other foodstuffs) were collected by the government and distributed according to status to the royal family, priests, bureaucrats, soldiers, artisans, and laborers who made up Egyptian society. Extensive scribal records document food payments according to social position. Large payments of many different foodstuffs were made to high-status individuals; the food was not meant for individual consumption but was to be redistributed to support their families, workers, and others under their control.

During the New Kingdom, religious communities became a competing center of wealth and land ownership. They similarly granted prerogatives to smaller landholders, effectively spreading wealth to larger numbers of Egyptians. Estimates suggest that New Kingdom elites probably ranged between 5 and 9 percent of the population; perhaps another 30 percent were lesser bureaucrats, highly skilled artisans, and lower priests, supported by government and religious entities. A new group of middle-class traders and craftsmen, who worked independently, supplied imported products and material goods demanded by these growing ranks of the well-to-do. The remaining folk were peasants, possibly tied to the land, and other low-skilled laborers, or slaves.

Slavery existed in Egypt but not on the same scale as found in the Greco-Roman world. Slaves frequently were foreigners or prisoners of war from the Levant or African hinterlands who performed menial household, agricultural, and construction work. Slavery did not become widespread until the New Kingdom, when even small landholders would have had slaves to work the property. From the earliest dynasties up until the New Kingdom, much of the hard and menial labor was performed through the corvée, a system of draft labor in which groups of Egyptian peasants, selected by the local communities, worked on the government's building campaigns, particularly during the season of Inundation, when no agricultural work could be done.

Beer and bread appeared on everyone's table and were the most common form of payment. The Egyptians measured quantities owed for services by the *psw*, or baking yield, of a given quantity grain; the higher the *psw*, the more loaves that could be produced from a set measure of grain. The *psw* varied from location to location, making it difficult to compare wages across Egypt, but some examples give a sense of the relative economic niches of different Egyptians. The standard wage of soldiers stationed at the fort at Uronarti during the Middle Kingdom was 10 loaves of bread plus one jug of beer per day; higher-ranking soldiers and bureaucrats received a multiple of this basic wage. New Kingdom workers on the tombs at Deir el-Medina received 4 *khar* of emmer (310 liters) and 1.5 *khar* of barley (115 liters) per month. Traders traveling on behalf of the pharaoh to Nubia or the Near East were credited with great quantities of grains and grain products, and they would pay those working under them by drawing against these reserves. Those managing great estates for the pharaoh would also receive more than was needed for their support; the excess was bartered for other products and luxury goods at lively markets for fruits, vegetables, fish, and other foodstuffs. Hunting, fishing, and foraging could supplement the basic allotment.

Payment was not limited to beer and bread. An Old Kingdom (ca. 2200 B.C.E.) record lists the wages of a laborer as 20 *deben* (about 4 pounds) of bread, two bundles of vegetables (no variety specified), and a roast of flesh (no quantity or animal specified.) Ramses II (thirteenth century B.C.E.) boasted of hiring 20 fishermen to supply fish to 40 workers and administrators building his tomb in the Valley of the Kings. Later pharaohs were less generous and suffered the consequences: workers building the tomb of Ramses III (twelfth century B.C.E.) staged a sit-down strike, claiming, "It is because of hunger and because of thirst that we come here. There is no clothing, no ointment, no fish, no vegetables. Send to Pharaoh our good Lord about it and send to the vizier our superior, that sustenance may be made for us."[2] Remains from the workers' village at Deir el-Medina show cooked or smoked and salted meats, chate melons (related to cucumbers), onions, fruits, coriander and sesame seeds, and honey; these may have been distributed directly by the government, grown privately in small gardens, or resulted from trading excess beer and breads.

Missing from the workers' village are oil and wine, although these items were paid to those higher on the social ladder. Pharaoh's messenger and standard bearer received "good bread, ox flesh, wine, sweet oil, olive oil, fat, honey, figs, fish, and vegetables."[3] Elites were expected to eat a greater variety of foods, and no one thought it odd to serve inferior food to a dinner guest of lesser status. An etiquette book, probably first written in Old Kingdom times, counseled a social inferior not to be jealous of the superior foods that the host would enjoy:

> *If you sit at the table of one who is greater than you, take what he gives you, what is set before you. Do not look [greedily] at what is in front of him, but only at what is in front of you. . . . Laugh when he laughs. . . . When a great man hosts, his actions depend on his humor, and a great man can be motivated by good humors to be more generous.*[4]

Analyses of mummies show that most Egyptians ate adequately, with relatively few nutritional deficiencies. Members of the elites often ate too well, or at least too much; their mummies show evidence of diseases related to obesity: diabetes, gallstones, and fat deposits in the arteries. In the earliest periods, only elite mummies showed dental cavities, attributable to a diet high in bread. This medical problem spread through all classes as government payments in flour filtered downward. The parasite *trichinella spiralis*, which causes trichinosis, has been found in mummies, including craftsmen and laborers at Deir el-Medina, showing that pork was widely eaten by the middle and working classes in the New Kingdom.

RECIPE SOURCES

No Egyptian cookbook has been found, nor are there detailed descriptions of Egyptian food written before the Hellenic period to suggest possible recipes. Medical papyri prescribed foodstuffs, mainly herbs and spices, as part of the Egyptian pharmacy, but how much medical practice influenced the kitchen is speculative. The fact that there is little food literature may suggest that Egyptians focused less on the gastronomic pleasures and perhaps had simpler foods than did their Mesopotamian contemporaries, who had a precise and extensive culinary vocabulary, descriptive literature, and complex recipes. Even so, Egyptians undoubtedly enjoyed food; one hieroglyphic expressed the related concepts of smell, taste, and pleasure.

Some practical evidence comes from food preparation and banqueting scenes that were included in elite Egyptian tombs to ensure bountiful eating in the afterlife. Because Egyptian religion equated the life of the gods and the dead with that of the living, the foodstuffs buried with the dead probably paralleled menus of the living. Archaeological digs have uncovered bureaucratic records, food-related implements, and food remains. Some of the food artifacts have been analyzed through electron microscopy, either to identify the foodstuffs more accurately or to reverse engineer cooking techniques by studying the chemical changes that took place in food processing. By following the steps in the artwork and trying to match the chemical evidence, archaeologists have learned more about ancient methods of processing grains, baking bread, and brewing beer.

Other evidence for the recipes comes from the technology available to the Egyptians for pounding, grinding, and cooking. Egyptian kitchens were well designed. Planned communities of workers' houses, such as those found in Amarna or Deir el-Medina and occupied by the laborers and lower craftsmen building various elaborate tombs, usually placed kitchens on the roofs to allow smoke, heat, and cooking odors to escape. Ventilation remained a problem in less-well-designed homes, as sooty beams and evidence of respiratory damage have been found in mummies. Most kitchens had *tannur*-style bread ovens fueled by charcoal or dried manure, querns for grinding, mortars, water jugs, baskets, pottery, and occasionally metal cooking vessels. Wealthier kitchens were larger with more ovens, potager stoves that could gently heat foods, and braziers. In palaces and temple complexes, whole kitchen wings with airy courtyards allowed cooking for large numbers.

The following recipes are hypotheses about the dishes that might have been eaten 5,000 years ago. They use ingredients and technologies (or their closest practical equivalents) known to have been available to ancient Egyptian cooks, but whether they taste anything like ancient food is unknowable. The lack of gastronomic literature leaves gaping holes in our knowledge of the subtlety with which Egyptian food may—or may not—have been seasoned. The recipes in this chapter tend to be a bit simpler than those in the other chapters, following the theory that the Egyptians' failure to write about food gastronomically signals less-complicated cookery.

BREADS AND GRAINS

Emmer and barley were Egypt's major grains, with barley predominate in the Old and Middle Kingdoms, while emmer was more widely used in the New Kingdom. These hulled grains required that the chaff be loosened by parching or pounding before threshing, a job that helped occupy some of Egypt's labor force. Curiously, although free-threshing bread wheat was known in pharaonic Egypt, it was seldom used and became widespread only when the Greeks gained influence in the fourth century B.C.E. The long dominance of hulled grains may be attributable to the underlying conservatism of Egyptian society; a more labor-efficient form of wheat would have disrupted the traditional labor chain by eliminating a key step in processing.

Although porridges were eaten, most records and other archaeological finds indicate that bread was preferred. More than 40 varieties appear in New Kingdom records. Leavened bread has been traced to Neolithic times with finds of porous bread; more regular leavening seems to date from late predynastic times and probably relates to the establishment of breweries. Excavations at predynastic Hierakonpolis revealed a bakery adjacent to a brewery. Leavened breads were often baked in elaborate molds to give interesting shapes, and possibly to convey symbolic meaning. The molds were usually made from clay and could be fired in the same ovens used to bake bread, so that the baker on a large estate or in a temple complex would make his tools as well as his bread. Although the molds were fragile and frequently broken, by coating the inside with fat and heating the mold several times, the baker might obtain a slick surface that would release the dough. These molds could either be placed in a larger oven for baking or turned onto a heated hearth, with hot ashes piled around the mold to provide heat from all directions. Other breads were baked free-form in large, preheated ovens.

A New Kingdom letter stated, "Don't let the granary be lacking in barley or emmer for it is upon its granary that a house stands firm."[5]

𓏲 39. BARLEY MEAL PORRIDGE 𓏲

An early elite tomb from the Second Dynasty contained barley porridge in an alabaster dish as one of the foods for the afterlife. Nigella (*nigella sa-*

tiva) was found mixed with linseed grains in Egyptian artifacts and presumably was used for flavoring. Nigella has an oniony flavor; if it is unavailable, substitute onion seed.

2/3 cup barley flour
1 1/2–2 cups milk or water
Salt to taste
1/2 teaspoon nigella seeds

Place the barley flour in a pot and stir in the liquid to moisten the flour. Bring to a boil, reduce heat, and simmer for 20 minutes, adding more liquid if the porridge becomes too thick. Season with salt and nigella.

𓏸 40. MATZOH 𓏸

Matzoh is the unleavened flatbread famously eaten by the Jews upon their exodus from Egypt, commemorated annually by the Passover holiday. To make matzoh kosher for Passover, the entire process, from the mixing of the dough to the baking, must be finished within 18 minutes. This short time eliminates the possibility of fermentation by wild yeasts, which would render the bread ritually impure. Quickly prepared from flour and water and baked on hot stones, these breads were likely a staple for slaves and poor Egyptians, and not just a food limited to the Jews who were enslaved in Egypt in New Kingdom times. Although matzoh is eaten throughout the year and often contains oil for flavor and texture, the Passover matzoh must be oil free. This lean bread would be consistent with slave rations in ancient Egypt.

Modern recipes sometimes recommend kamut flour for preparing matzoh. Kamut is a registered trade name of the Montana Flour and Grains Company for a strain of wheat brought back from Egypt in the 1940s by an American serviceman that is thought to be of ancient origin. The exact taxonomy of kamut is debated by scientists.[6]

2 cups kamut flour or barley flour
3/4–1 cup water

1. Place a griddle or baking stone on the lowest oven rack and preheat oven to 425°F.
2. Combine the flour and water to make a dough. Knead vigorously for 4 minutes. Divide the dough into 12 pieces and cover with a towel to keep moist while you work. Roll the first piece into a disk about 7 inches in diameter, keeping it as thin as possible. Prick with a fork and stretch slightly by hand to widen the holes.
3. Place the disk on your palm and transfer to the baking stone by inverting your hand just above the stone. Bake for 2 1/2–3 minutes, rolling the next matzoh while the previous one is baking.

ᛰ 41. SHAT *BREAD* ᛰ

Triangular-shaped emmer bread, probably called *shat,* has been found in tombs dating to the Second Dynasty, just before the start of the Old Kingdom.

2 cups semolina flour, plus more for kneading
1/2 teaspoon instant yeast
3/4 cup lukewarm water

1. Combine all of the ingredients to make a dough. Turn out onto a lightly floured surface and knead until the dough is elastic, about 5–7 minutes.
2. Pat the dough into a rectangle. Hold a knife at a 45° angle to the sides; starting at one of the short ends, make cuts to create six triangular breads.
3. Place the triangles on a baking sheet, pulling gently at each of the angles to elongate the dough and emphasize the triangular shape. Cover with a towel and let rise for 45 minutes. Meanwhile, preheat the oven to 425°F.
4. Bake the breads for 15–20 minutes, or until they sound hollow when tapped on the bottom.

ᛰ 42. EMMER BREAD WITH FIGS ᛰ

Archaeological analysis of loaves excavated at the workers' village at Deir el-Medina shows 15 different shapes of bread. Some of the loaves were flavored with fig paste. Workers at Deir el-Medina built and decorated the royal tombs in the Valley of the Kings and Valley of the Queens. As state workers on high-status projects, they may have received enhanced rations.

Studies of preserved bits of bread under an electron microscope show that some Egyptian loaves were made from sprouted wheat. This recipe uses the sprouting technique and requires several days' advance preparation. If *farro* is available, use it in place of wheat berries.

3 cups *farro* or wheat berries
3/4 cup dried figs, coarsely chopped
1 tablespoon instant yeast
1 teaspoon salt
Water, as needed
All-purpose flour for kneading
4 tablespoons vegetable oil

1. Place the *farro* or wheat berries in a 3-quart glass bowl and cover with room-temperature water. Soak overnight. Drain the berries

and rinse with lukewarm water. Shake out the excess moisture and return to the bowl; cover with cheesecloth and let stand overnight. By morning the berries should have begun to sprout; rinse and cover again, and continue to watch until the sprouts are about 1/3 as long as the berries, about 3 days.

2. Dry the berries with paper towels and divide into three portions. Place one portion in a food processor fitted with a metal blade and add 1/4 cup of the figs, 1 teaspoon of yeast, and 1/3 teaspoon of the salt. Pulse until the ingredients form a ball, adding a little water if needed. Remove and repeat the process with the next two batches. Knead each batch on a lightly floured surface for 3 minutes. Cover and let rest for 1 hour (or, wrapped in plastic, overnight in the refrigerator).

3. Preheat the oven to 325°F. Divide each ball in two and roll each half into a disk about 6 inches in diameter. Lightly oil two 12- by 18-inch baking trays with the vegetable oil. Place three disks on each of the trays and let rest for 30 minutes, covered with a towel.

4. Bake the breads for about 30–35 minutes. Serve warm or at room temperature.

𓏏 43. TA *(WHEAT BREAD)* 𓏏

Ta is the Egyptian word for bread. The Fifth Dynasty tomb of a high-level bureaucrat at the town of Sakkara is decorated with scenes of bread baking in small clay vessels resembling flower pots. This technique continued through at least the New Kingdom, although the shapes of the molds changed. Archaeologists have experimented with baking bread using ancient querns for grinding the grain and reproduction clay vessels that duplicate the size and shape of ancient pots. One even collected wild yeasts from Giza to leaven the bread in his experiments; he makes dried sourdough cultures incorporating the wild yeasts of Giza available commercially, along with instructions, if you want to try making an ancient sourdough.[7] This recipe combines aspects of the research and uses readily available small, unglazed terra cotta flower pots to simulate the process inexpensively.

2 unused terra cotta flower pots, 5 inches in diameter
1/2 cup lard
1 1/2 cups fine semolina
1/2 tablespoon instant yeast
2 tablespoons honey
5/8 cup warm milk or water

1. Preheat the oven to 300°F. Rub the inside of each flower pot with a thin coating of lard. Place the pots in the oven, turn off the heat, and let cool. Repeat the process.

2. Make a dough by combining the semolina, yeast, honey, and liquid. Knead until elastic, about 5 minutes, and set aside, covered, for 30 minutes.

3. Meanwhile, place the pots in the oven on a sheet pan, baking stone, or griddle. Preheat the oven to 425°F.

4. After 30 minutes, divide the dough in half and shape into soft balls. Carefully pulling out the oven rack that contains the flower pots, drop one ball in each pot. Using heavy potholders, invert the pots onto the baking sheet and quickly close the oven to maintain the heat. Bake for 5 minutes, then turn the oven off and let bake in the remaining heat for another 20 minutes. Carefully remove the hot flower pots and turn out the breads. If necessary, run a knife around the edges to loosen the breads.

☥ 44. FREEK *PILAF* ☥

Freek is often called green wheat because it is made from immature wheat grains, usually emmer. In Egypt, *freek* can be eaten raw and straight from the field without cooking, as the moist grains are palatable and are often part of first fruit festivals celebrating the new harvest. *Freek* imported into the United States has been dried for shipping. It must be cooked in liquid to be edible. The grains traditionally are smoked during processing, giving *freek* dishes a distinctive taste.

    5 teaspoons olive oil
    1 shallot, minced
    1 cup *freek*
    1/2 teaspoon crushed celery seed
    1 cup plus 2 tablespoons water
    Salt to taste
    2 tablespoons chopped chives

Gently heat the oil in a saucepan. Cook the shallot over low heat until soft. Add the *freek*, toasting it lightly in the oil. Add the celery seed, water, and salt. Bring to a boil, cover, reduce the heat, and simmer until tender, about 20 minutes. If any water is left, remove the lid of the pan and boil until dry. Stir in the chives and serve.

☥ 45. KUSH BREAD ☥

Egyptians called the area stretching from the Second to the Fourth Cataract (present-day Sudan) the land of Kush. Through much of its history, the Egyptians traded with the Kushites for exotic products such as gold, ivory, and ostrich feathers, although like so many neighbors, the Egyptians and Kushites often found themselves at war, with Egypt temporarily ruling northern parts of Kush. The Kushites pressed into Egypt on several occasions, ruling the country in the eighth and seventh centuries B.C.E. as the Twenty-fifth Dynasty, shortly before the Persians assumed control. The land and climate of Kush suited cultivation of millet. Traders or occupying forces may have encountered a simple bread such as this, which is a version of the injera bread that is ubiquitous in modern Ethiopia. Teff is the common name for millet flour.

Ethiopians use injera as their plates: placed on tables or trays, overlapping pieces of injera cover the surface. Chunky stews are placed on top, and diners then use additional pieces of injera instead of forks to grab bits of stew. When the stew is finished, the underlying bread will have soaked up some of the seasonings and is eaten. It is possible that some Egyptian households may have kept a vat of fermenting grain and made similar, quick-cooking breads for their daily fare, eating off of the bread in a similar fashion.

2 cups teff, ground into flour in a blender
3 cups water
1/4 teaspoon instant yeast

1. Combine the teff, water, and yeast in a bowl. Cover and let sit for 2–3 days to ferment, until the batter smells tangy and has the consistency of a thin pancake batter. If necessary, thin with a bit of lukewarm water.
2. Heat a nonstick skillet over medium heat. Ladle in a scant 1/2 cup of batter, starting at edges and moving into the center, tilting the pan in a figure-eight motion to create a thin film about 1/8 inch thick. Cover and cook over low heat for 2 minutes. The edges of the bread will begin to pull away from the sides of the pan when it is done. Peel off the bread with a wooden spoon, transfer to clean cloth towels, and roll up to keep warm. The texture should be soft and pliable. Pieces can be used to grab porridges or stews.

𓇬 46. KAMUT PORRIDGE 𓇬

Kamut grains are larger than bread or emmer wheat berries. They can be boiled until tender and bursting to make a porridge.

1 cup kamut
4 cups water
Salt to taste

Combine the kamut and water in a large saucepan and bring to a boil. Reduce the heat to a simmer and cook until the grains burst and break down, adding more water if the pan seems dry. Drain off any excess liquid. Serve with any of the condiments, if desired, or as a base for Boiled Beef Shanks (Recipe 49).

𓋹 47. BARLEY AND FISH SOUP 𓋹

One predynastic burial site dating to the late fourth millennium B.C.E. had corpses with unusually well-preserved stomach contents: one individual's last meal was a soup made of barley and tilapia, a firm, white-fleshed fish with large flakes. The stomach contents included bones, fins, and scales. This inelegant fare contrasts with the (admittedly later) Sumerian proverb that a loving husband removes the bones from fish for his wife.

1/2 cup barley
3 cups water
4 scallions, sliced
1 clove garlic, minced
1 whole tilapia, gutted (whole catfish or sea bream can be substituted)
2 tablespoons butter
Salt to taste

1. Rinse the barley under cold running water to remove some of the surface starch. Place the barley in a saucepan with the water. Bring to a boil and simmer for 30 minutes, skimming any starchy foam that rises to the top.
2. Add the scallions and garlic and boil another 10 minutes.
3. Cut the fish through the backbone into chunks, keeping on the skin and fins. Add the chunks to the barley base and cook 10 minutes more. Stir in the butter and salt to taste and serve.

DAIRY

Tomb paintings show Egyptian youths drinking milk straight from the cows' udders, and milk was part of the ritualized offerings for the dead. The earliest recorded reference to milk is in the funerary offerings for King Unas (Old Kingdom, Sixth Dynasty), who had "milk, three kinds of beer, [and] five kinds of wine" to quench his thirst in the afterlife. Milk is listed as part of the offerings in the *Book of the Dead*, written during the New Kingdom. There is scant linguistic evidence for either butter or cheese; several somewhat ambiguous artistic renderings have been interpreted as cheese making. Curds were used medicinally, but rather than being eaten, they were applied topically. Microscopic analysis of remains from jars buried in tombs predating the Old Kingdom shows remnants of a fresh cheese, but there is no evidence of added flavorings. The following recipe is speculative.

𝕪 48. FENNEL-FLAVORED CHEESE 𝕪

2 quarts cow's milk
1/2 cup yogurt
1/2 rennet tablet
2 tablespoons salt
1 tablespoon ground fennel

1. Warm the milk in a large saucepan to 110°F. Remove from the heat and stir in the yogurt. Cover the pan, wrap it in a towel to retain heat, and let ferment for 1 hour.
2. Crush the rennet with 1 tablespoon of water. Rewarm the milk mixture to 110°F on an instant-read thermometer and stir in the rennet. Cover the pan as in step 1 and set aside in a warm place for 1 hour; curds will form.
3. Return to a very low heat and gently slice the curd in the pan into small pieces; keep the curd at 110°F for 10 minutes.
4. Line a colander with three layers of cheesecloth and place over a bowl to catch the whey. Spoon the curd into the colander, sprinkling with salt and ground fennel. Tie the cheesecloth into a ball and let drain overnight in the refrigerator.
5. Transfer the curd to dry cheesecloth and let drain in the refrigerator another 24 hours. Serve.

MEATS AND FISH

The Nile Delta's pastures supported cattle; sheep and goats; and, to a lesser extent, pigs. The Egyptians favored cattle, domesticating several breeds and practicing animal husbandry, such as neutering bulls to create docile oxen that fattened readily. Egyptians liked fatty meats: cattle, ducks, and geese were force-fed by hand, often until the animals collapsed under their own weight, before slaughtering for elite tables. Chickens were introduced only in the first millennium B.C.E., but sophisticated artificial incubation soon developed that could hatch more than 10,000 chicks at a time. This technology would be lost and an alternative system that could produce as many hatchlings would not emerge until early twentieth-century America.

Wild game and birds were hunted and trapped, but exotic animals, such as water buffalo, giraffes, and various antelopes, although eaten in predynastic times, were relegated to very wealthy tables as a sport animal and had little effect on the average diet in dynastic times.

⚱ 49. BOILED BEEF SHANKS ⚱

In the Old and Middle Kingdoms, the pharaoh, as king and high priest of the land, owned all of Egypt's land and cattle, at least in name. As part of the dynamic between the pharaoh and his administrators, including the priests whose religious works helped ensure the gods' favor, these officials were granted land in the pharaoh's name and resources to raise cattle for their own use. Beef consumption thus was generally limited to the upper strata; those below the elites might eat beef as part of festivals hosted by the state or their superiors, or be given beef as part of rations. By the New Kingdom, the system had changed, and land ownership and the ability to raise large animals had spread beyond the most favored elites, although beef was still too expensive for most of the population to raise themselves.

Many artistic renderings show Egyptians spit roasting large joints of beef or boiling legs in large cauldrons. This recipe entails boiling beef shanks (a portion of the leg) that have been cut crosswise into individual servings about 1 1/2 inches thick, keeping the bone in. The Italians call this cut osso buco, or "bone with the hole," referring to the hollow, marrow-filled shank bone. The use of wine vinegar, made from turned wine, reinforces this as a potentially elite dish, since most Egyptians would seldom have had access to wine, nor would they have kept it around long enough for it to have turned into vinegar.

2 tablespoons vegetable oil
4 pieces beef shank, cut for osso buco
1/2 cup red wine vinegar
3 cups beef broth
1 cup water
3/4 teaspoon dried thyme
1 head garlic, separated into individual cloves, peeled
Salt to taste

1. Heat the oil in a sauté pan large enough to hold the beef in one layer. Add the shanks and brown on both sides. Add the vinegar, broth, water, and seasonings. Bring to a boil, reduce the heat to a simmer, cover, and cook for 2 1/2–3 hours, turning the meat once or twice, until tender.
2. Remove the meat from the pan and pull the meat away from the bones into bite-sized pieces. Strain the cooking liquid into cups, pressing down on the garlic cloves to force them through the sieve and into the liquid for sipping with the meat. Serve with a bread (Recipes 41, 43, or 45) or porridge (Recipes 39, 44, or 46).

> *The goddess Sekhat-Hor guaranteed a good supply of meat for the table and was depicted as a nursing cow.*

℣ 50. DRIED SPICED BEEF ℣

Meat spoils quickly in the hot Egyptian climate, so preserving part of slaughtered beef by drying was a frequent practice that was illustrated in many tomb paintings. The blend of curing agents is a mystery, although salt was long known to speed drying. Scientists have established that certain spices inhibit bacterial growth in meats, but whether the Egyptians had intuited this chemistry from years of observation is unknown. Because sun drying is impractical in most climates in the United States, the meat will be placed in a low oven to approximate the right environment. Archaeological remains show bones with evidence of butchery marks, suggesting that larger cuts were filleted.

1/4 teaspoon ground cumin
1/2 teaspoon ground coriander
1/4 teaspoon ground mustard
1/2 teaspoon ground nigella seeds
1/2 teaspoon ground sumac
1/4 teaspoon ground fennel
1/4 teaspoon ground fenugreek
1 teaspoon salt
1 chuck or flank steak, about 1 pound, sliced across the grain into
    strips no more than 1/2 inch thick

Preheat the oven to 200°F. Combine all of the spices together and toss with the strips of steak. Place the strips on a baking tray in the oven for 2 1/2 hours, or until the meat is dried and very chewy. Cool to room temperature and serve. If the meat has been thoroughly dried, it can be stored at room temperature.

℣ 51. GRILLED PORK CHOPS WITH SCALLIONS ℣

Although pigs were eaten by all social classes in Upper Egypt in predynastic times, the pig slowly lost status after the unification of Upper and Lower Egypt in the Old Kingdom. This very simple recipe is appropriate to laborers throughout pharaonic Egypt and to upper classes in earlier periods.

2 pork chops, about 3/4 inch thick
4 scallions
Vegetable oil as needed
Salt to taste

USING CURRENT FOOD HABITS TO INFER WHAT PEOPLE ATE IN THE PAST: A CAUTIONARY TALE

Scholars used to believe that pigs were taboo, based on statements by Herodotus, the fifth-century B.C.E. Greek historian, that any Egyptian who brushed against a pig would immediately plunge into the Nile for purification. Scholars also argued that because pork is forbidden by both Jewish and Islamic dietary law, the earlier ancient Egyptians must have considered them unclean. But once modern scholars deciphered temple records and went on extensive archaeological digs, pigs emerged as an important part of the Egyptian diet. Pig remains found throughout the predynastic site of Hierakonpolis suggest that all social classes ate pork. Pharaohs offered them at temples and for feasts, and some midden heaps have more pig bones than cattle, sheep, and goat remains. The role of pigs may have changed by New Kingdom times, when pork seems to have been considered a lower-class food: excavations at the workers' village built to house laborers creating the tombs in the Valley of the Kings have disproportionately more pig bones.

Preheat a grill pan until hot. Coat the pork chops and scallions with a light film of oil. Place the chops on the grill and cook, about 6–7 minutes per side. Halfway through the cooking, add the scallions to the grill, turning several times to soften. Sprinkle with salt before serving.

52. GRILLED QUAIL

Tomb paintings show high-status Egyptians nibbling quail; according to Herodotus, Egyptians ate them raw (after salting) or pickled. Raw quail may not be far-fetched: not only are many game birds eaten very rare in modern times, but the salt, if allowed to sit on the birds for an hour or more, would transform the texture of the small birds' flesh. This might be similar to the Swedish specialty gravalax, which is raw salmon cured with salt and eaten thinly sliced. Illustrations of quail and other game birds often show them spatchcocked, that is, with the backbone removed and the bird flattened and skewered on each side through the leg and the wing. It is a sturdy way of holding the birds for grilling, and the flattening helps them cook evenly.

4 quail
1/4 teaspoon ground fennel
1 tablespoon minced parsley
1 tablespoon *smen* (Recipe 10)

1 1/2 tablespoons olive oil
Salt to taste

1. Carefully remove the backbone from the quail by running a small knife down either side, starting at the neck opening. The bones are delicate, and you should encounter little resistance.
2. Combine the fennel, parsley, and butter in a small bowl. Slide your index finger between the skin and the breast meat of the quail. Smear a bit of the butter mixture over the breast meat. Rub the oil over the quail and sprinkle with salt.
3. Thread the quail onto two long metal skewers by piercing the wings and upper breast with one skewer and the thighs and lower tip of the breast with the other. Preheat a grill pan over medium heat. Grill the quail, skin side down, for about 5 minutes, or until golden brown. Turn and continue cooking for another 3 minutes. Serve immediately.

Note: Quail is best served pink, as it will have a more delicate flavor, but if you prefer it more well done, continue cooking until the desired degree of doneness.

৺ 53. EGYPTIAN CASSOULET: BROAD BEANS WITH SALTED MEATS ৺

Cassoulet is a traditional French dish made from beans cooked with salted meats that have been preserved in fat. Given the heavy use of dried beans by the Egyptians, as well as jars labeled preserved meat found in tombs, it is a short step to combine these two foods into one dish. Cassoulet is garlicky, which would be in keeping with Egyptian tastes. The beans could have been eaten by all social classes, yet the expense of using salt to preserve meats would probably make this dish too expensive for laborers' daily fare. The Tomb of Kha, a superintendent of public works in the New Kingdom, contained jars of salted birds. This dish requires two days to prepare.

Lupines (*lupinus albus*) were widely eaten in Egypt; the raw bean required soaking for several days to remove certain toxins. Italian markets sometimes carry broad beans under the name *lupini*, although they are not lupines. Fava beans or black-eyed peas, another African legume, can be substituted.

1 pound dried fava beans or black-eyed peas
1 pound pork riblets, separated into individual ribs
2 duck legs
1 head garlic, separated into cloves and peeled
1/3 cup kosher salt
1 bunch fresh thyme

2 cups duck fat (preferred), or lard or olive oil

1. Soak the pulses overnight in cool water that covers them by 2 inches.
2. While the pulses are soaking, combine the riblets, duck legs, and garlic. Coat with the salt and scatter the thyme over the mixture. Place on a rack over a flat pan in the refrigerator and let drain overnight.
3. The next day, wipe off the salt. Place the meats and seasonings in a heavy stewing pan and add the fat. Bring the pan to a gentle simmer and cook for 2 hours, turning the meats to cook uniformly. Remove the meat and garlic from the fat and let cool.
4. While the meat is cooking, drain the pulses and place in a large pan. Cover with water by 3 inches and bring to a boil. Reduce the heat to a simmer and cook until the pulses are tender, adding water if needed. Drain any excess water.
5. When the duck is cool enough to handle, pull the meat from the bones. Add the duck meat, the riblets, and the garlic to the pulses, plus a little of the cooking fat, if desired. Cook over low heat for 10–15 minutes to meld the flavors.

𓍿 54. ROAST DUCK WITH DATE STUFFING 𓍿

Dates have a high sugar content (70%–80% dry weight), which makes them ideal for storage because bacterial growth is inhibited. There is no direct evidence that Egyptians made stuffings, but they would have been a plausible use for leftover bread.

1 5-pound duck
1/4 cup water
1 onion, cut in half through the root end, peeled, and sliced into
    1/2-inch half moons
2 cups stale whole wheat bread cubes, or use any bread from this chapter
1 cup dried dates, coarsely chopped
3/4 teaspoon salt

1. Preheat the oven to 450°F. Remove the fat pads from inside of the duck, as well as any excess fat from the neck cavity.
2. Place the fat in a small saucepan with 1/4 cup water. Gently heat to a boil and reduce the heat to melt some of the fat. Cook until the water evaporates; you will know by a slight sizzling sound.
3. Heat 2 tablespoons of the rendered duck fat in a medium skillet (add a little butter or oil if there is not enough fat). Add the onions and cook over medium heat to soften.

4. Combine the onions, bread cubes, dates, and half the salt. Stuff into the cavity of the duck. Sprinkle the rest of the salt on the outside of the duck and place in a roasting pan at least 2 inches deep, breast side down.

5. Cook for 40 minutes. Remove the pan carefully from the oven (there will be hot fat in the bottom of the pan), and, using heavy tongs or a large kitchen fork, turn the duck breast side up. Return the duck to the oven for another 40–60 minutes, or until a meat thermometer inserted into the thigh reads 165°F.

6. Remove the stuffing from the duck cavity and serve on the side, with slices of the duck breast and the duck legs.

𝍪 55. FOIE GRAS WITH FIGS 𝍪

Tomb images show birds being force-fed to fatten them for the table, a process whereby the bird's neck is held and soaked grain is introduced into the bird's gullet so that it eats more than it would under confined barnyard circumstances. Birds also gorge themselves in the wild to fatten up for long, migratory flights so the cultivation techniques has precedents in nature. In both cases, the birds develop a thick layer of fat and their livers become enlarged. When a bird is slaughtered after fattening, the liver becomes the delicately flavored gourmet treat known to the modern world as foie gras, or fat liver.

Professional chefs pull out the sinewy vessels that run through the livers for aesthetic reasons, a step that requires patience, but is not difficult. If fresh foie gras is unavailable or too expensive, you can substitute tinned pâté de foie gras. The Egyptian record offers no guidance as to how foie gras was prepared; contemporary recipes often pair the liver with acidic fruits, and this recipe is inspired by modern practice. As a carefully cultivated meat product, foie gras would have been eaten by the wealthy, just as it is nowadays. The wine in this invented recipe makes it appropriate for elites; also, because fat was highly regarded, reincorporating the pan fat, which is done in many modern foie gras preparations, is also true to the spirit of ancient Egyptian cookery.

6 dried figs
1/4 cup pomegranate molasses
3/4 cup wine
1/2 pound fresh foie gras or tinned pâté de foie gras, cut into slices 3/4 inch thick
1/4 teaspoon ground cumin
Coarse salt to taste

1. Place the figs in a small saucepan and add the molasses and wine. Bring to a boil, reduce the heat to a simmer, and cook gently until

the figs are soft. Remove the figs and cut in half. Reduce the cooking liquid over high heat to a syrup. Reserve. If you are using tinned pâté de foie gras, skip to step 3.

2. Meanwhile, bring the fresh foie gras to room temperature to make cleaning easier. Gently poke along the edges of the liver to locate large veins. Pull or scrape them out, using your fingers or a paring knife. Slice the liver into medallions about 3/4 inch thick. Refrigerate for 30 minutes, or until ready to cook, to firm up the texture.

3. Preheat a small frying pan over medium heat for 1 minute. Sprinkle the liver with cumin and coarse salt. Sauté lightly on the first side, about 30 seconds. Fresh liver will give off lots of fat. Turn, and cook another 20–30 seconds. Remove the liver to serving plates and scatter with the poached figs. Add the syrup to the fat in the pan, stir briefly, and pour over the medallions. Serve with bread to soak up the sauce.

𓌙 56. PAN-FRIED KIDNEYS 𓌙

A dish of cooked kidneys was part of the funerary offerings in an elite Second Dynasty tomb (ca. 2890–2686 B.C.E.). The addition of sauce to this recipe is speculative. Modern cooks soak kidneys in milk to remove any whiff of ureic acid; how the Egyptians may have dealt with this culinary issue is unknown. Modern cooks also often pair kidneys with richly flavored sauces, especially mustard.

Mustard seeds have been found in Twelfth Dynasty tombs, and Roman writers prized Egyptian mustard. An herb believed to be parsley has been identified in medical texts as a cure for urinary incontinence; perhaps it was also used as a seasoning. Kidneys taste best when cooked no more than medium, that is, slightly pink on the inside.

1 pound lamb or veal kidneys
2 cups milk
4 tablespoons butter
Salt to taste
1 tablespoon ground mustard
1/4 cup vinegar mixed with 2 tablespoons water
3 sprigs parsley, chopped

1. Soak the kidneys in the milk in the refrigerator for 1 hour. Drain and dry thoroughly.
2. Preheat a large sauté pan over high heat and add the butter. Add the dried kidneys and cook on one side until a rich brown color, about 4 minutes; turn and continue cooking, another 2–3 minutes. Sprinkle with salt and remove from the pan.

3. Stir the mustard into the diluted vinegar and add to the butter remaining in the pan. Cook for 45 seconds, add the parsley, swirl to incorporate,, and remove from the heat. Cut the kidneys crosswise into thin slices and drizzle with the pan sauce.

☥ 57. GRILLED FISH WITH DILL ☥

By the first millennium B.C.E., some elite Egyptians began to consider fish taboo. Priests in particular might avoid fish as a defilement of their ritual purity, perhaps because fish defiled the god Osiris by eating his phallus after the god was killed and dismembered by his brother Seth. The taboo was not universally observed, as plenty of fish remains litter temple complexes. For most Egyptians, fish formed a regular part of the diet.

Fish were plentiful along the Nile, especially those that bred successfully in shallow waters, such as tilapia. Catfish also did well in the muddy waters.

4 sprigs dill
2 catfish fillets, or other meaty white-fleshed fish, skin on
Salt to taste
Jarred grape or fig leaves, as needed
4 teaspoons vegetable oil

1. Place 2 sprigs of dill on the flesh side of each fish fillet. Season with salt and wrap each fillet in the leaves to enclose. Rub each package with half the oil.
2. Preheat a grill pan until hot. Cook the fillets for 5 minutes, turn, and continue cooking until done, about another 3 minutes. Let each diner open the grape leaf wrapping at the table.

☥ 58. PICKLED MULLET ☥

The pharaoh Ramses III reigned for 31 years during the twelfth century B.C.E.; during that time, he provided 495,000 gutted, fresh, and pickled fish for public feasts to celebrate various holidays. The most esteemed fish was mullet.

2 whole shallots, peeled and thinly sliced
2 1/2 cups white vinegar
1 1/2 cups water
2 tablespoons salt
1/2 cup chopped cilantro
1 pound mullet filets, or other lean white fish, cleaned

Place the shallots, vinegar, water, salt, and cilantro in a pan large enough to accommodate the fish in one layer. Bring the mixture to a boil and simmer

3 minutes. Add the fish and turn off the heat. Let the fish rest in the hot liquid 10 minutes, or until cooked through. Carefully remove the filets from the pickle and serve hot or cold.

VEGETABLES

Vegetables leave little trace in the archaeobotanical record. Unlike charred cereals, animal bones, or even pits from fruits, vegetable tissues are soft and disappear, making evidence of vegetables rare in tombs and midden heaps. Nonetheless, vegetables played an important role in the diets of all Egyptian classes. For the elites, laboriously irrigated kitchen gardens supplied vegetables for the table. For the landless poor, wild weedy plants might be foraged among grain crops, in marshes, or in other marginal lands. Workers received vegetables as part of their rations, although ancient lists do not specify varieties; similarly, the *Book of the Dead* simply lists "green things such as were with [the deceased] on earth."[8]

☥ 59. BRAISED MOHLUHKIA ☥

Mohluhkia (*corchorus olitorius*) is a leafy green that is thought to have been introduced to Egypt from Syria in pharaonic times, although the first definitive evidence dates to Roman times. Modern Egyptians make one-pot stews from mohluhkia, often combined with lamb, rabbit, or poultry and chili peppers. Fresh mohluhkia is hard to find, but canned or frozen mohluhkia can be found in Middle Eastern markets in the United States. You can substitute spinach, beet greens, or sorrel, singly or in combination; the spinach and sorrel are anachronistic, but closer in flavor to mohluhkia, while the beet greens could have been eaten by Egyptians.

Mohluhkia probably grew wild in at least parts of ancient Egypt and thus was available to the poorest peasants. To reflect a dish suitable for the poor, this recipe is deliberately designed with a short cooking time to use minimal fuel and to maintain the onions and garlic in a state somewhere between raw and cooked, in keeping with the Egyptian habit of eating many of their onions raw.

2 tablespoons vegetable oil
1 large onion, peeled and coarsely chopped
3 cloves garlic, chopped
1 teaspoon ground coriander
1/2 teaspoon ground cumin
10 ounces canned or frozen mohluhkia or spinach, or 2 bunches fresh
    spinach, beet greens, or sorrel, washed and coarsely chopped
Salt to taste

Gently heat the oil in a large saucepan until warm, and add the onions. Cook for 15 seconds; they should just start to soften a bit. Add the garlic and spices and cook another 15 seconds. Add the greens of your choice and cook to wilt and warm through. Season with salt and serve, preferably with Kush Bread (Recipe 45) or Matzoh (Recipe 40).

Variation: Combine Braised Mohluhkia with Lentil Salad (Recipe 61) for a complete vegetarian dinner.

⚶ 60. LOTUS ROOT SALAD ⚶

The blue lotus flower symbolized rebirth to the Egyptians, as the blooms opened shortly after dawn only to close tightly by midday. The lotus was associated with banquets; the flower is intensely perfumed, and lotus petals and roots contain mildly narcotic alkaloids that are soluble in alcohol. Wines infused with lotus may have been especially intoxicating. Lotus roots are still used in Chinese cookery and can be found in Asian markets.

1 small onion
1 lotus root, about 1 pound
1/2 fresh pomegranate, preferred, or 1 cup red grapes
Salt to taste
Vegetable or olive oil to taste

Slice the onion and lotus root as thinly as possible. Remove and separate the fruitlets from the pomegranate, if available. Otherwise, cut the grapes in half and remove any pips. Combine the onion, lotus root, and fruit in a large bowl. Season with salt and drizzle with oil to taste, tossing to blend.

⚶ 61. LENTIL SALAD ⚶

Lentils are one of Egypt's oldest foods, found in predynastic tombs. One Greek writer noted that Alexandria was a "city full of lentil dishes."[9] Lentils were an important article of commerce. According to the *Tale of Wen-amon*, a late New Kingdom story, lentils were traded for Lebanese cedar. Lebanon would also have been a source for olives and olive oil in much of the pharaonic period.

Dill was brought to Egypt from Palestine, along with cumin and coriander, and easily adapted to the Egyptian climate. Herbs were used as insecticides and eventually were part of elite burial rites, found in various tombs from the Middle Kingdom forward, including that of the well-known New Kingdom pharaoh Tutankhamen. Their use in ancient Egyptian cooking seems likely.

1 cup lentils
1/4 cup chopped onion

1/4 cup olive oil

Salt to taste

2 tablespoons chopped dill

Place the lentils in a saucepan and cover with water by 2 inches. Bring to a boil and cook until the lentils are tender, about 25–35 minutes. Drain. Season with the remaining ingredients. Serve hot or at room temperature.

⸙ 62. CHOPPED SALAD ⸙

The types of lettuces available in ancient Egypt were limited to the cos family, long, leafy heads that tend to tough, sometimes bitter leaves. It is unclear whether the Egyptians actually ate these lettuces as a vegetable or simply cultivated them for their rich, oil-producing seeds. If they ate the lettuces, perhaps they were combined with flavorful herbs such as cress, and sweeter-tasting plants, such as fennel, to balance the bitterness. Dill sprigs were found in the New Kingdom tomb of Amenhotep. The evidence for the use of fennel or radishes, either in bulb form or as a spice or oil-producing seed, is inconclusive; scholars disagree about whether the translation of certain terms as fennel and radish is accurate or whether these mysterious terms referred to less familiar plants. Radishes were not indigenous but were introduced at an unknown date. According to the Roman writer Pliny the Elder, they were an important and profitable oil and vegetable crop by classical times.

The Egyptians undoubtedly had plenty of vinegar, resulting from wine oxidizing in air-permeable pottery containers. Whether they shared the modern taste for vinaigrette-dressed salads is impossible to know from the current archaeological record.

2 cups cleaned, coarsely chopped chicory

1 bunch watercress, tough stems removed, coarsely chopped

2 cups chopped romaine leaves

1/2 onion, thinly sliced

1 head fennel, stalks and core removed, thinly sliced

4 radishes, cleaned and thinly sliced

1/4 cup dill sprigs

Salt, vegetable or olive oil (about 1/3 cup, more or less), and vinegar
  (about 3 tablespoons, more or less) to taste

Combine the greens, vegetables, and dill in a bowl. Season to taste with salt, oil, and vinegar, tossing thoroughly.

Lettuce symbolized fertility to the Egyptians because ancient lettuces exuded a milky sap reminiscent of semen. Min, the god of vegetation and procreation, is often shown in a lettuce field, with Pharaoh offering a lettuce plant to the god.

ϗ 63. SAVORY MELON SALAD ϗ

Chate (*cucumis melo* var. *chate*) is closely related to the cucumber (*c. sativus*). Scholars disagree about exactly when the cucumber reached Egypt. Most think that it was relatively late, around classical times, although some place it back in the Middle Kingdom. All agree that its cousin, chate, was found in pharaonic Egypt. Part of the confusion arises in the artistic record: small oval melons that could be either cucumbers or chates appear in tomb paintings. Neither cucumber nor chate is sweet, and because chate is difficult to find in the United States, this recipe substitutes the similar cucumber for the ancient Egyptian fruit.

12 mint leaves, chopped
1 tablespoon honey
1 1/2 tablespoons vinegar
1 large cucumber, washed and thinly sliced
1/2 onion, chopped
Salt to taste

Combine all of the ingredients and toss thoroughly.

ϗ 64. SWEET MELON SALAD ϗ

In addition to savory melons, the ancient Egyptians enjoyed sweet musk-melons (similar to honeydew or cantaloupe) and may have enjoyed watermelon, although there is some debate as to whether the latter was cultivated mainly for its oil-rich seeds.

Sweet melon likely was eaten plain on many occasions. This invented recipe uses seasoning that would have been available in Egypt and makes a refreshing salad.

1 cantaloupe or honeydew, cut in half, seeds discarded, and flesh cut
    into bite-sized cubes
1/2 teaspoon ground sumac
2 tablespoons chopped cilantro
1/2 onion, thinly sliced
1 teaspoon nigella seeds

Combine all the ingredients and toss thoroughly.

CONDIMENTS

ϗ 65. DUKKAH (NUT AND SPICE BLEND) ϗ

Modern Egyptians still make snack and seasoning blends such as *dukkah* from ingredients that were indigenous or imported to ancient Egypt. *Duk-*

kah can be eaten with flatbreads, by either dipping the breads' edges in the mix or sprinkling it on the surface and holding it like a slice of pizza. With the fats and proteins from the nuts and seeds, *dukkah* can make a subsistence diet for the poor. Similar foods using local ingredients may have been important in pharaonic times.

1/2 cup sesame seeds, toasted in a 350°F oven for 8 minutes
2 tablespoons dried mint
1 tablespoon dried marjoram
1/4 cup coriander seed
1 tablespoon cumin seed
1/4 cup blanched hazelnuts, toasted in a 350°F oven for 8 minutes
1 teaspoon salt

Combine all the ingredients in a mortar and pound with a pestle to pulverize. Serve as a dip for hot flatbreads, either dry or brushed generously with olive oil, or as a seasoning for simply prepared dishes.

℣ 66. BATAREKH *(DRIED ROE)* ℣

Batarekh is the salted and gently dried egg sacks (roe) of fish, usually mullet, but tuna and cod roes are traditionally preserved this way as well. *Batarekh* is known by different names, including the French *boutargue,* the Italian *bottarga,* and the Greek *tarama.* Pungent, salty, and rich, the roe flavors bland carbohydrates and remains popular around the Mediterranean. Modern Egyptians slice *batarekh* thinly and serve it on bread brushed with butter or olive oil. It may have been served the same way in pharaonic times to enliven bread, legumes, or porridge.

Salted, dried roe can be purchased at well-stocked ethnic and gourmet markets, but it is easy to make if you have access to fresh roe, and the flavor is vastly superior: salty, earthy, and not too funky.

1 pair of shad or other roes, with the thin membrane covering the
    eggs intact, about 1 1/2 pounds
1 cup or more kosher salt
Flatbreads, olive oil, onion, and parsley for serving

1. Gently dredge the roe in the salt, trying not to break the encasing membrane. Place on a triple layer of paper toweling on a plate and place in the refrigerator. The eggs will begin to give off liquid. Replace the toweling as the paper gets wet, two or three times a day, turning the roe over to absorb moisture from all sides. Keep sprinkling with a thick layer of salt to remove as much moisture as possible.

2. Once the roe stops leaching water (after about 3 days), air-dry the roe by preheating an oven to 200°F. Turn the oven off. Place the

roe in the turned-off oven and let the oven cool down completely. Repeat the process, removing the roe while heating the oven. The roe should be firm, but not hard.

3. To serve: Brush a flatbread generously with olive oil. Sprinkle with 2 tablespoons finely minced onion and 1 tablespoon finely minced parsley. Slice or grate as much *batarekh* as you like on top. Cut the flatbread into wedges and serve. Alternatively, grate the roe over any cooked legume. *Batarekh* can be stored at room temperature, sealed in wax, or refrigerated.

𓇳 67. CHICKPEA DIP (HUMMUS) 𓇳

Faience (glazed, fired pottery) models of chickpeas appear in New Kingdom tombs, but there is little evidence of how they might have been processed for food. In addition to hummus, modern Egyptians eat roasted chickpeas tossed in salt or sugar. Ancient Egyptians might have eaten them with salt, although sugar would be anachronistic.

2 cups chickpeas, soaked overnight in 2 quarts water, or two 15-ounce
    cans chickpeas, drained
2 cloves garlic, minced
2 tablespoons white vinegar
1/2 cup tahini (sesame paste)
1 1/2 teaspoons ground cumin
1 teaspoon ground coriander
1 tablespoon ground sumac
Water, as needed
Salt to taste
Olive oil and chopped cilantro, for garnish

1. If using dried chickpeas, drain them and place in a pot with water to cover by 3 inches and boil until tender, about 45 minutes. Drain.
2. Working in batches, combine the chickpeas (canned or just cooked), garlic, vinegar, tahini, cumin, coriander, and sumac in a mortar and pound with a pestle to purée. Alternatively, combine in one batch in a food processor and pulse. Thin with water as needed, and season with salt to taste. Garnish generously with olive oil and cilantro.

𓇳 68. RAW ONION RELISH 𓇳

Onions were common on offering tables from the Fourth Dynasty forward, usually accompanying bread. During the Late Period (ca. 664–332 B.C.E.), priests sometimes avoided eating onions, which, like fish, became another food considered taboo for those maintaining the sanctity of the temples. This priestly shunning may also have been a way of asserting class distinctions given that the social hierarchy was in flux during that time. The Romans, who annexed Egypt as a Roman province in the first century B.C.E., mocked the local Egyptian tradition of eating raw onions.

The optional olive oil in this recipe is designed to make the relish a little more appealing to contemporary palates and to offer a variation suitable for the wealthier classes of ancient Egyptian society: olive trees grew successfully in relatively small areas and could not have satisfied all of Egyptian demand. Imported oil was another option, again, a luxury available to the landholding and administrative classes.

> 1 yellow onion, finely minced
> 4 scallions, thinly sliced, white and light green parts only
> 2 cloves garlic, finely minced
> 1/2 cup coarsely chopped parsley
> Salt to taste
> Optional: 3–4 tablespoons olive oil

Combine all the ingredients. Serve with warm flat breads.

℣ 69. YOGURT AND TAHINI SAUCE ℣

There is no archaeological or textual evidence for this recipe, yet given the use of very traditional ingredients, ancient Egyptians may have enjoyed sauces like this. Today, with the addition of lemon juice and red chilies, ingredients unavailable to ancient Egyptians, it is popular in modern Egypt.

> 2 tablespoons tahini
> 1/4 cup yogurt
> 1 tablespoon pomegranate molasses or vinegar
> 1 tablespoon water
> 1 clove garlic, finely minced
> Salt to taste

Combine all of the ingredients and stir to blend. Serve with meat, fish, or poultry or as a dipping sauce for breads.

SWEETS AND PASTRIES

℣ 70. CAROB CAKE ℣

Carob is also known as locust bean and may be the "locusts" of John the Baptist's desert sojourn. When modern pods are freshly picked, they are tender, although some scholars question whether the tender pods are the result of selective breeding. They suggest that the pods in the ancient world were tough and fibrous, requiring stone grinding and seeming much more like the dried pods that are imported into the United States. Carob pods have been found in tombs at least as early as the Twelfth Dynasty of the Middle Kingdom.

Almonds have been found in a few New Kingdom tombs; there is little evidence for cultivation of almonds in the Nile Valley, so these would have been a luxury. This recipe uses chicken eggs, anachronistic to ancient Egyptians. Cakes could have been made with the eggs of ducks or other birds available to the Egyptians.

> 1 cup carob powder
> 1/2 cup whole wheat flour
> 1 cup ground almonds
> 1/2 cup raisins
> 5/8 cup carob molasses (substitute honey if carob molasses is
>   unavailable)
> 2 eggs
> 1/4 cup vegetable oil, plus more for the pan

1. Preheat the oven to 325°F. Mix the carob powder, flour, nuts, and raisins.
2. Combine the carob molasses or honey, eggs, and vegetable oil, beating thoroughly. Stir the mixture into the dry ingredients to moisten uniformly. Scrape the mixture into an oiled 8-inch cake pan. Bake for 30–35 minutes, or until a skewer inserted in the middle tests clean.

𓍼 71. TIGER NUT CAKES 𓍼

The tiger nut, *Cyperus esculentus,* has edible rhizomes rich in protein and carbohydrates, with a sweet, nutty taste. Also called earth almonds, tiger nuts continue to be popular in Africa as an ingredient in sweet puddings, beverages, and jellies. Tiger nuts have been found at predynastic sites, making them one of the earliest foods identified in Egypt. The New Kingdom tomb of the vizier Rekhmire shows workers preparing offering cakes from what is believed to be tiger nuts. The entire process is illustrated, from grinding the rhizomes to shaping the dough into triangles, panfrying them, and delivering the cakes. Part of the scene illustrates beekeeping and jars of honey being delivered to the tomb, so it is possible that the cakes were eaten with honey, something like dense pancakes.

> 1 1/2 cups tiger nuts, ground (or substitute chestnut flour)
> 1 1/2 cups whole wheat flour, plus additional for rolling
> 1/3 cup milk

2 eggs, lightly beaten

3 tablespoons melted butter, plus more for frying

1/2 cup honey

1. Combine the ground nuts, flour, milk, eggs, and melted butter and knead briefly to make a dough. Cover and set aside for 30 minutes.
2. On a lightly floured surface, pat the dough into a square 1/2 inch thick. Divide the dough into four equal quadrants and cut each quadrants in half diagonally to yield 8 triangle-shaped cakes.
3. Melt 2 tablespoons butter over medium heat in a frying pan. Cook the dough triangles for about 3 minutes on the first side; turn and cook an additional 2 minutes. Pour the honey into the frying pan and cook an additional 30 seconds. Turn the cakes and cook 30 seconds more. Remove to a platter and pour the honey and fat from the pan over the cakes. Serve immediately.

Honey was an expensive luxury; Egyptians believed that honey was divinely inspired when a tear from the god Rē turned into a bee. The bee flitted from flower to flower, creating sweetness out of sadness.

𓏏 72. STEWED FIGS 𓏏

Stewed figs were one of the dishes found in a Second Dynasty tomb of an aristocratic woman. The wine suggested in this recipe would have been very luxurious at this early date and makes the recipe appropriate for Egyptian elites. By substituting beer or water for the wine, the dish can suit lesser tables.

1 cup dried figs

3/4 cup water

3/4 cup wine, any type

Combine all of the ingredients in a saucepan. Bring to a boil, reduce the heat, and simmer for 15 minutes or until the figs are softened. The exact time will depend on how dry the figs are.

BEVERAGES

𓏏 73. BOUSA (FERMENTED BARLEY BEER) 𓏏

Bousa is a lightly fermented beer that has bits of grain floating in the liquid. It is described by contemporary imbibers as a thick, yeasty beverage or a thin, yeasty porridge and is consumed in Egypt by the poor, as it is cheaply made at home. The archaeological evidence suggests that the basic manufacture of this staple food has changed little in 5,000 years. Pottery shards discovered in tombs and village excavations show grains of barley or emmer mixed in with the liquid residue. This gruel could have fueled manual laborers building the Great Pyramids or digging irrigation canals, as the live yeasts yield more protein than a comparable amount of bread (the heat kills the yeast, destroying the protein) and also valuable B vitamins. Like the many varieties of bread, this brewed staple also came in different varieties, including "dark," "iron," "garnished," friend's," and others.

Most scholars have believed that Egyptian beer was made with lightly baked breads, as found in Mesopotamia and documented in the *Hymn to Ninkasi* (see recipe 38). Recently this conventional wisdom has been called into question by an archaeologist who examined beer residues under an electron microscope. Based on the amount and pattern of fusion in the starch molecules, she concluded that certain Egyptian beer was made using a lightly cooked porridge.[10] This recipe is inspired by that research.

> 2 cups barley, coarsely ground in a grain mill
> 2 cups sprouted wheat berries (see Recipe 42, Emmer Bread with Figs,
>   for sprouting instructions), coarsely ground in a grain mill

Combine the barley with 6 cups water in a saucepan. Bring to a boil and simmer until thickened into a porridge. Remove from the heat and add 6 cups room-temperature water and the ground wheat berries. Set aside for 3 days at room temperature to ferment. Strain the liquid through a medium sieve to remove the coarsest grain, if desired, or drink through a straw.

☥ 74. POMEGRANATE SHANDY ☥

The pomegranate is one of the oldest cultivated fruit trees and had strong associations with Egypt throughout the classical world. Known to the Latin-speaking world as the Carthage apple, its many fruitlets containing seeds were a fertility symbol in both Egyptian and Greco-Roman mythologies. Plenty of artistic and archaeological evidence points to the cultivation of pomegranates, but nothing suggests how the pomegranate was used. With its sweet-tart flavor, it may have been used to make wine. Like the Mesopotamians, the Egyptians flavored their beers with fruits, spices, and herbs, so the following recipe might be one way in which Egyptians consumed the fruit. The term shandy refers to a mix of beer and lemonade, so it seems a fair invented name for this drink.

> 1 bottle nonalcoholic beer or 12 ounces of *bousa* (Recipe 73)
> 1 cup pomegranate juice or 2 tablespoons pomegranate molasses

Combine the liquids and serve in chalices.

3
ANCIENT GREECE

Greek civilization was born in the Aegean Sea. In the third millennium B.C.E., Minoans established a thriving culture on the island of Crete that spread to other islands and possibly the Greek mainland. The scale and wealth of Minoan culture, while impressive, pale in comparison to those found in contemporaneous Mesopotamia and Egypt. Various disasters, including the calamitous eruption of the volcano Thera on the island of Santorini in 1628 B.C.E., devastated Minoan life. The Mycenaeans, centered on the Greek mainland and peninsula known as the Peloponnese, succeeded the Minoans and colonized sites throughout the Aegean and the eastern Mediterranean along the coast of Anatolia. The Mycenaeans are the heroes of the *Iliad,* the poet Homer's epic recounting of the Trojan War, although he calls them Achaeans. Little is known of the victorious Mycenaeans after the Trojan War concluded in the mid-thirteenth century B.C.E.; although the Minoans and Mycenaeans were literate (their proto-Greek languages, Linear A and B, respectively, have not yet been deciphered), the Greeks plunged into the illiterate Dark Ages as more internecine wars broke out, barbarians invaded, and plagues reduced the population.

Stability returned when city-states emerged in what is known as the Archaic Age, lasting from approximately 750 to 500 B.C.E. City-states (known in Greek as *polis*) were self-governing, independent urban centers with populations that lived off the surrounding farmland and countryside. The city-states were loosely confederated but never developed into a cohesive Greek nation; much of Greece's landmass is mountainous and difficult to trans-

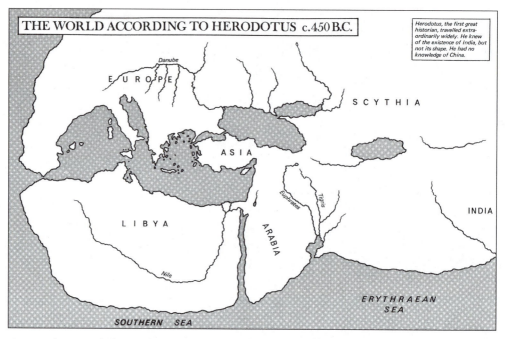

THE WORLD ACCORDING TO HERODOTUS c.450 B.C.

Herodotus, the first great historian, travelled extraordinarily widely. He knew of the existence of India, but not its shape. He had no knowledge of China.

From: The Routledge Atlas of Classical History, *Michael Grant, Copyright (© 1994), Routledge. Reproduced by permission of Taylor & Francis Books UK.*

verse, making communications hard and centralized government unmanageable. Each city-state thus retained its distinctive politics, culture, and even food preferences. City-states had limited local resources, so as their populations grew, Greeks searched the Mediterranean for sites to colonize. Greeks settled in southern Italy (known as Magna Graecia), Sicily, along the Black Sea and the Aegean coast of Anatolia, and even in isolated outposts in Spain and France, although Greece civilization centered in the eastern Mediterranean and Aegean.

During the fifth and fourth centuries B.C.E., known as Greece's Classical Age, the most powerful city-states were Athens, which controlled the lands known as Attica on the mainland, and Sparta, which controlled the region of Laconia in the Peloponnese. United by the Greek tongue, the city-states and colonies banded together when threatened by outsiders, most notably to defeat the Persian king Xerxes. Nonetheless, intense rivalries continued within the Greek world, resulting in the Peloponnesian War in the late fifth century B.C.E. in which Sparta defeated Athens. Skirmishes between various Greeks and with Persia continued, leaving a power vacuum in the fourth century B.C.E. filled by the Macedonians and Alexander the Great, who extended Greek control over Egypt and Persia up to the border with India. Through Alexander's eastern campaigns, Greeks learned of previously unknown foods, such as the citron, that became part of the Mediterranean diet. Greek political rule collapsed shortly after Alexander's death, although Greek influence continued throughout the Mediterranean and beyond for centuries. Well-educated Romans read both Greek and Latin and emulated much of Greek culture, including its food. Theater, experiments in democracy, the foundations of Western philosophy, and the Olympics are all Greek legacies.

Unlike with Mesopotamia and Egypt, Greek culinary literature abounds. The Greeks invented the art of gastronomic writing, never tiring of discussing food and cookery from a critical perspective. The word *gastronomy* combines two Greek roots meaning *stomach* and *laws*; modern English defines gastronomy as the art and science of good eating, evoking the legendary Greek appreciation of fine cuisine. By the fifth century B.C.E., Greeks had linked food to medicine in learned treatises; had written cookbooks, fragments of which survive; had founded cooking schools; and even had made wily cooks stock characters in Greek comedies.

FOODSTUFFS AND AGRICULTURE

- Barley and pulses were common staples; emmer and bread wheat were appreciated for bread when available.
- Grapes thrived in the Mediterranean climate and were used for wine, vinegar, raisins, and syrups; other fruits included figs, apples, pears, peaches, and plums.
- Olive oil was the major cooking fat; animal fats, while important, played a lesser role.
- Cheese was an important ingredient in gourmet cooking as well as eaten on its own; there is little discussion of milk and yogurt, but yogurt would have been another way to preserve milk.
- Sheep and goats were valued for their milk and meat; cattle were more valuable as work animals but were eaten at major sacrifices. Pigs were another common meat source. Game, such as deer and wild boar, and a range of birds were appreciated.
- An astounding array of fish and seafood were a significant part of the diet. Fish could be fresh or preserved. Large fish, such as tuna, were more prestigious; smaller fish were cheaper and considered less desirable. Small, fried fish were a common street food in the *agora* (marketplace). *Garum* (fermented fish sauce, known to the Greeks as *garos*) was a common seasoning.
- Vegetables such as lettuces, leafy cabbages, onions, asparagus, roots, pulses, and lupines were widely eaten. Gardens and field agriculture supplied cultivated vegetables. Wild varieties were foraged from the

lands immediately surrounding Greek villages, towns, and cities as part of the economy of the city-state. Wild vegetables were especially important for the poor, although more affluent Greeks ate certain varieties that were considered gourmet treats. With the exceptions of truffles and a few varieties of mushrooms, only the poor ate foraged fungi.

- Local herbs and spices flavored foods. Ingredients such as silphium, sumac, and dates were imported from Egypt, North Africa, and the Near East. Cinnamon, sugar, and other spices from the Far East were not yet imported into the Mediterranean for culinary uses but were rare and costly medicines. Long pepper *(Piper longum)* from northern India entered limited culinary use in the early Classical period. Honey and dried fruits were the sweeteners.

In Neolithic times Greece was covered with forests, including vast stands of oak trees. Prehistoric peoples used acorns, which could be boiled or roasted and ground into flour, as a staple food. Climate shifts in the late Neolithic and exploitation of the environment for shipbuilding deforested much of the land, although the land clearing made it possible to cultivate grains in some areas. Erosion impoverished the limestone soils, making barley and pulses, especially nitrogen-fixing lentils, best suited to the Greek environment by the second millennium. Greece had no great river with annual floods for irrigation, so Greeks depended on seasonal rains for winter cereal crops that were harvested in the spring. Although some areas could support the ancient wheats, einkorn, emmer, and spelt, Greeks imported much of their wheat, especially bread wheat, from more fertile colonial outposts in modern-day France, Spain, Egypt, the Balkans, and the areas around the Black Sea. Barley continued as an important grain for all social classes and an indispensable part of religious sacrifices. Unlike the Mesopotamians and Egyptians, the Greeks did not use grains to make beer but ate them in breads, cakes, and porridges.

Next to cereals and pulses, olives and grapes were the signatures of the Greek diet. Although these crops originated in the Near East, once the crops reached the Greek Aegean, the Greeks spread olives and grapes through the Mediterranean, where they thrived in the favorable climate. Domesticated olives and oil were part of the Minoans' diet by 2000 B.C.E.; at an uncertain time, the trees spread to mainland Greece, and then to Italy and other parts of the Mediterranean as Greek influence grew in the first millennium B.C.E. Evidence of the consumption of wild grapes in Greece dates to the late Paleolithic, about 11,000 B.C.E.; domesticated grapes have been confirmed at sites dating to 2,500 B.C.E., and perhaps date to the fifth millennium B.C.E. The Minoans had well-developed wine industries by the dawn of the second millennium B.C.E. and preserved wines by resinating them: sticky tree resins were spread over the insides of clay amphorae, elongated bulbous jugs, that made the vessels air-tight and lent a distinctive flavor. Archaeological evidence for a similar prac-tice has been found in the Levant and Egypt, but only the Greeks continue this tradition in their modern wine *retsina*, to which resin is added to give the wine an assertive piney taste.

The fruits and vegetables of the Greeks were similar to many enjoyed by the Mesopotamians and Egyptians, although date trees would not fruit in the Mediterranean climate. Date fruits were imported but did not play the central role in Greece that they did in Mesopotamia and Egypt. Beekeep-ing and honey were developed by the Minoans on Crete, making honey the Greek sweetener of choice, although dried fruits and syrups played a smaller role. By the Classical period, orchards boasted apple, pear, quince, cherry, apricot, peach, and fig trees. Many vegetables were foraged; in addition to most of the vegetables found in Mesopotamia and Egypt, the cooler Greek climate supported asparagus, salsify, and parsnips. Acorns gathered from oak trees continued as a hedge against famine when crops failed; in historic times, they were considered food for barbarians or the desperately poor.

Greece's extensive coastlines made fish an important component of the Greek diet. Much was salted and preserved, with industries stretching from colonies in Spain to the Black Sea. Greeks, especially Athenians, were pas-sionate lovers of fish; some thought the appreciation bordered on madness or obsession.[1] Well-to-do Greeks preferred larger fish, while small fish sold cheaply in the markets. The mountains were suitable for raising sheep and goats, prized as much for their renewable milk and wool as for their meat, which was an expensive delicacy. Cattle tended to be an elite dish and very popular for sacrifice, while the efficient pig was more commonly eaten. Wild game, such as deer, boars, hares, asses, bears, and even lions, were hunted. Large and small birds, such as geese, ducks, pigeons, pheasants, larks, and quail were eaten throughout Greek history; the chicken reached Greece in the Classical period, around 500 B.C.E.

CUISINE AND SOCIAL CLASS

- Meal structures centered on the *sitos* (staple grains), enhanced by flavorful *opson* (side dishes or relishes made from meats, fish, veg-etables, fruits, pulses, and dairy). By the Classical Age, formal meals were generally eaten without wine; wine appeared in the sympo-sium (drinking party) after the main eating was completed. The symposium could range from reflective discussion to wild drinking bouts complete with musicians, party games, courtesans, and licen-tious behavior. Informal meals would include wine.
- Public banqueting and feasting tended to be segregated by gender; adult men reclined while boys and other men of lesser status in

attendance sat and ate those foods the principal males chose to give them. These dependents were called *parasitos*.

- Food was served on small tables shared by at most two or three diners; knives and spoons were used; platters, bowls, and individual drinking vessels were made of clay or metals such as silver, gold, or bronze.
- Professional cooks could be freemen or slaves; a few famous cooks were known by name and prestigious reputation. Unless they were wealthy, women typically prepared foods in homes without slaves.

The main, and sometimes only, meal was the *deipnon*, an evening dinner. Some Greeks also enjoyed the *ariston*, a light midday brunch, comprised of leftovers from the *deipnon*, with the possible addition of fresh breads. All meals were divided between the *sitos*, and the *opson*. *Sitos* formed the bulk of most Greeks' diet and took the form of breads, porridges, and legumes or pulses. *Opsa* were everything else—meat, fish, fruits and vegetables, cheeses, and nuts. For the poor or for everyday meals, *opsa* might be limited to vegetables. Greek meal structures are comparable to the traditional Chinese menu where tastes of different meat and vegetable dishes enhance a bowl of rice as the main source of calories. Some estimates suggest that cereals accounted for 80 percent of the calories typically consumed in the Greek world, and the fifth-century B.C.E. philosopher Socrates criticized gluttons who ate more *opsa* than *sitos*.

A *deipnon* for the poor would include bread, porridge, or pulses, plus greens or root vegetables; livestock was typically too valuable to slaughter for the table, although hunting, fishing, and foraging could expand the diet. For those above subsistence, a greater variety of *opsa* enhanced *sitos* and might include some poultry, fish, or meats, especially salted pork and sausages. Beef was a rare treat, usually the result of a sacrifice connected with a festival and sponsored by a wealthy landowner who could afford to raise large animals and offer them for public consumption. For the wealthier classes, a *deipnon* took the form of a banquet and was typically divided into two or three courses with a great variety of foods presented sequentially in platters on portable tables. Individual plates were not used: descriptions from Homer and other sources tell of "well-scrubbed" tables, and solid foods selected from the common serving plates that were eaten directly or placed on any of the varieties of breads that were offered at banquets. Diners complained that they had to be quick to snatch their preferred morsels from the serving platters. Knives cut off bits of meat or cheese, and spoons made from materials ranging from simple woods to rich gold were used to eat porridges and soupy dishes from shallow bowls or cups.[2]

An elite *deipnon* might open with appetizers, called *propomata*; these were small, sharply seasoned dishes such as salt fish, pickled vegetables, or other items designed to whet the appetite. Fish often preceded meats as main courses, and all were accompanied by a variety of breads. For most formal dinners, both the appetizers and main courses were served without wine; eating required sober attention. The final course was the "second table," when wine was introduced and *tragemata*, "things to chew with wine," were served. *Tragemata* could include fruits, often dried, and sweet pastries as well as savory items, such as fresh beans, tiny birds, nuts, and cheeses. This is when the meal shifted from a dinner to a symposium, or drinking party. The wine was almost inevitably diluted with water, a custom that the Greeks thought distinguished them from barbarians; indeed, the Macedonians, always of questionable elegance to Attic Greeks, were critiqued for drinking their wine neat. The drinking might continue well into the night, with the god Dionysus's gifts loosening tongues for discussions of arts and politics, or helping the guests to appreciate music and dancing. The Greeks also thought that mild inebriation brought tipsy mortals closer to the gods, although outright drunkenness was frowned upon.

These elaborate private banquets would most often be prepared by slave cooks. Slave ownership penetrated deeply into Greek society, although for Greeks of modest means, slaves worked in the field rather than in the kitchen. As wealth rose, the slaves might pound grains and perform more laborious kitchen chores; there are many terra-cotta models of women cook-

ing and grinding grains for household use, but whether they were slaves or housewives is unclear. Employment of professional cooks, whether free or slave, indicated significant wealth.

Wealthy Greeks also sponsored public feasts as part of their civic duty and desire to impress their compatriots. Greeks of more limited means could occasionally hire specialized professional cooks, known as *mageirosi*, at the market to prepare special meals that included the religious sacrifice of an animal. These professionals were males, as respectable women seldom ventured into the public sphere.

The Consequences of Too Much to Drink, depicted on a Fifth Century B.C.E. kylix, or wine cup. Inv. No. 3880. Courtesy of the Department of Classical and Near Eastern Antiquities, National Museum of Denmark.

RECIPE AND COOKERY SOURCES

No detailed cookbooks from Greece survive, but many recipe fragments and evocative descriptions of Greek foods guide recipe reconstructions. The most famous and useful source is Athenaeus's *Deipnosophists,* or *Philosophers at Dinner,* which is set at a dinner party at which the guests (all men, in keeping with Greek tradition) discuss the food, drink, and dining customs of the Greek world stretching back to Homeric times. Although Athenaeus wrote in third-century C.E. Egypt, *Deipnosophists* is laced with quotations attributed to Greek authors of the fifth and fourth centuries B.C.E., and in many cases preserves snippets of literature that otherwise would be lost. The most important of these are *The Life of Luxury* by Archestratus of Gela, written in the fourth or third century B.C.E., and *Banquet* by the early fourth century B.C.E. poet Philoxenus. Most of the recipes in this chapter are inspired by passages in Athenaeus.

Other sources for Greek foods come from medical and agricultural writers. Hippocrates, the fifth-century B.C.E. physician and author of *On Regimen* and *On Regimen in Acute Diseases,* and Galen, the second-century C.E. physician and author of, most importantly, *On the Properties of Foods,* largely based on Hippocrates, were the most important medical writers, and their texts have been preserved and translated. Erudite Greeks were conversant with these and other medical works by physicians such as Diphilus of Siphnis, writing around 300 B.C.E. These sources are freely quoted in Athenaeus and influenced concepts of the ideal Greek diet. The philosopher Theophrastus wrote several treatises in the fourth century B.C.E. on food plants and agricultural techniques; his work remained influential until the early modern world. The poet Hesiod, writing in about 700 B.C.E., collected farming advice in *Work and Days* that reflects Greek practices shortly after it emerged from the Dark Ages; it is the earliest deciphered Greek work dealing specifically with food.

Playwrights, too, gave a sense of the conviviality that was part of Greek dining. One character from Aristophanes recited a dinner menu that included breads, split-pea soup, a whole roasted ox, pies, stewed birds, and sweet wine, concluding with the entreaty, "Now come in, because the cook was just about to take the fish off the grill, and they're bringing in the tables."[3] Others of his characters wagered "thyme-seasoned salt" or barked directions to pull roasted meat from the skewers, giving a sense of festive Greek food.[4]

A final written source for Greeks' attitude toward food, rather than specific recipes, comes from the philosophers. In addition to the comments on the *sitos-opson* dichotomy, Plato's *Republic* investigated the nature of justice by debating the merits of a bucolic, simple, and vegetarian lifestyle versus the more luxurious, meat-eating culture that required physicians and consumed more than it produced.[5] Plato's *Gorgias* critiqued the misuse of intricate cookery in place of medicine and rued the human tendency to prefer the intemperate pleasures of the palate to healthful foods.[6] Epicurus, whose name has been misappropriated in the word epicurean, opined that pleasure was the absence of pain, not the gourmand sensuality that is now associated with his name. For those above subsistence, Greek dining might be hedonistic pleasure, balanced moderation, or frugal restraint.

Rounding out the sources for Greek recipes are the archaeological finds of cooking equipment. The small, portable dome-topped clay *clibanus* baked foods ranging from breads to fish and meats. Metal frying pans and grills, as well as metal molds that resemble modern muffin pans, allowed high-heat cookery, while ceramic braziers could be used for stewing and simmering. Much cooking took place outdoors.

As with the Mesopotamian and Egyptian recipes, the exact balance of tastes is speculative, but the literature gives general ideas about flavors pleasing to the Greek palate. Even among ancient Greek cooks who might have had access to the now-lost cookbooks, recipes were not an immutable formula. Each cook was entrusted with the serious business of creating delicious food. As instructed by Athenaeus:

> [Y]ou can't go wrong when your organs of sense are clear. Cook, and taste often. Not enough salt; add some. Something else is required; keep tasting it again until the flavor is right; tighten it, as you would a harp, until it is in tune. Then, when you think that everything is by this time in harmony, bring on your chorus of dishes.[7]

Sitos: Breads, Grains, and Pulses

℣ 75. BARLEY PORRIDGE WITH SESAME ℣

Now [set before us] the cheerful barley-porridge, full of sesame.

Anonymous[8]

Although originating in India, the sesame was cultivated in the Near East by the second millennium and moved to the Mediterranean by classical times. Unlike the Mesopotamians and Egyptians, who pressed oil from the sesame, the Greeks tended to use the seeds whole, as a flavoring.

1 cup barley flour
2 cups water
Salt to taste
1/2 cup sesame seeds, lightly toasted

Combine the flour and water in a saucepan. Bring to a boil and cook for 7–8 minutes, or until thickened. Season with salt, sprinkle with the sesame seeds, and serve.

⚕ 76. AMOLGAIA *(HEARTY BARLEY CAKES)* ⚕

Hesiod calls another kind of barley-cake amolgaia, "a hearty barley-cake and milk from goats just running dry," meaning the shepherd's cake full of strength.[9]

These nourishing dry cakes date back at least to Greece's Dark Ages, given the attribution to Hesiod. They have good keeping qualities, suitable for travelers and shepherds without easy access to freshly baked bread.

2 cups pearl barley
2 cups buttermilk
3/4 cup water
2 cups barley flour
1 teaspoon salt

1. Soak the pearl barley in the buttermilk overnight.
2. Preheat the oven to 350°F. Line an 8-inch square baking dish with baker's parchment, or rub the inside with butter and dust with flour, shaking out the excess, so the barley cake will not stick.
3. Place the soaked barley mixture in a food processor and add the water. Pulse to break up the grain. Add the water, the barley flour, and the salt, pulsing briefly to combine. Pour into prepared pan and bake for 30–40 minutes, or until firm but not completely dry.
4. Turn the barley cake out from the pan and cool. Reduce the oven to 325°F. Cut the cake into 1-inch slices and toast for 10 minutes per side, or until dried out.

⚕ 77. MAZA *(TOASTED BARLEY CAKES)* ⚕

Scholars disagree about the nature of *maza.* Some believe *maza* were thin cakes cooked on a griddle, similar to the matzoh in the Egyptian chapter (Recipe 40). Others believe the cakes were not baked but were made from toasted barley flour kneaded with hot liquids. According to this camp, the term *maza* derives from the verb *masso,* to knead, and is similar to the Tibetan staple *tsampa.* This recipe follows the latter theory, although you could also use Recipe 40 in a Greek meal. The key to flavorful kneaded *maza* is to toast the barley flour. *Maza* are very filling because they absorb moisture and contribute to feelings of satiety.

1 1/4 cups barley flour
1/2–3/4 cup warm water
1/2 teaspoon salt
2 tablespoons olive oil

1. Place the flour in a large skillet and toast over medium heat, stirring frequently. The flour is ready when it gives off a very nutty fragrance and turns a light brown.

2. Transfer the flour to a bowl and stir in 1/2 cup water, the salt, and the olive oil to form a dough that holds together when you squeeze it. You may need to add more water, depending on the age and grind of your flour. Mash the dough until it holds together: it cannot be kneaded like wheat dough.

3. Shape the dough into 8–10 small balls. Nibble the balls with your choice of *opson*, dipping them into sauces.

The sixth-century B.C.E. *Athenian ruler Solon passed a law requiring every bride to have a* phrygetron, *or barley roaster.* Maza *was daily fare in classical Greece, with wheat breads baked for the many festivals that crowded the Greek calendar.*

⚕ 78. GRIDDLE CAKES STUFFED WITH CHEESE ⚕

Athenaeus described a dinner treat of "griddle cakes" and "cheese bread."[10] This invented recipe combines the two and is suitable for a banquet or special meal. Best served hot from the pan, this type of cake might have been cooked throughout a meal by slaves or professional cooks, replenishing bread baskets as needed. Similar stuffed breads are still part of the Near Eastern and Central Asian diet.

3/4 cup cottage cheese
4 cups all-purpose flour, plus more for rolling the dough
2 teaspoons salt
1 3/4 cups warm water
2 cloves garlic, minced
1 1/2 teaspoons ground coriander
1/4 cup chopped parsley
Olive oil, as needed, for cooking the cakes

1. The day before you wish to make the bread, place the cottage cheese in a colander lined with dampened cheesecloth. Allow to drain overnight in the refrigerator.

2. Also the day before, make the dough by combining the flour and salt in a bowl. Make a well in the center and slowly stir the water in with a fork until all the flour is moistened. Turn the dough out on a lightly floured surface and knead briefly. Wrap in plastic and store overnight in the refrigerator.

3. Season the drained cottage cheese with the garlic, coriander, parsley, and salt. Divide into four portions.

4. Divide the dough into eight pieces. On a lightly floured surface, roll each piece into a disk about 6 inches in diameter. Spread half of the disks with a portion of the cheese, leaving a border of about 1 inch. Cover with the remaining disks and pinch the edges together tightly to seal. Gentle press the breads to distribute the filling.

5. Preheat a heavy frying pan over medium heat. Add 2 tablespoons olive oil and ease in one of the cakes. Cook for 3–4 minutes, or until golden brown. Turn the cake with a large spatula to finish cooking on the other side, about 2–3 minutes, adding more oil as needed to prevent sticking and burning. Repeat with the remaining cakes. Serve hot.

৬ 79. FOLDED WHEAT BREAD ৬

Athenaeus praised light, pliable loaves that could be folded and served with honey and soft cheeses; perhaps supple breads were spread with honey and cheese and then rolled up or folded like a thick crepe.[11] This bread's elasticity and chewiness, compared with that of the cakier pitas in the next recipe, demonstrates the different potentials of wheat and barley. This and the next several bread recipes use commercial yeast to leaven the bread. The ancient Greeks would have used sourdoughs, incorporating a bit of reserved unbaked dough from the previous batch as the leavener. Sourdough breads are tangier, but the leavening process is trickier to control.

1/2 tablespoon instant yeast
1 1/2 cups whole wheat flour, plus more for kneading
2 cups all-purpose flour
1 teaspoon salt
1 1/2 cups plus an additional 1/4 cup lukewarm water
1 tablespoon olive oil, plus more for greasing the bowl
Curds and Honey (Recipe 86) (optional)

1. Combine the yeast, flours, and salt in a bowl. Make a well in the center. Combine 1 1/2 cups water with the oil. Slowly stir the liquid into the flour to form a dough. Turn out onto a lightly floured surface and knead for 10 minutes.

2. Place the dough in an oiled bowl. Cover and let rise for 1–1 1/2 hours, until doubled in volume. Pour in the remaining 1/4 cup water and knead into the dough. Cover and let rise again for 30–45 minutes, until doubled.

3. Press the air out of the dough and divide into four pieces. Preheat a griddle or skillet. With wet hands, pat each bread into a round and place on a work surface sprinkled with water. Pull and stretch each piece into rounds about 7–8 inches in diameter. Place on the hot

skillet and cook for 3 minutes, lowering the heat to avoid scorching. Flip and cook on the second side another 3 minutes. Reheat the pan for each bread, so that the moist bread is placed in a very hot skillet before the heat is lowered.

4. If desired, spread the bread with Curds and Honey (Recipe 86), or some cottage or farmer's cheese drizzled with honey, and fold in half.

ᛦ 80. PITA BREAD ᛦ

Athenaeus claimed that priestesses ate pitas for dinner.[12] Barley, as Greece's traditional grain, would be appropriate to include in dishes offered to religious officiants, although used alone it would make a very dense bread. Many breads were made from a blend of barley and emmer, resulting in a lighter loaf. This recipe combines semolina, to emulate emmer, with barley flour; even with the semolina, the pitas will be denser than modern ones made exclusively from bread flour.

1 1/2 teaspoons instant yeast
1/2 cup barley flour
1 cup fine semolina
2 tablespoons milk
1/4 teaspoon salt
2 tablespoons olive oil, plus more for greasing the bowl
1/2 cup water, or a bit more or less as needed

1. Combine the yeast with the flours. In separate bowl, combine the milk, salt, olive oil, and water. Slowly stir the liquid mixture into the flour mixture to create a thick dough. Knead the dough until it is smooth and elastic, about 5–8 minutes. Place the dough in an oiled bowl, cover, and let rise until doubled in volume, about 1 hour.

2. Gently press the air out of the dough and divide into four to six portions. Shape each into a round ball. Cover with a lightly floured cloth and let rise for 30 minutes.

3. Place a baking stone or cast iron griddle in the center rack of the oven. Preheat oven to 500°F for at least 45 minutes.

4. While the oven is heating, roll each ball into a circle about 7 inches in diameter and about 1/8 inch thick. Place on a floured cloth, cover with another floured cloth, and let rest for 20 minutes.

5. When the oven is hot and the pitas have rested, use heavy potholders to partially pull out the racks holding the baking stone or griddles. Carefully transfer 2–3 flat breads to the cooking surface. Push the racks back in and close the oven. Work as quickly as possible to minimize the heat lost by opening the oven door.

6. Bake the pitas for 4–5 minutes. If they have been rolled to the correct thickness, they will puff up; if they do not puff, they will still be tasty. Remove the cooked pitas and keep in a warm place.

7. Repeat steps 5 and 6 with the uncooked breads, keeping the baking surface as hot as possible to allow for a quick heat transfer that will cause the pitas to puff. Serve the pitas warm.

𝆣 81. CAPPADOCIAN SALT-RISING BREAD 𝆣

Athenaeus identified a soft bread from Cappadocia (part of present-day Turkey) that included milk, oil, and "sufficient salt" in its ingredients.[13] Before the days of pasteurized milk and commercial yeast, salt was added to sourdoughs made with raw milk, as the salt prevented the milk's bacteria from destroying the dough's gluten structure. The salt also improved the dough's texture. Absent raw milk, use beaten yogurt with active cultures, plus a bit of yeast, to simulate the process.

This bread is baked in a large loaf form, which Hippocrates considered the most nourishing "because the moisture of these is least consumed by the fire."[14]

1 teaspoon instant yeast
3/4 cup lukewarm water
1/2 cup yogurt at room temperature
1 teaspoon salt
2 1/2–3 1/2 cups whole wheat flour, plus additional for rolling
1 tablespoon olive oil, plus more for the bowl

1. Combine the yeast, water, yogurt, and salt in a bowl and stir to liquefy. Add 1 cup of flour to make a sponge and stir for 2 minutes. Cover and set aside for 30 minutes.

2. Add the oil to the sponge. Add as much of the remaining flour as needed to make a dough. Knead for 10 minutes. Transfer to an oiled bowl, cover, and let rise until doubled, about 1 hour or more.

3. Press the air out of the dough and shape into a round loaf. Place on a floured baking sheet. Cover and let rise 30 minutes, or until doubled.

4. Meanwhile, preheat the oven 450°F. Bake the bread for 15 minutes and then reduce the heat to 375°F. Continue baking for 25–35 minutes, or until the loaf sounds hollow when tapped on the bottom.

𝆣 82. DICE BREAD 𝆣

One of the long-lost cookery books mentioned by Athenaeus is Heracleides's *Art of Cookery*, which contained a recipe for dice-shaped bread flavored with anise, cheese, and oil.[15] This followed the ancient tradition of baking pan breads in distinctive shapes; a modern 9- by 5-inch loaf pan will give a brick-shaped loaf that can be cut in half to approximate two dice.

> 1 tablespoon anise or fennel seeds, lightly toasted and then coarsely
>   ground in a mortar with pestle
> 1/4 cup olive oil, plus more for greasing the bowl and pan
> 3/4 cup grated sheep milk cheese, such as pecorino
> 2 cups whole wheat flour, plus more for kneading
> 1 1/3 cups white flour
> 1 1/2 teaspoons instant yeast
> 1 cup lukewarm water
> 1 tablespoon honey

1. Combine the anise or fennel seeds with the olive oil and cheese. Set aside.
2. Combine the flours, yeast, water, and honey in a bowl and stir to form a dough. Add the cheese mixture, stirring to incorporate thoroughly. Turn out onto a floured surface and knead for 5–7 minutes until elastic, adding flour if needed to prevent sticking. Turn into an oiled bowl, cover, and allow to rise for about 1 hour and 15 minutes, or until doubled.
3. Press the air out of the dough and form into a brick shape about 8 inches long. Grease a 9- by 5-inch loaf pan with additional olive oil and place the bread in the pan. Cover and let rise until nearly doubled, about 30–45 minutes.
4. Meanwhile, preheat the oven to 375°F. Bake the loaf for about 30–40 minutes, or until it begins to shrink from the sides of the pan. Remove from the pan and let cool on a rack before unmolding. Cut in half to approximate the dice shape.

Ψ 83. CHEESE PIZZA Ψ

In his play *Acharnians*, the late-fifth-century B.C.E. playwright Aristophanes described as "delicious" a round pizza covered with cheese.[16]

Kasseri cheese is Greek string cheese and is similar to mozzarella, so if kasseri is unavailable, mozzarella can be substituted. *Plakuntos* was another form of ancient pizza seasoned with oil, garlic, and herbs, and this recipe borrows a bit from that dish.

> 1 recipe Folded Wheat Bread (Recipe 79), prepared through step 2
> 2 tablespoons coarse semolina
> 3 cups shredded kasseri cheese
> 2 cloves garlic, thinly sliced
> 2 teaspoons dried oregano or marjoram

1. Place a baking stone on the lowest rack of the oven and preheat to 450°F.
2. Deflate the dough and divide into two pieces. On a lightly floured surface, roll the dough into rounds each about 12 inches in diameter. Sprinkle 1 tablespoon semolina on a pizza paddle or on the back of an inverted cookie sheet and ease one round onto the surface. Spread half of the remaining ingredients on the pizza's surface.
3. Working carefully, open the oven and slide the pizza onto the baking stone, shaking and jerking the paddle or pan to transfer the dough. Bake for 13–16 minutes, or until the bottom crust is golden brown and the cheese bubbling. Repeat with the second pizza.

ᛦ *84. ACORN OR CHESTNUT CAKES* ᛦ

Acorns were a significant part of the prehistoric Greek diet; the nuts could be boiled or roasted before being ground into flour for dense cakes and porridges. Chestnuts, probably introduced in Mycenaean times, could be used similarly. Homer mentioned acorns as part of the diet of the heroes, harking back to a time when great men did not work the fields but were hunter-gatherers. Attitudes changed, and by the Classical Age, most Greek writers looked down on acorns as famine food, suitable only for foreigners or the very poor. Socrates was a notable exception, and he listed acorns as part of the menu for the ideal city, which also was vegetarian, contrary to the preferred diet of most Greeks.[17] Butter is another "barbarian" food, making this dish suitable for barbarians on the fringes of Greek society.

1/2 pound frozen, canned, or jarred chestnuts
4 tablespoons butter, melted
1 egg, beaten

1. Mash the chestnuts into a paste. Stir in 2 tablespoons of the melted butter and egg and blend thoroughly.
2. Preheat a skillet over medium heat. Divide the chestnut mix into four portions and flatten into disks. Add the remaining butter to the skillet and add the chestnut cakes. Cook for 2 minutes, lowering the heat if necessary to prevent scorching. Turn and cook 90 seconds more. Serve warm.

OPSON: ANYTHING TO ACCOMPANY *SITOS*

Opson is a catch-all term, often translated as relish, for any foods that accompany the basic grain *sitos* at the core of the Greek diet. In this context, relish means anything that enhances or enlivens flavors; it does not mean a finely chopped texture, as in modern pickle relishes. The role of *opson* in the Greek diet was a source of philosophical as well as practical concern. In the *Republic,* Plato ascribed to Socrates a prescription for diet in the ideal Greek city: in addition to *sitos:*

> [T]hey will have opsa—*salt, of course, and olives and cheese, and . . . they will boil up bulbs and other vegetables, as they now do in the country. And perhaps we will serve them desserts, figs and chickpeas and beans, and they will parch myrtle-berries and acorns in the ashes, and will drink moderately with their meals. And with a peaceful and healthy life of this kind, they will no doubt reach old age and pass on a similar style of life to their offspring.*[18]

Other sources, especially *Deipnosophists,* catalogued a dizzying array of meats and fish that served as relish. Again Socrates condemned those who ate *opson* too eagerly, and later writers came to associate this gluttonous behavior especially with eating fish.[19]

DAIRY

Cheese was a common food for the Greeks, and the Sicilians in particular were noted for the excellence of their fresh cheeses and their tendency to cook with cheese.[20] Some gourmets considered the Sicilian penchant for cheese excessive.

⚶ 85. FRESH CHEESE WITH OLIVE OIL AND HERBS ⚶

Athenaeus listed fresh cheese as one of the constituents of a dinner in Sparta, along with roasted goat, honey cakes, and sausages.[21]

2 quarts milk (goat or sheep milk preferred)
5 tablespoons white vinegar
4 tablespoons extra virgin olive oil
Chopped fresh herbs of your choice, to taste

1. Place the milk in a large saucepan and bring just to a boil. Make sure that the pan is no more than half full, as the milk will tend to boil over quickly. Add the vinegar and simmer gently for 15 minutes. The whey should take on a yellowy color.
2. Line a colander with a double layer of dampened cheesecloth and ladle in the curds to drain. Bring up the sides of the cheesecloth and gently squeeze out excess liquid.
3. Turn the cheese onto a serving dish and drizzle with the oil and chopped herbs. Season with salt and pepper, if desired.

⚔ 86. CURDS AND HONEY ⚔

The addition of cream to the milk more closely approximates the fat content of sheep or goat milk, which would have been the preferred milks for making cheeses. These curds might accompany Folded Wheat Bread (Recipe 79).

2 quarts milk of any type, preferably unpasteurized
1 cup heavy cream
1 rennet tablet, dissolved in 1/4 cup warm water
1 teaspoon coarse salt
2 tablespoons honey

1. Place the milk and cream in a large saucepan and heat to 90°F. Stir the dissolved rennet into the warm mixture and hold at about 90°F over very low heat until the milk curdles.
2. Line a colander with a double layer of dampened cheesecloth and ladle in the curds to drain. Bring up the sides of the cheesecloth and gently squeeze out excess liquid. Sprinkle with the salt.
3. Drizzle the curds with the honey before serving.

⚔ 87. TOASTED "GALLIPOLI" CHEESE ⚔

Athenaeus described dishes served at the feast of Amphidromia, which was held five or seven days after the birth of a child and was the day on which the child was named. Among the celebratory dishes were toasted slices of Gallipoli cheese.[22] Modern-day Greeks continue to grill slices of cheese as part of appetizer courses, using kasseri or haloumi, Greek cheeses available in many supermarkets or specialty shops. Gallipoli is on the western coast of Turkey, an area periodically under Greek domination, so Gallipoli cheese may have been an ancestor to these modern Greek varieties. If neither is available, substitute a firm mozzarella.

4 slices kasseri or haloumi, each about 1/2 inch thick
1 tablespoon extra virgin olive oil (optional)
Freshly ground long pepper (optional)

Preheat a frying pan over medium heat. Add the cheese and toast on one side until it takes on a little color; the Greek cheeses will not melt very much and are ideal for grilling. Turn and cook briefly on the other side. Remove to a serving platter, drizzle with the olive oil and pepper, if desired. Serve with bread.

FISH AND SEAFOOD

Homer's heroes preferred meat and ate fish only when necessary, and fisherman and fishmonger were low-status occupations. By the Classical period, however, Greeks seemed inordinately fond of fish, so much so that the term *opson* moved from its association with any food eaten to perk up bland *sitos* to a term dedicated to fish. Some judged the Greek preoccupation with fish as mildly crazy, as shown by this excerpt from Athenaeus:

> *The fishes . . . set before us were numerous and extraordinary in size and variety. Myrtilus [a grammarian] remarked: "It is no wonder, my friends, that among all the specially prepared dishes which we call an opson fish is the only one which has won its way, on account of its excellent eating-qualities, to be called by this name, for people are so mad for this kind of food. Anyway, we give the name "relish-eaters," not to those who eat beef, like Herakles . . . not to the fig-lover either, such as the philosopher Plato . . . no, we give the name rather to people who gad about among the fishmongers.*[23]

⍦ 88. PEPPER-FRIED SCALLOPS ⍦

According to the third-century B.C.E. physician Diphilus of Siphnis, scallops were good for the digestion and bowels when seasoned with cumin and pepper.[24] Mentions of pepper in comedies or medical texts date to the late fifth or early fourth centuries B.C.E., but this may be the earliest Greek culinary recipe to use pepper. The pepper is the long pepper *(Piper longum)* rather than the round pepper, *P. nigrum,* more common nowadays.

1/2 pound scallops, foot muscle removed
1 teaspoon coarsely grated black pepper (long pepper, if available)
1/2 teaspoon ground cumin
3/4 teaspoon sea salt
2 1/2 tablespoons olive oil

1. Pat the scallops dry. Mix the pepper, cumin, and salt and toss the scallops in the spice mix.
2. Preheat a frying pan until it is very hot. Add the oil and immediately add the scallops. Let cook for 60–90 seconds, or until scallops no longer stick to the pan. Turn to cook on the other side, about 30–60 seconds, depending on the size. If they are very large, lower the heat and cook a few minutes longer. Serve as is, or with Silphium Sauce (Recipe 119).

𝈝 89. HONEY-GLAZED SHRIMP 𝈝

Philoxenus, a fourth century B.C.E. poet, describes an elaborate meal in his poem *Banquet* that includes many fish and seafood dishes, among them cuttlefish, squid, honey-glazed shrimp, an enormous tuna steak, and a whole sea bream "as big as a tabletop."[25]

3 tablespoons white grape juice
1 1/2 tablespoons honey
1 1/2 tablespoons white wine vinegar
1 tablespoon *garum*
1/4 cup chopped basil
3 tablespoons extra virgin olive oil
1 pound shrimp, cleaned and deveined

1. Put the grape juice, honey, vinegar, and *garum* in a small saucepan. Bring to a boil and reduce until the sauce is thickened to a glazing consistency. Stir in the basil and reserve.
2. Preheat a frying pan until hot. Place half of the olive oil in the pan and add half of the shrimp. Sauté until the shrimp turn barely opaque in the center. Remove and repeat with the remaining shrimp.
3. Pour the sauce over the shrimp and serve immediately.

> *Among the Laws of Solon was a rule prohibiting fishmongers in the agora from pouring water over fish with the intent to make them appear fresher than they actually were.*

𝈝 90. ROASTED TUNA 𝈝

Archestratus, a Greek living in Sicily in the fourth century B.C.E., wrote the lost cookbook *The Life of Luxury* that survives only in fragments collected by Athenaeus in *Deipnosophists*. In Fragment 38 of *The Life of Luxury*, Archestratus offered cooks practical information on cooking tuna: select a female tuna and roast it with a bit of finely ground salt and baste it with olive oil. He praised the plain dish as suitable for the immortal gods but acknowledged that some might like a sauce of pungent brine. He disapproved of sprinkling the dish with vinegar, claiming it would ruin the good fish.

2 tuna steaks, about 6 ounces each
Extra virgin olive oil
Salt to taste
Pungent Brine Sauce (Recipe 122) (optional)

Preheat the oven to 500°F. Coat the tuna steaks with olive oil and season lightly with salt. Place on a pan and roast in the oven to the desired degree of doneness. The time will vary according to the thickness of the tuna steaks, but assume 7 minutes for a 1-inch steak cooked medium rare. Remove and slice into strips. Serve plain or with Pungent Brine Sauce.

ϒ 91. SALT-BAKED SEA BASS ϒ

The Milesian [bass], my friend, are amazing in their excellence. Descale them and bake them well whole, until tender, in salt. When working on this delicacy do not let any Syracusan or Italian come near you, for they do not understand how to prepare good fish. They ruin them in a horrible way by "cheesing" everything and sprinkling with a flow of vinegar and silphium pickle . . . little dishes which are cheap and sticky and based on nonsensical seasoning.[26]

The different ethnic tastes and regional cooking styles shine through in this excerpt from Archestratus's *The Life of Luxury*. Cooking whole fish in a salt crust remains a popular technique.

1 whole, round white fish, such as Mediterranean sea bass (bronzino) or sea bream, cleaned and gutted, about 1 1/2 pounds, or a larger whole, round white fish, such as snapper
2 sprigs fresh thyme
2 pounds kosher salt, or as much as needed to coat the fish entirely
1 cup water
4 egg whites, lightly beaten
Extra virgin olive oil for serving

1. Preheat the oven to 400°F.
2. Rinse and thoroughly dry the fish. Place the thyme sprigs in its belly cavity.
3. Spread a thick layer of coarse salt on the bottom of a baking sheet and place the fish on top. Combine the remaining salt with the egg whites to form a paste that holds together. Mold this mixture around the fish, enclosing it completely. Place in the oven and bake until an instant-read thermometer inserted into the thickest part of the flesh registers 130°F, about 25 minutes for sea bass and up to 45 minutes for larger fish such as snapper. Let cool slightly. Crack the salt case and remove, brushing off any salt that clings to the fish. Remove the skin from the fish, drizzle with olive oil, and serve.

ϒ 92. CHEESE-STUFFED MACKEREL ϒ

But if it is yellowish-brown in appearance and not too big, roast it after poking holes in its body with a straight, newly whetted butcher's knife. And baste this fish with a large amount of cheese and olive oil, for it likes to see people spend money, since it lacks self-control.[27]

Archestratus identified the "lyre-fish" for this recipe, but it is unclear what fish that was. Oily fishes generally were thought appropriate for rich sauces, in the Greek mindset, but large tuna and swordfish, oily fishes that were highly valued, were deemed too refined for this treatment.

1 whole mackerel, gutted
2 tablespoons *garum*
2 tablespoons chopped fresh mint
2 tablespoons chopped fresh parsley leaves
2 tablespoons chopped fresh dill
1/4 cup finely minced yellow onion
1/2 teaspoon asafetida
1/4 cup grated pecorino
3 tablespoons extra virgin olive oil, plus extra for drizzling
Freshly ground pepper, preferably long pepper

1. Preheat the oven to 400°F. Rinse the mackerel and slash three diagonal incisions on each side.
2. Combine the remaining ingredients. Stuff a bit of the cheese mixture into the slashes, placing any remaining mixture in the belly cavity, and secure with toothpicks. Place the fish on a roasting rack in a baking pan and roast for about 18–20 minutes, or until the cheese has melted and the fish has cooked through. Remove to a platter and serve drizzled with additional oil and freshly ground pepper.

⚓ 93. FRIED WHITEBAIT ⚓

Athenaeus described cooks (he called them "disciples of Archestratus") quickly panfrying tiny fish, called "small fry."[28] Their tiny size and rapid cooking time made them ideal street food, easy to munch with one's fingers while shopping in the agora. These low-status fish were appropriately served with a sprinkling of vinegar, unlike Roasted Tuna (Recipe 90).

2 cups pure olive oil, for frying
1/4 pound tiny whitebait (silversides, sand lances, etc.), left whole
1 cup all-purpose flour
1 tablespoon salt
Sea salt and white wine vinegar for serving

1. Preheat the oil in a deep pot (the oil should come up no more than one-third of the side) until it registers 375°F on a deep-fat thermometer.
2. While the oil is heating, rinse and dry the fish very thoroughly. Combine the flour and salt and toss the fish in the flour, shaking off the excess. Working in three or four batches, gently lower the fish

into the hot oil. Cook until lightly browned, about 20–30 seconds, and drain on paper towels. Serve immediately, with a light sprinkling of sea salt and vinegar.

⚓ 94. BAKED SHARK OR SWORDFISH WITH POUNDED SAUCE ⚓

In Fragment 23 of *The Life of Luxury,* Archestratus advised travelers that:

In the city of Torone you must buy the underbelly of the dog-shark, the hollow part below. Then sprinkle them with a little cumin and bake with a little salt. Add nothing else my dear except perhaps some yellow-gray oil. And when it is baked, then add your pounded sauce and the trimmings. Now whenever you stew something within the sides of a hollow cooking pot, do not add water or wine vinegar, but pour on it only oil and dried cumin together with fragrant leaves. Stew it over the heat of the charcoal without bringing it too close to the flames, and stir often in case it burns without your noticing. There are not many mortals who know of this divine food...[29]

1 pound shark steak or swordfish steak
1/2 tablespoon ground cumin
1 teaspoon sea salt
1 tablespoon extra virgin olive oil
8 basil leaves, left whole
1/2 cup walnuts
2 cloves garlic, smashed
1 cup basil leaves
1/4 cup parsley leaves
1/4 cup extra virgin olive oil, or more as needed
Salt or *garum,* as needed

1. Preheat the oven to 450°F. Trim the fish into 1-inch slices and pat dry. Sprinkle with the ground cumin and sea salt.
2. Place the fish in one layer in a heavy pan. Add the 1 tablespoon olive oil and the 8 whole basil leaves. Cover and bake until the fish is cooked, about 10 minutes. Remove from the heat, transfer the fish to a warm platter, and cover with foil.
3. Turn the oven off and toast the walnuts in the oven's residual heat for 5–7 minutes, stirring occasionally.
4. Pound the nuts with the garlic in a large mortar and pestle (preferred) or in a food processor until they are almost a paste. Add the remaining 1 cup basil leaves and the parsley leaves and pound or process, adding the 1/4 cup extra virgin olive oil as needed to make a coarse puree. Adjust the seasoning with salt or *garum* and spoon over the fish.

⚓ 95. PEA PORRIDGE WITH SALT FISH ⚓

Athenaeus compiled several dishes that paired salt fish with vegetables and pulses such as cabbage, dried peas, or lentils. Marjoram was the recommended herb to brighten the taste of stale salt fish.[30] Such combinations could be very common fare for Greeks of most social classes, often using preserved tuna or mackerel. Cod, a North Atlantic fish, is easily found salted in ethnic markets under the name *bacala* or *bacalao*. If you have access to salt tuna, available in some gourmet markets as an expensive delicacy, place a few slices on the pea porridge for a truer version of this dish.

> 1 cup dried yellow or green split peas
> 3 cups water
> 1 teaspoon salt
> 1/2 pound salt cod, soaked in two changes of water overnight to
>   remove excess salt
> Olive oil, as needed
> 1 tablespoon chopped marjoram

1. Combine the peas, water, and salt in a saucepan and bring to a boil. Reduce the heat to a simmer and cook until the peas disintegrate and thicken the liquid, about 45 minutes.
2. Preheat a grill pan over medium heat. Dry the cod and rub with the olive oil. Grill to heat through, about 4 minutes per side. Flake the fish into the pea porridge, drizzling both with additional olive oil to taste and chopped marjoram.

MEAT AND POULTRY

⚓ 96. SLICED EGG HORS D'OEUVRES ⚓

Sliced eggs would have been part of the hors d'oeuvres at many tables; Athenaeus described a particularly luxurious appetizer platter of many different foods displayed as the constellations, "while slices of egg represented the stars."[31] The Greeks debated the quality of different birds' eggs, judging peacock (or, more appropriately, peahen) eggs superior to all others, with chicken eggs ranking third.

> 4 eggs
> 2 anchovy fillets, rinsed
> 1/2 teaspoon capers
> 1 sprig dill
> 1 1/2 tablespoons extra virgin olive oil

1. Place the eggs in a saucepan and cover with cold water by 1 inch. Bring to a boil, cover the pot, and remove from the heat. Let the eggs

cook off the heat for 13 minutes. Drain, rinse in cold water, and peel the eggs. Cut the eggs in half.

2. Mince together the anchovies, capers, and dill. Stir the mince into the olive oil and spoon over the eggs to season.

⚕ 97. CHICKEN IN THE POT ⚕

Chickens were introduced to the Mediterranean during the first millennium B.C.E. and were held in considerable culinary esteem. One of Athenaeus's guests related a tale of a fellow who refused to go to the public baths while boiling a fowl, lest the slaves steal the broth. A friend suggested that the fellow's mother guard the pot, to which came the reply, "Am I going to trust chicken broth to my mother?"[32] The addition of the herbs, dates, oil, and honey to flavor the broth is based on the description of *hypotrimma*, an enriched broth, found in medical texts.[33]

1 3-pound chicken, cut into 8–10 pieces and fat pads removed
2 leeks, dark green tops removed, split in half and rinsed thoroughly
6 dates, split in half
4 cloves garlic, peeled but left whole
2 tablespoons honey
1 tablespoon olive oil
1 bay leaf
3 sprigs fresh thyme, or 1 teaspoon dried
1 teaspoon salt
6 cups water, or more as needed

1. Place all the ingredients in a pot wide enough to hold the chicken in one layer. Cover with water. Bring to a boil, reduce the heat to a gentle simmer, and cook for 1 hour, covered. Remove the chicken, leeks, dates, and garlic to a serving platter.
2. Add more salt to the broth, if desired. Strain the broth to remove any bits of herb or chicken meat and serve in cups along with the chicken.

⚕ 98. CAPON IN VINEGAR-OIL SAUCE ⚕

Another guest at Athenaeus's dinner party praised capon in a vinegar and oil sauce as a lovely dish.[34] A capon is a rooster that has been castrated for fattening and can be ordered from the butcher's department in many supermarkets. Otherwise, substitute a large chicken. The original Greek suggests that the vinegar-oil sauce was beaten, perhaps in the nature of a thick vinaigrette. A bit later on, the text debates whether *opson* should be served hot, warm, room temperature, or cold; thus, this dish might be a chicken salad.

1 capon or large chicken
1 1/2 cups wheat berries
1/2 cup raisins or dried currants
1/2 cup finely chopped onion
Salt to taste
1 recipe Vinegar and Oil Sauce (Recipe 121)

1. Place the bird in a deep pan and cover with cold water by 2 inches. Bring to a boil and simmer until cooked through, about 15 minutes per pound. Remove the bird from the water and let cool.
2. Add the wheat berries to the chicken cooking water (or cook the grain in a separate pot simultaneously) and bring to a boil. Cook until tender, about 35–45 minutes. Drain. Toss the grain with the raisins, onion, and salt.
3. Pull bite-sized pieces of meat off the chicken and combine with the wheat berries. Dress with the vinegar and oil sauce and toss to combine. Serve at room temperature.

♆ 99. QUAIL BAKED IN FLAKY PASTRY WITH POMEGRANATE MOLASSES ♆

In ancient Greek mythology, the pomegranate symbolized Persephone, goddess of spring, whom Hades abducted and brought to the underworld. While there, she ate six pomegranate fruitlets. Her mother, Demeter, the goddess of grain, begged Hades to release Persephone; Hades compromised, demanding that Persephone return to the underworld for six months each year, one month for each pomegranate fruitlet; these six months became the winter season.

The poet Philoxenus's *Banquet* included "baby birds in flaky pastry" and inspired this invented recipe, which uses purchased filo dough. When working with a sheet of filo, keep the remaining filo covered with a piece of plastic wrap that is then topped with a damp towel. This system prevents the dough from either drying out or getting too soggy.

4 boneless quail
1/2 cup white grape juice
1/4 cup pomegranate molasses
2 tablespoons *garum*
For the stuffing:
1/4 cup bulgur wheat
1 tablespoon extra virgin olive oil
1/4 cup finely chopped onion
1/2 teaspoon ground fennel
6 leaves Swiss chard, stemmed and chopped

1/4 cup dries currants
1/4 cup chopped fresh mint
1/4 cup chopped fresh parsley
1 tablespoon *garum*

For the pastry:

8 sheets filo dough
3/4 stick butter, melted

1. Remove the wing joints from the quail and discard. Mix the grape juice, pomegranate molasses, and *garum* and pour over the quail. Refrigerate while assembling the stuffing.
2. Put the bulgur in a bowl and cover with 1 cup boiling water. Let sit for 20 minutes and then drain in a colander, pressing hard to squeeze out the excess water.
3. Meanwhile, heat the olive oil in a sauté pan and sweat the onion to soften. Add the ground fennel and toast about 30 seconds. Add the chard, currants, mint, and parsley and toss to wilt the greens. Drain any excess liquid from the pan and stir in the bulgur. Season with *garum* and let cool. Divide the filling into four portions.
4. Preheat the oven to 375°F. Place one portion of the filling in the breast cavity of each quail. Place a piece of filo on a smooth surface and brush with some of the melted butter. Cover with a second piece of filo. Place the quail in the center of the dough and fold up the edges to enclose the quail, brushing any edges with butter to make the dough adhere. Transfer the packages to a baking sheet. Repeat with the remaining ingredients. Bake in the preheated oven for 40–45 minutes and serve. If desired, boil the marinade for 10 minutes and serve it as a dipping sauce with the quail pies.

Note: Boneless quail will retain bones in the leg. Old fashioned meat pies often were made with meat still on the bone, with the diner nibbling the meat off the bones.

♆ 100. BOILED MIXED DINNER ♆

Following these viands platters were passed around containing many kinds of meats prepared with water,—feet, head, ears, jawbones, besides guts, tripe, and tongues, in accordance with the custom in shops at Alexandria called "boiled meat shops." [35]

This excerpt from *Deipnosophists* follows a lengthy discussion of shellfish and mollusks, suggesting that a fish course preceded the meat course at certain dinners, resembling the practice at contemporary formal dinners. The variety of boiled meats has been used historically in many different cuisines and has been associated in recent times with peasant cuisines. Long, gentle simmering tenderizes these flavorful meats; these dishes need little attention during the cooking process, making them easy to prepare. This dish was a regional specialty of the Egyptian city of Alexandria, controlled by the Greeks under the Ptolemies starting in the fourth century B.C.E.; it may be flavored with Silphium Sauce (Recipe 119).

2 pig or sheep trotters, split
1 pound beef tripe (part of the lining of the stomach), cut into strips
   about 1 by 2 inches
1 beef or calf tongue
1/2 pound slab bacon, in one piece
3 onions, peeled and quartered
2 bay leaves

1. Place the trotters, tripe, tongue, and slab bacon in a large pan. Cover with cold water by 2 inches. Bring to a boil, reduce heat to a simmer, and cook for 2 hours. Add the onion and bay leaves and continue simmering until tender, about 60–90 minutes longer, adding water to cover if the liquid begins to boil away.

2. Remove the meats from the liquid. Strain the liquid into a clean saucepan and boil to reduce to 1 cup. Slice the tongue and bacon into pieces about 1/2 inch thick and serve on a platter with the trotters and tripe, moistened with the reduced broth.

⚓ 101. SPIT-ROASTED HARE (OR PIGEON OR GOSLING) ⚓

Archestratus acknowledged several ways to prepare roasted hare in *The Life of Luxury*, but admitted in Fragment 57 that his favorite was to serve it hot off the spit, cooked rare, seasoned only with salt. He advised, "Do not let it distress you to see the divine *ichor* [blood of the gods] dripping from the meat, but eat it greedily."[36]

Hare is a dark-fleshed member of the same family as the domesticated rabbit. Concerns about possible parasites in hare, which has never been domesticated, caution against eating it rare. To prepare this recipe safely, substitute dark-fleshed goose, duck, or pigeon, also known as squab. Other references to meats in Greek texts suggest that most, including pork, were roasted rare or medium rare to maintain juiciness. In another recipe fragment, Archestratus recommended roasting a gosling (baby goose) in a similar fashion.[37] These can be difficult to find, so if you use a larger duck or goose, the roasting time will increase significantly, to a little over one hour for a duck and to at least two hours for a goose, depending on the exact size.

Check with a thermometer for an internal temperature in the thigh of at least 165°F for these larger birds.

1 pigeon, 3/4 to 1 pound
Salt to taste

1. Preheat the oven to 450°F or prepare an outdoor fire for spit roasting. Remove any entrails in the bird's cavity, If roasting outside, place the bird on a spit over a dripping's pan to catch the juices as it roasts. If oven roasting, place the bird on a roasting rack in a pan.
2. Roast the bird 20–25 minutes, or until a meat thermometer registers 125°F–130°F when inserted into the thigh. Sprinkle with salt. Let rest a few minutes before eating so that you can pull the meat and joints off with your fingers.

⚓ 102. GRILLED LAMB OR MUTTON CHOPS WITH CABBAGE ⚓

According to Athenaeus, another of the dishes traditionally served at the feast of Amphidromia to celebrate the birth of a child was lamb or mutton chops, grilled and served with boiled cabbage, glistening with oil.[38]

Mutton is meat from a sheep older than one year and weighing more than 100 pounds. Mutton is difficult to find in the United States, as most sheep are slaughtered as lambs, which are younger, smaller animals with more delicately flavored flesh. Mutton is more expensive to raise, and only commercial cheese makers are interested in sheep's milk. Moreover, modern consumers have generally rejected stronger-tasting mutton. Ancient Greeks, however, appreciated both mutton and lamb. Many people raised sheep for their milk and then slaughtered them for a feast once their milk-giving days were over.

4 tablespoons olive oil
1 tablespoon chopped fresh rosemary, or 1 teaspoon dried
4 lamb or mutton shoulder chops, each about 3/4 inch thick
1/2 head white cabbage, cored and thinly sliced
Salt to taste

1. Combine 1 tablespoon olive oil with the rosemary and rub over the lamb or mutton chops. Set aside.
2. Heat the remaining olive oil in a frying pan over low heat and add the sliced cabbage. Cook, stirring often, until soft, about 20 minutes. Season with salt and set aside.
3. Preheat a grill over high heat. Season the chops with salt and place on the grill, cooking about 4 minutes per side for rare to medium-rare chops, a bit longer for more well done. Serve the chops on the wilted cabbage.

⚚ 103. ODYSSEUS'S SACRIFICIAL LAMB ⚚

Dark blood gushed forth, life ebbed from her limbs—they quartered her quickly, cut the thighbones out and all according to custom wrapped them round in fat, a double fold sliced clean and topped with strips of flesh. And the old king burned these over dried split wood and over the fire poured out glistening wine while young men at his side held five-pronged forks. Once they'd burned the bones and tasted the organs, they sliced the rest into pieces, spitted them on skewers and raising points to the fire, broiled all the meats.[39]

Although *The Odyssey* is filled with feasts and sacrifices, it gives a misleading picture of the diet of most Greeks. Meat was not daily fare; some estimates of average per-person consumption range from two to five pounds annually, although the elites would eat much more.[40] Shepherds and farmers in the countryside likely ate more meat than poor city dwellers, who generally could not afford to purchase meat. Even the poor received some meat at holidays: the annual Athenian festival Panathenaia, honoring Athena "of the city," concluded with a sacrifice of a hecatomb of cattle (100 heads) on the Acropolis. Meat was distributed according to status, with proportionally more given to the politically powerful.

This recipe uses leg of lamb to make it easier to cook in modern ovens, although a large beef roast could be substituted. The organs are represented by sweetbreads and chicken livers, wrapped in fatty pancetta, an unsmoked bacon.

1 bottle red wine
1 cup honey
1 teaspoon asafetida
5 cloves garlic, minced
2 tablespoons ground coriander
Leaves from 2 sprigs marjoram or oregano, coarsely chopped
Leaves from 3 sprigs fresh rosemary, coarsely chopped
1 leg of lamb, boned, about 5 pounds
1 pound veal or lamb sweetbreads
1 pound chicken livers
Salt to taste
1/4 pound thinly sliced pancetta
Wooden skewers soaked in cold water for 30 minutes

1. Mix the wine, honey, asafetida, garlic, coriander, marjoram, and rosemary in a large pan for the marinade. Meanwhile, trim the lamb of excess fat and cut into two sections, the thigh end and the shank end. Cut the shank end into cubes approximately 1 1/2 inches square. Place the meat in the pan with the marinade mixture and let sit for 30 minutes at room temperature, turning once halfway

through to make sure that all portions absorb some marinade, or overnight in the refrigerator to absorb more flavor.

2. While the lamb is marinating, soak the sweetbreads in cold running water for 10 minutes. Peel any tough membrane off the sweetbreads. Bring 2 quarts of salted water to a boil and add the sweetbreads. Reduce the heat to a simmer and cook the sweetbreads gently for 10 minutes. Drain and refresh in cold water to stop the cooking. Break the sweetbreads into chunks and dry them. Reserve in the refrigerator.

3. Preheat the oven to 450°F. Remove the meat from the marinade and pat it dry. Tie the thigh portion of the meat into a neat roast, sprinkle generously with salt, and place on a roasting rack in the oven for 1–1 1/2 hours, depending on the size, or until deeply browned and the internal temperature reaches 130°F for medium rare, 140°F for medium, or 155°F for well done. Remove to a cutting board and let rest 15 minutes before slicing.

4. While the meat is roasting, bring the marinade to a boil on top of the stove and reduce to about 1 cup. Strain and keep warm.

5. Thread the sweetbreads, livers, cubes of lamb shank, and pancetta on skewers. Heat a grill pan and grill the skewers for 6–8 minutes, turning several times, or until the meats are just slightly pink in the center. Place the skewers on a platter with the sliced lamb and pour the reduced sauce over all.

VEGETABLES

Vegetables played an important part in Greek cuisine. Greek writers such as Pythagoras, Plato, and Empedocles advocated a vegetarian diet for different reasons, among them better digestion. In addition to being a source of foraged food for the poor, vegetables could be artfully seasoned; they could be served as *paraopsides* (delicate appetizers) to precede more substantial meat and fish dishes enjoyed by wealthier Greeks.

ᛃ *104. CRAZY RADISH HORS D'OEUVRES* ᛃ

Part of elite Athenian's passion for fish and disdain for most vegetables is reflected in a comment from an obscure poet: that anyone who considered radishes more of a delicacy than fish was utterly crazy.[41]

1/2 shallot, finely minced
1 teaspoon *garum*
1 tablespoon white wine vinegar
2 tablespoons olive oil

2 sprigs fresh coriander, cleaned and chopped
12 radishes, cleaned, stems trimmed to 1/2 inch in length

Combine all the ingredients except the radishes in a bowl and stir to blend. Serve as a dipping sauce for the radishes.

⸾ 105. STUFFED VINE LEAVES ⸾

Stuffed fig leaves were listed by Athenaeus in an inventory of dishes to be served at a grand feast.[42] Some commentators consider them the predecessor of modern *dolmades*, grape leaves stuffed with seasoned rice. Because rice was unavailable in ancient Greece, barley is substituted to invent a prototype. Use widely available jarred grape leaves in place of fig leaves.

24 grape leaves in brine
1/2 cup pearl barley
2 shallots, finely chopped
2 cloves garlic, finely chopped
2 tablespoons extra virgin olive oil
1/2 cup white grape juice
2 tablespoons raisins or dried currants
2 tablespoons chopped dill
1/4 cup chopped walnuts
4 tablespoons *garum*
1/4 cup white wine vinegar

1. Carefully separate the grape leaves and cut out the coarse central stem. Rinse under cold water and set aside.
2. Rinse the pearl barley in a colander to release some of the surface starch. Place the barley in a small saucepan, cover with water by 2 inches, and bring to a boil. Reduce the heat to a simmer and cook until tender, about 35 minutes. Drain and refresh under cold water.
3. Meanwhile, gently sweat the shallot and garlic in the olive oil. Set aside.
4. Heat 1/4 cup of the white grape juice and pour over the raisins to plump. Let sit for 15 minutes, drain the raisins, and add them to the shallot mixture, along with the dill, walnuts, and *garum*. Mix in the cooked barley.
5. Place a tablespoon of the barley mixture in the center of each grape leaf and fold the sides over the edge of the filling. Fold the bottom up to enclose the filling, and roll the leaves into tight bundles. Place them, seam side down, in a large skillet in one layer. Pour in the remaining grape juice and the white wine vinegar and add enough water to come halfway up the leaves. Simmer gently for 45 minutes,

carefully turning once during the cooking. Remove from the cooking liquid and serve warm or at room temperature.

𝒴 *106. GREEN HERB SALAD* 𝒴

Uncooked greens formed part of the menu of the Spartans' Cleaver feast, most likely in honor of Apollo. The Spartans also celebrated with tall barley cakes, wheat bread, a bit of boiled pork, broth, figs, nuts, and lupines.[43] Gourmets ranked Spartan cuisine among the worst in the Greek world, as evidenced by this miserly menu.

3 stalks celery, with leaves, if possible, cleaned and thinly sliced
1 bunch parsley, washed, dried, and coarsely chopped
1 bunch fresh coriander, washed, dried, and coarsely chopped
1 bunch sorrel or arugula, washed, dried, and torn into small pieces
Leaves from one bunch of tarragon
1/4 cup coarsely chopped chives
3 tablespoons extra virgin olive oil
1 tablespoon white wine vinegar
1/2 tablespoon *garum*

Combine all of the ingredients in a large bowl and toss gently to coat the leaves with the dressing.

𝒴 *107. GRILLED ASPARAGUS* 𝒴

The Greeks enjoyed several different varieties of asparagus and also considered them a universal tonic for "internal complaints."[44] Greek literature does not identify the cooking techniques used for vegetables, so grilling is speculative but fits the available technology.

1 bunch asparagus
Extra virgin olive oil, as needed
Salt to taste

Preheat a grill pan. Brush the asparagus with oil and grill, turning occasionally, until tender, about 3 minutes for thin asparagus, longer for thicker ones. Season with salt.

𝒴 *108. MARINATED BEETS* 𝒴

Beets with herbs were a common hors d'oeuvre, as they were thought to whet the appetite and to balance heavier foods.[45]

1 bunch beets
1 teaspoon salt

1 tablespoon wine vinegar
3/4 teaspoon *garum*
1/2 teaspoon ground coriander
2 tablespoons extra virgin olive oil
1 clove garlic, finely minced
Freshly ground pepper to taste, preferably long pepper
Chopped fresh chives

1. Cut off the beet greens. Wash, but do not peel, the beets. Place them in a pot, cover with water by 1 inch, and add the salt. Bring to a boil and cook until tender, about 45 minutes to 1 hour. Drain and, when cool enough to handle, slip off the skins. Cut into slices about 1/2 inch thick.
2. Combine the remaining ingredients and toss with the warm beets. Serve warm or at room temperature.

Three Recipes for Wild Plants

Athenaeus considered only a few wild greens to be suitable for cooking: dark green lettuces (such as romaine or chicory), watercress, mustard greens, onions, and cilantro.[46]

ϡ *109. WILTED GREENS* ϡ

2 bunches watercress, tough stems cut off and coarsely chopped
1 bulb fennel
3 tablespoon extra virgin olive oil
1/4 cup chopped cilantro
Salt to taste

1. Remove the stalks from the fennel, reserving 1/4 cup of fronds, if available and in good condition. Cut the fennel bulb in half, cut out the core, and slice thinly.
2. Heat the olive oil in a sauté pan and add the fennel. Cook until tender, about 3 minutes. Add the watercress, cilantro, and fennel fronds. Cook for 20–30 seconds and season with salt. Serve warm.

ϡ *110. MUSTARD GREENS* ϡ

Modern recipes for cooked mustard greens often incorporate pork fat to help smooth out the slightly bitter flavor of the greens. The Greeks used different forms of pork fat freely; the Greek word *lardion* indicates some form of salt pork, which has been incorporated into this speculative recipe.

2 tablespoons olive oil
2 tablespoons minced salt pork
2 cloves garlic, peeled and thinly sliced
1 bunch mustard greens, washed, tough stems cut out, and chopped
Salt as needed

Heat the oil in a deep skillet over medium heat. Add the salt pork and garlic and cook for 30 seconds to soften. Add the mustard greens. Reduce the heat and cook until tender, about 10 minutes. Drain any excess liquid and season with salt.

⚜ 111. GRILLED SCALLIONS ⚜

Unlike the Mesopotamians and Egyptians, who relished raw onions, Athenaeus advised cooking them.

2 bunches scallions
4 teaspoons olive oil
Salt

1. Clean the scallions by stripping off any unsightly outer leaves. Cut off the roots and the dark green leaves. Toss with the oil and salt.
2. Preheat a grill pan over medium heat and cook, turning periodically, until tender, about 4–6 minutes.

⚜ 112. WISE LENTIL SOUP ⚜

Lentils were a common food but were considered inelegant; they would probably not appear on wealthy, status-conscious tables. The late-fifth-century B.C.E. playwright Strattis wrote, "When you cook lentil soup, don't add perfume," meaning expensive spices, reinforcing the lentil's poor connotations.[47]

Nonetheless, lentil soup on a chilly night was compared to ambrosia, the mythological food of the gods, and even the philosophers were alleged by Athenaeus to take seriously the wise seasoning of lentil soup, adding just a bit of coriander.[48]

2 cups brown lentils
6 cloves garlic, minced
1 teaspoon coriander seeds, crushed in a mortar and pestle
1/2 cup extra virgin olive oil
1/2 teaspoon dried thyme or oregano leaves
Salt to taste

Place the lentils, garlic, and coriander in a saucepan and cover with water by 3 inches. Bring to a boil, reduce the heat to a simmer, and cook for

40–50 minutes, or until the lentils disintegrate into a smooth soup. Add the remaining ingredients to season.

ᛣ 113. DRIED FAVA BEANS ᛣ

Fresh, tender beans were considered a dessert; dried beans were boiled or roasted and served as a vegetable.[49] Boiled beans, called *pyanepsia*, were served to celebrate the start of the growing season in the month of *Pyanepsion*, dedicated to Demeter. Bean dishes and their effect on the digestive tract elicited comic comment:

> [F]inding a heap of beans, I grabbed some and ate them up. But when the donkey saw us, like Cephisodorus on the platform, he let forth wind . . . and celebrated Bean-Festival as a windy holiday.[50]

1/2 pound dried fava beans
3 tablespoons extra virgin olive oil
1 tablespoon minced thyme leaves
Salt to taste

Bring a large pot of water to a boil. Add the beans, reduce the heat to a simmer, and cook until tender, about 1 hour. Drain and toss the beans with the remaining ingredients.

ᛣ 114. PICKLED TURNIPS IN MUSTARD ᛣ

Another hors d'oeuvre frequently listed were turnips pickled in vinegar and mustard.[51]

1 cup water
2 tablespoons salt
1/2 cup white wine vinegar
1 pound turnips, peeled and shredded with a coarse grater
Reserved pickling brine, as needed
1 tablespoon ground mustard
1 clove garlic, minced
2 tablespoons honey

1. Place the water, salt, and vinegar in a saucepan and bring to a boil. Pour over the turnips and set aside overnight. Drain, reserving the brine.
2. Stir 1/4 cup of the brine into the mustard. Add the garlic and honey, and more of the brine, if needed, to form a sauce that will lightly coat the turnips. Stir in the turnips.

ψ 115. MUSHROOMS WITH THYME ψ

Our dinner is a barley cake bristling with chaff, cheaply prepared, and perhaps one iris-bulb or a dainty dish of sow-thistle or mushroom or any other poor thing that the place affords us poor creatures. . . . Nobody eats thyme when meat is to be had, not even they who profess to be Pythagorean vegetarians.[52]

The Greeks were skeptical of mushrooms because of the risk of eating poisonous varieties. Medical writers prescribed antidotes of potions of vinegar, honey, and salt, followed by induced vomiting. To avoid such unpleasantness, several recipes recommend cooking mushrooms with vinegar or honey as a prophylactic against poison.[53] With the exception of a few identifiable mushrooms enjoyed by gourmets, mushrooms were most important to the poorest Greeks, who were forced to forage for much of their diet.

2 tablespoons olive oil
1/2 pound white button mushrooms, cleaned and cut into quarters
1/2 teaspoon salt
1 1/2 teaspoons chopped thyme leaves

Preheat a frying pan over high heat and add the oil. Immediately add the mushrooms, salt, and thyme. Cook, stirring occasionally, until the mushrooms are lightly browned and have given off their liquid, about 5 minutes. Serve hot or at room temperature.

ψ 116. OLIVES IN BRINE ψ

Olives in brine were another hors d'oeuvre identified by both Archestratus and Athenaeus.[54]

If you can find raw olives, preserve them at home; the process is simple but takes two months. Otherwise, use dishes of olives packed in brine as part of the Greek first table.

1 pound ripe, raw olives
1/4 cup coarse salt

1. Rinse the olives thoroughly. Place them in a bowl and cover with water. Let soak for 2 days, then drain and repeat the process for a total of 40 days. The repeated soakings remove many of the bitter tannins from the olives.
2. After 40 days, transfer the olives to a glass or earthenware jar. Sprinkle with the salt and cover with water. Seal and set aside for at least 3 weeks before tasting. The olives will last 2 years.

Harvesting Olives, depicted on a Sixth Century B.C.E. amphora. *Courtesy of the American School of Classical Studies at Athens.*

℣ *117. FLAVORED OLIVES IN BRINE* ℣

The playwright Aristophanes, in *Frogs*, made fun of stingy Athenian masters who came home and immediately ranted "at the slaves, demanding to know . . . 'Where's that garlic from yesterday? Who's been nibbling olives?'"[55]

If you cannot cure your own olives, you can make a flavored brine in which to add some purchased olives.

3 cloves garlic, minced
1 tablespoon chopped marjoram or other herb
1/2 teaspoon salt
2/3 cup red wine vinegar diluted with 1/3 cup water
1/2 cup black olives
1/2 cup green olives

Combine the garlic, herb, salt, and diluted vinegar. Pack the olives tightly in a jar and pour the liquid over the olives. Let soak overnight to absorb the flavors. Store indefinitely in the refrigerator.

CONDIMENTS AND SAUCES

The exact nature of Greek sauces is unclear. References to broth and gravy suggest that Greeks used the liquid in which meats and poultry were boiled as a sauce base. Oil, vinegar or wine, and brine or *garum* also could form the base. Physicians opined that meats prepared in piquant sauces of ingredients pounded together—like a pesto—were too "oily, fiery, [and] warm," while "preparations in brine or vinegar are better."[56] "Warm" is a reference to humoral medicine, not to the literal temperature of the sauce. Sauces were presented at table in small dishes in which diners would dip their foods.

⚚ 118. SPICED SAUCE ⚚

Athenaeus quoted a line from a satirical play in which the people of Delphi were called "spiced gravy makers." Delphi was home to the famous Oracle that Greeks would consult to learn the future; to ensure a good prophesy, sacrifices and offerings would be left. Thus the people of Delphi would have had access to plenty of meat, both to eat and to use as a base for spiced gravy.[57]

1/2 cup beef broth
1 teaspoon crushed fennel seeds
1/4 teaspoon crushed cumin
1/2 teaspoon crushed peppercorns, preferably long pepper
1/2 teaspoon dried rosemary
1 teaspoon *garum*
1 tablespoon honey
2 teaspoons red wine vinegar

Combine all the ingredients in a saucepan and bring to a boil. Reduce heat to a simmer and reduce the liquid by half. Strain out the solids.

⚚ 119. SILPHIUM SAUCE ⚚

Silphium was a wild plant in the Umbelliferae family that grew in Cyrenaica, modern-day Libya, and was colonized by Greeks in the seventh century B.C.E. The plant was a popular export, noted for its culinary and medicinal properties. Overharvesting led to extinction during the Roman Empire; the declining supply led Roman writers to recommend substituting asafetida, also in the Umbelliferae family, with a garlicky-oniony flavor.

Silphium sauce was popular. Theophrastus, the fourth-century B.C.E. philosopher and natural historian, suggested that silphium juice was key to the sauce.[58] Many writers mentioned the practice of combining silphium with vinegar and, possibly, cumin. As seen already in Recipe 91, the chef Archestratus critiqued Italian and Syracusan cooks who "ruined" good fish by sprinkling them with silphium-flavored broth. Others praised pork preparations enhanced by silphium sauce, especially sow womb; pig paunch, trotters, snout, and cheeks; and tripe.[59] Lacking fresh silphium to juice or infuse into vinegar, you can substitute the bottled garlic and onion juices that are available in Middle Eastern markets. If these are unavailable, omit them and double the asafetida.

1/2 cup chicken or beef stock
3 tablespoons onion or garlic juice
3 tablespoons vinegar
1/2 tablespoon *garum*
2 teaspoons sweet wine or grape must

1/2 teaspoon asafetida
1/2 teaspoon ground cumin

Combine the stock, onion or garlic juice, vinegar, *garum*, wine, asafetida, and cumin in a saucepan. Bring to a boil and reduce by half. Serve hot or at room temperature, especially to accompany the Boiled Mixed Dinner (Recipe 100).

ᛣ 120. CHEESE SAUCE ᛣ

In the recipe for Spit-Roasted Hare (Recipe 101), Archestratus explained his favorite way of preparing hare: simply roasted. Other anonymous cooks, however, made complicated sauces that "are, in my opinion, much, much too elaborate—sauces made of sticky things and over-rich in oil and cheese, as if they were preparing the dish for a weasel."[60] This rich cheese sauce might be of the type Archestratus alluded to.

1/4 cup loosely packed fresh dill, coarse stems removed
1/4 cup finely crumbled feta cheese
2 tablespoons extra virgin olive oil
1 tablespoon honey
1 tablespoon *garum*
Water, wine, or vinegar as needed to thin the sauce

Place the dill and feta in a mortar and pound with a pestle to blend, or place in the bowl of a food processor and pulse to combine. Stir in the remaining ingredients and serve as a dipping sauce for roasted meats and fishes, or as a dip for bread.

ᛣ 121. VINEGAR AND OIL SAUCE ᛣ

Athenaeus mentioned "vinegar and oil sauce" for capon with no further description. These seasonings are selected from the list of pantry ingredients provided by the fourth-century B.C.E. playwright Antiphanes: "Raisins, salt, boiled must, silphium, cheese, thyme, sesame, soda, cumin, sumac, honey, oregano, green herbs, vinegar, olives, bitter greens for a pungent sauce, capers, eggs, preserved fish, cress, fig leaves, fig-rennet."[61]

5 tablespoons red wine vinegar
3/4 cup olive oil
6 olives, pitted and chopped
2 tablespoons chopped capers
2 tablespoons chopped parsley
2 hard-cooked eggs, peeled and finely chopped
Salt to taste

Combine all the ingredients and serve as a dressing for cold meats, fish, or vegetables.

♆ 122. PUNGENT BRINE SAUCE ♆

This sauce accompanies Roasted Tuna (Recipe 90).

1 clove garlic
2 anchovy filets, rinsed and patted dry
2 teaspoons fresh marjoram or oregano leaves
1 leaf mustard greens or kale, or 3 leaves arugula, chopped
1 tablespoon finely chopped raisins
1/4 cup extra virgin olive oil
2 tablespoons water
2 tablespoons *garum*

Combine the garlic, anchovies, marjoram, mustard greens, and raisins in a mortar and pound to purée with a pestle. Stir in the olive oil, water, and *garum*. Set aside for at least 30 minutes before serving to allow the flavors to blend. The sauce will separate; stir it immediately before serving.

SWEETS AND PASTRIES

Tragemata were the "second tables" and marked a distinct shift in the meal: in addition to fresh tables brought in bearing foods that contemporary Americans might eat for dessert, such as fresh and dried fruits, sweet breads, and cheeses, this is also when the wine would begin to flow, at least in the Classical Age. The *tragemata* ("things to chew with wine") might also contain savory snacks that could be nibbled with wine once the drinking party started, much like the grazing foods served at contemporary wine bars.

Pastries, especially cheesecakes, were the mark of elite desserts. "All other common desserts are a sign of dire poverty—boiled chickpeas, beans, apples, and dried figs."[62]

♆ 123. POOR PERSON'S DESSERT TABLE ♆

1 pound fresh fava beans
1 cup cooked chickpeas
Salt to taste
2 apples, sliced
1 cup dried figs

Fresh fava beans are found seasonally in the United States and are more delicately flavored than the dried favas. If possible, use fresh (or frozen) favas in this recipe. Very fresh chickpeas can be eaten raw, although they are diffi-cult to find in the United States. Canned or dried chickpeas are the practical substitute, but the flavor is quite different. Edible raw chickpeas are some-times found in Italy and the Middle East.

1. Bring a pot of water to a boil. Remove the fava beans from their pods and plunge the beans into the boiling water for 2 minutes. Drain and rinse in cool water. Slip the favas out of the thin casing surrounding each bean.
2. Toss the chickpeas and fava beans with salt to taste. Arrange in small bowls next to the sliced apples and dried figs.

𝖄 124. CHEESECAKE 𝖄

Athenaeus praised Athenian cheesecakes, or, as second best, suggested drenching whatever cheesecake was at hand in Attic honey.[63] There are many different styles of cheesecake, from very rich ones based on dense cream cheese to lighter versions made from curds bound with starch or eggs. This cake will rise in the baking and then compress as it cools.

2 tablespoons oil, preferably almond or walnut
2 pounds ricotta cheese
5 eggs
1 cup all-purpose flour
1 cup honey

1. Preheat the oven to 350°F. Rub the inside of a 10-inch springform pan with the oil and set aside.
2. Place the ricotta in a large bowl and beat with a whisk to smooth out its texture. Add the eggs one by one, beating just long enough to incorporate the eggs. Gently stir in the flour.
3. Pour the batter into the prepared pan and bake in the center of the oven about 50 minutes, or until the cake is nearly set in the center; a small area about the size of a quarter should still be a bit loose. Remove from the oven and place the cake on a rack in its pan to cool. Pierce the top of the cake with a skewer repeatedly and im-mediately pour over the honey so that it can be absorbed while the cake is hot. Unmold the cake only after it is thoroughly cooled.

𝖄 125. BRAZIER BREAD 𝖄

And when they are tired and sated with eating, they then introduce a most delightful allurement in what is called smeared brazier bread. It is a soft and delectable compound dipped in sweet wine, with such harmonious effect that a marvelous result comes to one whether he will or no; for just as the drunken man often becomes sober again, so the eater of it grows hungry again with its delicious flavor. [64]

9 ounces chapati or whole wheat flour, plus additional for kneading
　　and shaping the breads
1 teaspoon salt
7/8 cup water
Walnut oil, as needed
Sweet wine or cooked grape must, for dipping

1. Combine the flour and the salt in a bowl and slowly add the water to form a dough. Turn the dough out onto a floured surface and knead for 8–10 minutes, until the dough is smooth. The dough will be sticky. Cover and reserve for 10 minutes.
2. Divide the dough into 12 equal portions. Roll each into a smooth ball and keep covered with plastic wrap.
3. Heat a griddle over medium-high heat. Working with just a few pieces of dough at a time, roll the balls into very thin rounds, about 8 inches each in diameter, dusting with flour to prevent sticking. Brush off the excess flour and place the dough directly on the griddle. Cook until the bread is spotted brown on the underside, about 1 minute, and turn over with tongs. Finish cooking on the other side for about 25–30 seconds and remove from the griddle.
4. Smear a thin coat of walnut oil over one side of each bread. Fold in quarters and keep warm in aluminum foil. Serve with small dishes of sweet wine for dipping.

♆ 126. HONEYED PANCAKES WITH FIGS OR PEARS ♆

The oil is put in a frying pan resting on a smokeless fire, and when it has heated, the wheat flour, mixed with plenty of water, is poured on. Rapidly, as it fries in the oil, it sets and thickens like fresh cheese setting in baskets. And at this point the cooks turn it, putting the visible side under, next to the pan, and bringing the sufficiently fried side, which was underneath at first, up on to the top. . . . Some mix it with honey, and others again with sea-salt. [65]

This recipe, from the Greek physician Galen, was written in the second century C.E., but references to pancakes antedate the Roman period.

1 1/4 cups all-purpose flour
1/4 cup whole wheat flour
1 cup water

1/4 cup olive oil
2 eggs, lightly beaten
2 tablespoons honey
Olive oil for sautéing, as needed
8 ripe figs or 4 pears
1 cup honey
4 tablespoons white grape juice

1. Place the flours in a bowl, stir to combine, and make a well in the center. Combine the water, 1/4 cup olive oil, eggs, and honey, stirring to blend. Slowly whisk the liquid into the flour to make a batter and let rest for 30 minutes.
2. Meanwhile, make the fruit sauce: Slice the figs or pears in quarters or eighths, depending on size. Warm the honey and white grape juice in a small saucepan. Add the fruit, cooking to soften if the fruit is not ripe. Reserve.
3. Preheat a small nonstick skillet until it is warm but not hot. You will have to make each pancake individually. Add about 1 teaspoon of oil and 2 tablespoons of batter for each pancake. Gently sauté until lightly browned on the first side, about 1 1/2 minutes; flip them over and finish the cooking, about another minute longer. Remove to a warm platter and continue cooking until all the pancakes are made.
4. Rewarm the fruit sauce and place a small amount on each pancake. Roll or tuck the edges of the pancakes under to create a neat package that can be eaten with the fingers. Serve immediately.

ϒ 127. WALNUT AND FLAXSEED CONFECTION ϒ

Athenaeus mentioned a "confection made of honey and flaxseed," with no other details.[66] This speculative recipe uses nuts, a frequent addition to the second tables, to help bind the mixture.

1 cup honey
1 1/2 cups chopped walnuts
1 cup flaxseeds or sesame seeds
Vegetable oil, as needed

1. Combine all the ingredients in a saucepan and bring to a boil. Reduce the heat and cook for 15 minutes.
2. Line a baking sheet with olive oil. Rub a metal spatula with oil. Carefully pour the hot honey mixture onto the sheet, spreading it with the spatula. Let cool to room temperature and cut into bite-sized pieces before it hardens.

BEVERAGES

⚓ 128. KYKEON ⚓

In this cup the woman skilled as a goddess mixed them a strong drink with Pramnian wine, over it shredded goat cheese with a bronze grater and scattered barley into it, glistening pure white, then invited them to drink.[67]

Among the most famous ancient Greek foods is *kykeon*, consumed at the Eleusinian Mysteries, a festival shrouded in secrecy that was held every five years to celebrate Persephone's return from the underworld. *Kykeon* thus became a metaphor for rebirth. In the *Iliad*, *kykeon* refreshed tired warriors; Athenaeus described *kykeon* as a lightly thickened mixture, part food, part drink, to be served from cups.[68] Most of the recipes specified Pramnian wine, believed to be dark colored and strong. It was often flavored with pennyroyal, an herb in the mint family.

The mixture of barley and wine reinforced the sacramental nature of the drink. The barley will absorb some of the liquid, like *maza*, making the drink gritty. This sort of loose porridge was easy to prepare and nourishing, even if the texture is alien to contemporary Americans.

2 cups wine or grape juice
1/4 teaspoon dried mint
2 ounces firm goat milk cheese, finely grated
1/4 cup barley flour

1. Combine the wine or grape juice with the dried mint in a saucepan and bring to a boil. Remove from the heat and let cool. Strain the wine into two chalices or bowls.
2. Sprinkle each portion with half the goat cheese and half the barley and serve.

The writer Hesiod, in his Work and Days *written around 700 B.C.E., warned that it was bad luck to place a ladle on top of a serving bowl at a drinking party.*[69] *He gave no reason for the superstition.*

⚓ 129. ATHENIAN WINE ⚓

Red and white wines were available in the ancient world, although most scholars believe that most red wines were not the inky deep purples of many modern wines, but were much paler, like modern rosé. Wine was drunk throughout the day and many Greeks, especially the Athenians, whose grapes ripened well on the hot plains of Attica, diluted their wines in a ratio of two or more parts water to one part wine. Others, including the Macedo-

A Greek Symposium, depicted on a Fifth Century B.C.E. *kylix, or drinking cup, similar to the ones portrayed here. Courtesy of the American School of Classical Studies at Athens.*

nians, were noted for drinking their wine neat. One theory for this difference is that grapes ripened poorly in the mountainous Macedonian vineyards. Underripe grapes would have had less natural sugar that would be available for fermentation and would yield wines with lower alcohol levels than their Athenian counterparts, allowing the Macedonians to drink more without getting drunk. On the other hand, the Macedonians did have a reputation for drunkenness.

Many Greeks coated the insides of porous clay amphora with resin to make a watertight container that also minimized the effects of oxygen on the stored wines. The tradition continues in modern resinated wines, although with the development of glass bottles for wine storage, the use of resins is a matter of taste, not preservation. Not all Greeks used resin to preserve wine; amphorae from Rhodes and other locations show no traces of resinated pitch coatings, although some of these wines have salt water added to them, a practice that the Romans also used for lesser-grade wines.

1 bottle (750 milliliters) wine, ideally a *retsina*, any color
2 bottles (1,500 milliliters) water

Combine the two liquids and serve.

⚕ 130. OXYKRATON ⚕

So-called sour wines were widespread in the Aegean and could be made from several different products, wine either turned to vinegar or directly pressed from unripe or underripe grapes, similar to the contemporary product verjuice. The tart flavor was refreshing, much like lemonade, and could be sweetened with honey if desired. *Oxykraton* was relatively inexpensive and a common drink for poorer Greeks.

1/2 cup verjuice or 1/4 cup wine vinegar
Water as needed
Honey to taste (optional)

Add water and honey, if desired, to the verjuice or vinegar until the drink reaches a pleasing tartness.

4
ANCIENT ROME

Legend holds that King Romulus founded the eponymous Rome in 753 B.C.E. on the Palatine Hill, one of the seven hills that still form the heart of the modern city. Through war, slave labor, and brilliant engineering and administrative prowess, Rome expanded from a kingdom centered in the Italian peninsula to a vast empire stretching from present-day Scotland in the northwest, encompassing western and central Europe to the Rhine and Danube rivers, all of the lands touching the Mediterranean, including Egypt's Nile River Valley, and culminating in the east in Anatolia and the Levant. The empire was so large and diverse that by the third century C.E., it became impossible to manage centrally from Rome. Several administrative solutions were tried, eventually leading to the division of Rome into the western and eastern empires, respectively headquartered in the cities of Rome and Constantinople. The western empire fell under pressure from invading Goths, Vandals, and other tribal groups in the fifth century C.E., signaling the start of the European Middle Ages. The eastern empire continued, evolving into the urbane Byzantine empire that lasted until 1453 C.E., when Constantinople fell to the Ottoman Turks and the city was renamed Istanbul.

The kingdom of Rome was a period of hereditary aristocracy marked by frequent wars, both internecine and with neighboring clans. The historian Livy (59 B.C.E.–17 C.E.) described a rebellion in the late sixth century B.C.E. that led to the founding of the Roman republic. Under the republic, Roman society divided into three broad groups: patricians, plebeians, and slaves. Pa-

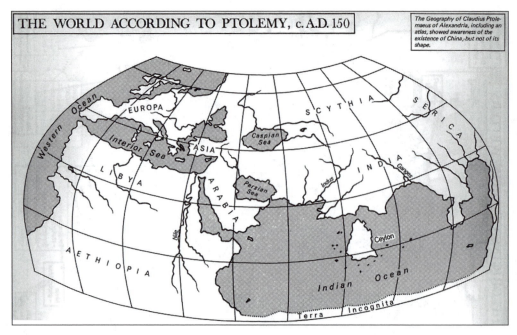

THE WORLD ACCORDING TO PTOLEMY, c. A.D. 150

The Geography of Claudius Ptolemaeus of Alexandria, including an atlas, showed awareness of the existence of China, but not of its shape.

From: The Routledge Atlas of Classical History, *Michael Grant, Copyright (© 1994), Routledge. Reproduced by permission of Taylor & Francis Books UK.*

tricians were descended from the hereditary aristocracy and owned substantial country estates. They were the original high office holders and knights, but notwithstanding these duties, these elite Romans prided themselves on being farmers and raising their own food (albeit that the labor and day-to-day management was performed by others). Patricians typically owned homes in the city of Rome to facilitate their government service; it was the mark of a noble Roman to supply his town house with food from his country estate. This privileged elite was a tiny fraction of the population, perhaps 1 percent.

Plebeians were numerically a much larger and more diverse group than the patricians and were professionals, tradesmen, craftsmen, laborers, or landowning peasants. Lacking inherited social status, plebeians originally were forbidden to marry patricians or to serve as consuls or senators, although they held lower offices. Within a few generations, as some plebeians accumulated fortunes, the laws were changed to permit intermarriage among the classes and to open more offices to plebeians. By the founding of the empire, there were only a few practical differences between patricians' and plebeians' political power and legal rights, although social distinctions remained.

Slaves were crucial to Rome's success, providing much of the agricultural and construction labor for Roman farms and cities. Slaves were not citizens but were prisoners of war, foreigners, victims of piracy, or disenfranchised debtors. Some were highly educated or skilled artists and craftsmen, although many were unfortunate grunts captured in battle. Slaves might receive their freedom as a gift from a benevolent master or by earning enough money through side endeavors to purchase their emancipation. Many slaves, however, were indentured for life with bleak prospects: The patrician Cato the Elder (234–149 B.C.E.), in his treatise *De Agricultura*, recommended selling or decreasing the food rations of old and sickly slaves as a necessary part of managing a farm.[1]

FOODSTUFFS AND AGRICULTURE

- Grains were a significant part of the Roman diet; depending on where they lived, Romans might eat emmer, bread wheat, spelt, barley, oats, rye, and millet, although emmer and bread wheat were preferred. Barley was thought medicinal, but it lacked the status of the wheats. Wheat was so fundamental to Roman identity that soldiers were punished with rations of barley in place of wheat.
- Olive oil was the preferred cooking fat, although in the northern regions of the empire, where olives could not grow, butter and animal fats supplemented imported olive oil.
- Wine was the preferred drink, although again in fringe areas, climate dictated that beer be consumed in addition to imported wine.
- Pork, both fresh and cured, was the most popular meat of the Romans and a centerpiece of the Saturnalian holiday. Sheep and goat were common, but beef less so, in part because of the value of cattle as draft animals. Both land birds and waterfowl were eaten; the chicken was thoroughly domesticated in the Mediterranean by the Roman period.
- Freshwater and saltwater fish and shellfish were regular parts of the Roman diet, and Romans pioneered aquaculture; even so, they lacked the Greeks' passion for fish.
- Romans ate cabbages and other members of the brassica family; lettuces, usually bitter varieties; bulbs such as beets, turnips, radishes, onions, and garlic; stem vegetables such as carrots, parsnips, celery, and asparagus; and beans and peas. Vegetable gardens were cultivated by most Romans with access to a plot of land. With a very few gourmet exceptions, wild foods were eaten by those lowest on the socioeconomic ladder or in times of famine.
- Romans ate the same fruits popular in Mesopotamia, Egypt, and the Greek Mediterranean; in addition, Romans in the northern reaches of the empire had berries that could not tolerate the hotter, drier Mediterranean. The Romans mastered cultivation of the apricot,

peach, and quince, and continued the Greek cultivation of the citron, a cousin of the lemon, that had reached the eastern Mediterranean by the fourth century B.C.E.

- Romans used dairy products in the form of cheeses, from fresh curds
  to dried and smoked cheeses. Milk was sometimes used in baking
  breads and grains; it was seldom drunk in the Mediterranean, other
  than by shepherds, but was more common in northern areas.
- Honey and dried fruits liberally sweetened foods; cane sugar was
  known but was used only as a medicine.
- Local herbs and spices, especially cumin, coriander, and lovage, were
  widely used. East Asian spices such as cassia and cinnamon were
  used in medicines and perfumes but entered cookery only toward the
  end of the Classical period. Black pepper (round and long species) was
  an ingredient in many recipes. While still expensive, Asian spices
  became more available through the discovery of the monsoon winds
  that shortened shipping times and required fewer middlemen.

The Roman empire's vast terrain had different climates suitable for different crops and dining customs, making sweeping generalizations about the
Roman diet impossible. Romans living in Britain ate differently from those
living in Egypt, who ate differently from those on the Italian peninsula. In
the northern geographic fringes of the Roman empire, beer, oats, millet, and
butter formed important parts of the diet, especially for the less affluent,
while beer remained important in Egypt. On the Italian peninsula and among
the moderately affluent throughout the non-Mediterranean portions of the
empire, the Mediterranean staples of wheat bread or porridge, wine, and olive
oil were main constituents of the diet, as either local products or imports. In
Roman Europe, agriculture was dependent on rainfall and modest irrigation.
Agricultural treatises explained techniques such as grafting and preserving
to an increasingly literate audience. The invention of greenhouses allowed
Mediterranean crops to grow in marginal climates. Aqueducts increased the
water supply to cities and supported larger urban populations.

The government's extensive and well-maintained road system was the
single greatest manmade resource of the Roman empire. Private merchants
explored water navigation in the Mediterranean and beyond. One way for a
foreigner to gain Roman citizenship was to bring grain via ship into Ostia, the
seaport nearest Rome, to help supply the *annona*, the state-run system that
started under the republic and continued through the empire to distribute
grain to Rome's needy urban citizens and to insure survival in the provinces
in times of famine. Beginning with *lex Sempronia frumentaria* (123 B.C.E.),
which granted Roman citizens the right to purchase monthly rations of grain
at below-market prices, the system evolved into complex governmental distributions of bread, wine, oil, and meat. The scale of the undertaking was

phenomenal: estimates place the city of Rome's population at one million during the empire, and many urban dwellers depended on the dole.

The discovery of the monsoon winds in the first century B.C.E. influenced Roman cuisine. The monsoons shift direction seasonally and allowed traders to sail east to India from the Levant in the summer and return west with exotic bounty in the winter. Romans thus could circumvent some of the overland middlemen who had limited the amount and inflated the price of spices for previous civilizations. The most important addition to the Roman pantry was pepper. Although the long pepper *(Piper longum)* of northeastern India had been imported in small quantities by the Greeks, the Romans greatly increased the trade and also imported the familiar round black pepper *(P. nigrum)* of southern India. Unlike in any of the previous civilizations, pepper appears regularly in Roman recipes, although the recipes do not specify which species was used. Long pepper is hotter and was more expensive, so it was probably used by those who could afford the greater luxury.

Trading records from the first century C.E. identify taxes on cooks, elephant trainers, fortune-tellers, and eunuchs imported from the East. Spices to be used in cookery, medicine, and perfumery formed nearly half the items listed as subject to taxation, in addition to silk, gemstones, and exotic animals.

CUISINE AND SOCIAL CLASS

- Romans generally preferred cultivated fruits and vegetables to wild varieties and developed greenhouses and aquaculture to increase the range of foods available to gourmets.
- Romans typically ate three meals per day. Many urban Romans, particularly plebeians, did not have kitchens in their apartments and thus ate in taverns and snack shops regularly, or bought prepared foods from cookshops that could be rewarmed over charcoal braziers at home. Commercial bakeries baked bread in cities and towns.
- Hand washing was part of formal dinner etiquette; small forks may have been used at very casual taverns and snack shops that did not offer hand washing or in more formal settings to extract snails or seafood from shells. Large cuts of meat were cut into finger food in the kitchen or at table by skilled servers.
- Well-to-do Romans dined in *triclinia*, rooms furnished with three couches on which diners reclined and took food from platters on a common table. Ideally, each couch held three diners, and each different space could signify one's status at the dinner, from host to

guest of honor to least important guest. Mixed-gender dining was common.

Romans viewed themselves as civilized farmers; they disdained hunters as barbaric and held shepherds in low esteem. The Roman diet centered on domesticated fruits, grains, and vegetables as well as animal husbandry. A few wild foods, be they game animals, vegetables, or fungi, were gourmet treats for elite tables, but Romans preferred farm-raised foods. Gathering and eating most wild foods was a task for the poorer ranks who needed to supplement their diet. Fish and seafood were exceptions to this generalization, but even there, the Romans explored basic aquaculture. The scientist Pliny the Elder (23–79 c.e.) described fish and oyster ponds for cultivating seafood,[2] while part of the vast market set up in central Roman by the early second century c.e. emperor Trajan purportedly contained tanks for live freshwater and saltwater creatures.

Romans tended to eat more frequently than Greeks, enjoying an *ientaculum* (breakfast) of bread and cheese, and a *prandium* (alternatively translated as lunch or snack) of cold meats, fruits, vegetables, and bread. *Cena* (dinner) was the day's most elaborate meal and started before sunset. For those above moderate economic means, dinner was divided into three courses, each accompanied by wine: the *gustatio*, comparable to extensive appetizers and salads; the *primae mensae*, more substantial dishes of roasted, grilled, or stewed meats and more complicated made dishes; and the *secondae mensae*, or dessert, comprised of *bellaria* (sweet) and *mattea* (savory) offerings. The *mattea* follows the Greek tradition of concluding meals with small birds or other savories that would be stretched into symposium fare.

Roman writers described the foods consumed by slaves, peasants, urban plebeians, and patricians. Some of the poetry and literature may not be literally true in all details, as some authors exaggerated behavior for social commentary, yet many descriptions seem true at their core, as they discuss foods and preparations that are corroborated in cookbooks and scientific treatises. Recipes are provided for most of the dishes discussed in the following examples of the diet of the different social classes.

Evidence of the staple diet of slaves and poor freemen employed on large farms comes from Cato, who directed masters to supply wheat, watered-down wine, salt, and olives.[3] The quantity of food varied with the season and was calculated to add calories when required by heavier work. Cato assumed that the slaves and laborers would supplement their diet by foraging, hunting, or fishing, and approved of landowners cutting back on bread rations when sugary-rich figs ripened. He recommended bonus wine during the Saturnalia and Compitalia holidays in December and additional amounts for the chain-gangs who performed the most arduous tasks.

The diet of the poor was described by poets. In his *Metamorphoses,* Ovid (43 B.C.E.–18 C.E.) told the story of Baucis and Philomen, elderly peasants who offered the most lavish table possible to their station when strangers (gods in disguise) stop by their hut. The couple had no slaves to help in the preparations but served endives, radishes, fresh cheese, olives, coddled eggs, and fruit preserved in wine as *gustatio.* The single main course was braised cabbage flavored by a bit of bacon and washed down with cheap wine. Fresh and dried fruit, nuts, and honey were the dessert.[4] The successive courses and variety of humble foods were an extravagance for the poor couple and identify the best foods that the poor might be able to supply for themselves. In *Moretum,* a poem attributed with reservation to Virgil (70–19 B.C.E.), the peasant Similus breakfasted on bread and herbed cheese, a typically Roman breakfast, although the great quantity of garlic in the cheese identifies Similus as a lower-class peasant.[5] Significantly, Similus is a bit more prosperous than Baucis and Philomen; he has a slave housekeeper who prepared his bread while he made the cheese.

Moving up the socioeconomic scale, Martial (40–104 C.E.) portrayed urban plebeian life in the early empire. Martial was a master of the dinner invitation, a Roman literary genre that mimicked the real-life practice of listing at least part of the dinner menu to entice guests to attend. Martial's *gustatio* included lettuce salads, fish garnished with hard-cooked eggs and rue, smoked cheese, braised pork bellies flavored with *garum,* and bowls of olives. The multiple dishes of the *mensa prima* might include chicken, duck, a "ham that has already survived three dinners," and a "kid, snatched from the jaws of a savage wolf, morsels requiring no carver's knife, workman's beans, and early greens."[6] Romans believed that animals bitten by wolves became more tender, so this dish would have been a gourmet treat.[7] Martial juxtaposed this dish with dismal leftovers and workman's beans, suggesting the social climbing aspirations of the pleb class.

Roman elites often dined extravagantly. As early as the second century B.C.E., sumptuary laws tried to regulate behavior at banquets, limiting the number of guests, the dishes that could be served, or the richness of the tablewares. These laws were often flaunted, to the chagrin of commentators such as Cato and Pliny. The Christian theologian Clement of Alexandria (ca. 150–215 C.E.) offered specific guidance on dining, giving a clear picture of the well-to-do, but not excessive, Roman table in the empire. He approved of semiprecious alabaster cups but condemned gold, silver, and jewel-encrusted goblets: not only were they ostentatious, but they also made it impossible to drink hot beverages and ruined the taste of cold ones. (Elite Romans had scads of precious tablewares, evidenced by the Roman law that had attempted to limit the weight of silver tablewares to 100 pounds.) Clement emphasized a diet of "rich and wholesome variety" of vegetables, olives, and dairy products and only occasional consumption of meat. He discouraged spicy preparations that aroused the appetite and caused people to overeat but was not a killjoy: he approved of wine, honey, and pastries in moderation. He even discussed table manners, instructing diners to take from the communal dishes only in turn, to avoid seeming gluttonous.[8]

Among the most famous dinner parties of all times is Trimalchio's Feast, recounted as a chapter in Petronius's incomplete tale *Satyricon*. Petronius (d. 66 C.E.) was the Emperor Nero's "arbiter of taste," and some thought that Petronius was critiquing the lavishness of Nero's table in thinly veiled fiction. Trimalchio is a freed slave who has made a vast fortune; he spends huge amounts on food, wine, and elaborate tablewares, but his table manners are simultaneously boorish and pretentious. Although some doubt that Trimalchio's Feast truly describes elite Roman dining, recipes for dishes similar to those served by Trimalchio can be found in ancient cookbooks, suggesting that some wealthy Romans ate in the spirit of Trimalchio. A few excerpts give a sense of the meal:

> [T]hey brought us really swell hors d'oeuvres. . . . On the relish platter was a donkey made of Corinthian bronze, and he was wearing little dishes in the form of saddlebags containing black olives on the one side, white on the other. Two other platters (with Trimalchio's name and the weight of the silver inscribed on the rim) flanked the donkey. On one were welded little bridges, receptacles for cooked dormice that were dipped in honey and sprinkled with sesame seed. On the opposite platter was a toy silver grill, sausages on top and Syrian plums and pomegranate seed underneath standing for hot coals. . . .
>
> [There came a dish whose] novelty drew everyone's attention. It was a round platter with the twelve signs of the zodiac on it, above each of which the architect of the thing had placed an appropriate food. Above the Ram there were "ram's head" chickpeas, above the Bull, a piece of beef, above the Twins a pair of testicles and a pair of kidneys . . . As we glumly approached this crude repast, Trimalchio said, "C'mon, let's dine. It's fine to dine."
>
> No sooner was this said than there was a honk of music and four Mars dancers rushed out and snatched away the top layer of the platter. This revealed fattened fowls and sows' udders and a hare that had been fitted with wings to make it look like a tiny, furry Pegasus. . . .
>
> A platter followed, with a gigantic boar on it—a freedman's cap on its head, no less. . . . Set up to look as if they were pressed to the udders were little piglets made of biscuit dough; obviously it was a mother sow.[9]

All of the meals thus far have been situated in private homes. Public feasts, underwritten either by the government or by politically prominent wealthy individuals, were also significant. Most commemorated holidays, the most famous being Saturnalia, celebrated in mid-December when little agricultural work could be done and animals that could not overwinter had been slaughtered. Boar and pig were particularly popular, along with sweets. The

feast lasted several days and temporarily suspended social and class norms; slaves were generally permitted to feast and play dice and the classes, ages, and genders mixed with greater freedom than at any other time of the year.

The poet Statius (45–96 C.E.) recounted the Saturnalian treats offered by the emperor Domitian: sweetmeats, dates, breads swaddled in white napkins, unnamed luxurious delicacies, and abundant wine, concluding that "One table served every class alike, children, women, people, knights, and senators: freedom had loosed the bonds of awe. Now everyone, be he rich or poor, boasts himself the Emperor's guest."[10] In an effort to promote the temporary fiction of a classless Roman citizenry, patricians might don the freedman's cap, a simple cloche worn by former slaves to indicate their status. Drinking abounded, but at the end of the holiday, everyone returned to his or her normal station.

RECIPES SOURCES

Hundreds of sources depict Rome's culinary habits. Already mentioned are some of the philosophical, legal, and religious works that condemned gluttonous behavior; poetry that portrayed lower- and middle-class dining; satirical literature that poked fun at the gastronomic pretensions of the newly rich; and agricultural treatises that advised landowners and their estate managers on everything from diluting wine with seawater for the slaves' tables to plowing fields, constructing villas, and making sacrifices for the health of the farm animals. Most spectacularly, a Roman cookbook commonly attributed to Marcus Gavius Apicius, *De Re Coquinaria* (On Cookery), survives with nearly 500 recipes.

Little is known of Apicius. Several figures bear that name from the first century B.C.E. through the second century C.E., and all appear to have been wealthy gastronomes. It is unlikely that the recipes were actually written by any Apicius; perhaps parts were written by anonymous cooks in his service, or perhaps publishers took advantage of his association with gourmandise to attribute the work to him. No Roman-era copy of the manuscript has survived, but copies made in the ninth century at European monasteries are owned by the Vatican and the New York Academy of Medicine. Judging from differences in the style of Latin used in different recipes, Apicius was compiled from different sources over several centuries; many of the recipes are in the vulgar Latin that may date to the late empire. Unlike the well-educated Athenaeus, whose *Deipnosophists* is an intellectual parlor game of gourmet literature, Apicius was probably written by practicing cooks, as it lacks erudite references to the works of poets, physicians, philosophers, and playwrights. The recipes are generally just lists of ingredients and mention of basic cooking techniques, written for experienced cooks.

Apicius is divided into 10 books, most focusing on categories of ingredients such as fish or birds or vegetables. Many recipes are for sauces to accompany the underlying ingredient. Because many of the recipes are untitled, modern translators have adopted a system of identifying recipes by number indicating the book, chapter, and, when necessary, the paragraph within Apicius. Similar systems identify passages in other classical works.

Two of Apicius's books deserve special attention. The first book, called *The Careful Housekeeper*, gives many basic preparations that will be needed in subsequent recipes, much the way modern cookbooks might give a recipe for basic chicken stock that will be used to make soups, stews, and sauces. This building block approach to cookery contemplates a kitchen where basic formulas can be used in many different dishes and allows the cook greater flexibility and creativity, as various combinations made up in advance are ready to enhance a dish on a moment's whim. Key recipes from *The Careful Housekeeper* are grouped herein as "Pantry Staples" and are identified with the numerical prefix 1. The seventh book, titled *Gourmet*, has complex recipes; all have the numerical prefix 7, and several have been adapted to illustrate the complex elite cookery of the empire. Nonetheless, what makes Apicius especially instructive is that many of the recipes are very simple and use common, inexpensive ingredients. Many of the vegetable and egg dishes could have been used by plebeians or peasants, making Apicius an unusual document that illustrates the cuisine enjoyed by all Romans but the destitute.

Scattered recipes also can be found in Cato's *De Agricultura* (On Farming) and Pliny's *Historiae Naturalis* (Natural History). These tend to be for grain-based and cheese dishes, preserved foods, and wine rather than the sauce-oriented cuisine of Apicius. Physicians such as Galen (131–201 C.E.), author of *On the Powers of Foods*, and Oribasius (ca. 320–400 C.E.), author of *Medical Compilations*, wrote lengthy descriptions of foods as well as their effect on the health of the diner, and gave occasional recipes. Both Galen and Oribasius were born in Pergamum in Anatolia. Oribasius's writings frequently referenced foodstuffs from the Black Sea and other areas under the control of the eastern empire and offer insight into the cookery that formed the foundations of the more exotic cuisine of the Byzantine empire.

THE ROMAN PALATE AND COOKERY TECHNIQUES

- Roman recipes range from complex, highly seasoned preparations with sweet and sour flavors to very simple dishes.
- Cooking techniques changed little from those found in Mesopotamia, Egypt, and Greece. Well-to-do Romans might have had elaborate, permanent kitchens with ovens, raised hearths, or metal stands that supported pots for frying, boiling, and stewing. These could be fu-

eled by charcoal or wood, and pots could be metal or clay. Many dishes are described as cooked *sub testu,* or under a preheated clay dome.

- Rome boasted a number of cooking and carving schools to train professional cooks and servers to work in elite households.

Roman food has a bad reputation. From Tobias Smollett's eighteenth-century novel *Peregrine Pickle,* in which a guest who tasted the food at an "authentic" Roman dinner party fled the dining room "puking and crossing himself," to the advice of a contemporary classicist to have a supply of hamburgers to eat after a Roman dinner party, those who read Apicius's recipes are often baffled by the unusual herbs, spices, and condiments that can seem like nasty combinations.[11] Quantities are missing in many Roman recipes, requiring the cook to season to taste. When recipes specify quantities, however, they often are tasty, such as Honey-Spiced Wine (Recipe 206). Indeed, if cooks followed Oribasius's advice, many dishes would have been carefully and delicately seasoned to ensure easy digestion:

> One ought to make things pronounced with seasonings as rarely as possible; this is because whatever has been seasoned in this way is noticeable even in the stomach. The best seasonings are those which have been mixed in from the beginning; the worst seasoning is anything that has been mixed in later; the reason for this is that the cooking is not even.[12]

Roman food was often sweet. Many recipes, especially for sauces that accompany meat and fish, use dried fruits and honey. This sweetness was usually balanced by sour flavors from wine or vinegar. Pepper (either round or long) or mustard added hot bite. Salt appears in some recipes but more often was added in the form of *liquamen,* a fish brine discussed in detail in connection with Recipe 141, for homemade *garum.* Most herbs were used in dried or seed form, although recipes occasionally specify "green" (meaning fresh) varieties. Bitter herbs such as rue presumably were used in small quantities, just as a contemporary cook uses only a bit of rosemary, bay, or oregano: more would overwhelm a dish. These latter herbs will substitute for rue, which is both difficult to find and reputed in folk medicine to be an abortifacient.

Breads and Staple Grains

Porridges and breads were the core of the Roman diet. Porridge recipes abound, but although Roman literature describes a large repertory of breads, fewer bread recipes survive; Apicius has none. Most of the breads found in the preceding chapters might also have been eaten by Romans in Italy, and surely by those living in the Levant, Egypt, or the eastern Mediterranean.

Physicians and scientists analyzed grains, flours, and breads for their digestibility and laxative properties. Galen was intrigued by cookery. He claimed that the choice of baking technique affected nutritional value, that dough made from the whitest flour was stickier and required more yeast, more vigorous kneading, and a greater time in the oven than bran or mixed-grain breads.

The excellence of the finest kinds of bread depends principally on the goodness of the wheat and the fineness of the bolter. Some persons knead the dough with eggs or milk, and butter even has been employed for the purpose by nations that have had leisure to cultivate the arts of peace, and to give their attention to the art of pastry-making.

Pliny, 18.27[13]

🔱 131. SILIGNITES *(WHITEST BREAD)* 🔱

According to Galen, Romans throughout the empire ate *silignites*, the whitest wheat bread, whenever possible. He considered *silignites* the most digestible and bread baked under a dome (*sub testu*) the healthiest. His second choice for baking was a tile-lined oven with a moderate, rather than intense, fire: he strongly disapproved of the dark, burnt crusts that hot ovens created, resembling a shell that encased a raw or undercooked crumb.[14]

Silignites ideally should be baked under a clay dome such as those available from La Cloche. The cloche approximates the *testum* used by Romans, although the shape and size differ somewhat. The Romans preheated the *testum* by creating a fire underneath the dome on a baking stone. Once the dome was heated, the ashes were swept away, the bread was placed on the hot stone, the dome was replaced, and the flattened top was mounded with hot coals to maintain heat. A modern alternative is to preheat the cloche and baking stone, place the bread on the stone, and cover with the cloche. You could also use a relatively flat, unglazed terra cotta flowerpot along with its drip tray to simulate the *testum*, but it will be deeper than the authentic *testum* and the heat will not penetrate the bread as quickly. If using a cloche or flowerpot, handle carefully with thick, dry potholders. If neither a cloche nor a flowerpot is available, the bread can be baked normally in an oven, in keeping with Galen's second choice of cooking techniques.

This recipe borrows from Pliny to use milk, resulting in a soft loaf. You could also use the whey left over from making Homemade Fresh Cheese (Recipe 147). The mix of white and whole wheat flour approximates the extraction rate of the finest ancient flour.

2 1/4 cups all-purpose white flour, preferably stone-ground, plus more
    for kneading
1/2 cup whole wheat flour
1 teaspoon salt
1 teaspoon instant yeast
1 cup plus 2 tablespoons lukewarm milk
Olive oil as needed
2 tablespoons millet

1. Combine the white and whole wheat flours, the salt, and the yeast. Make a well and stir in the milk to make a slightly sticky dough. Dust a work surface lightly with flour and turn the dough out. Knead until smooth and elastic, about 7–8 minutes, adding flour only as needed. If the dough is too sticky to work with, let it rest, covered, for about 15 minutes, which will make it more manageable. Continue kneading until smooth but slightly sticky. Lightly grease a clean bowl with olive oil, add the dough, cover, and set aside in a warm place until doubled, about 1 1/2 hours.
2. Deflate the dough and shape into a round ball. Sprinkle millet on a baking sheet or pizza paddle to prevent sticking, and place the dough on top. Cover with a floured cloth and let double, about 45 minutes.
3. While the dough is rising, adjust an oven rack to the lowest portion of the oven. Place the baking stone and clay dome, if using, on the lowest rack in a cold oven. Preheat the oven to 425°F.
4. When the bread has risen, carefully slash the top of the bread with a knife or razor blade held at a shallow angle to make incisions no more than 1/4 inch deep, to allow the dough to expand in the oven. Place the baking sheet on the lowest rack (or shake and jerk the dough from the paddle to the baking stone) and carefully cover with the dome. Bake for 15 minutes and reduce the heat to 400°F. Bake for another 20–30 minutes, or until the loaf sounds hollow when tapped on the bottom. Let cool before cutting to firm up the crumb.

Note: If no cloche is available, increase the baking time by about 10–15 minutes.

⚓ 132. CRACKER BREAD (CATO 74) ⚓

Wash your hands and a bowl thoroughly. Pour meal into the bowl, add water gradually, and knead thoroughly. When it is well kneaded, roll out and bake under a crock.[15]

The emphasis on rolling the dough after kneading and on washed hands and bowl suggests that this recipe is for a crackerlike bread: the cook is to avoid introducing yeasts or traces of sourdoughs that might cause the dough to rise. Baking under a crock introduces heat from both the top and bottom. If a cloche is unavailable, the crackers can be turned in the oven to cook both sides. If using a cloche, have very thick, dry potholders to handle it.

1 1/2 cups fine semolina
1/2 cup all-purpose flour, plus additional for kneading
1 teaspoon salt
About 5/8 cup water, or as needed

1. Combine the semolina, flour, and salt in a bowl. Slowly add as much of the water as is needed to make a coarse dough. Turn onto a lightly floured surface and knead until the dough is elastic. Depending on the fineness of the semolina, the dough may be slightly gritty. Let the dough rest, covered, for at least 30 minutes so that the gluten will relax and the dough can be rolled thinly.
2. Place a baking stone or sheet and the dome, if using, in the middle of a cold oven and preheat to 450°F. Divide the dough into six pieces and roll into rounds no larger than the diameter of the dome, or about 10 inches. Let the rounds rest 10 minutes.
3. Working one at a time, place a round on the preheated stone or sheet and cover with the dome. Let cook for 3 minutes and check for doneness under the cloche. If necessary, turn the bread with a large spatula or tongs to cook both sides. Eat hot or at room temperature.

♆ 133. WATER BREAD (PLINY 18.27) ♆

It is not so very long since that we had a bread introduced from Parthia, known as water bread, from a method in kneading it, of drawing out the dough by aid of water, a process which renders it remarkably light, and full of holes, like a sponge.[16]

This chewy, spongy bread results from the high ratio of water to flour. It is baked on an inverted wok (metal handles only!) to yield large, flat loaves; if no wok is available, make the breads smaller and bake them on a griddle on top of the stove.

1/2 teaspoon yeast
2 1/2 cups stone-ground all-purpose flour, plus more for kneading and rolling
1 teaspoon salt
1 tablespoon honey
1 cup lukewarm water, or as needed
Vegetable or olive oil, as needed

1. Combine the yeast, flour, and salt in a bowl. Make a well in the center. Combine the honey and the water and slowly stir into the flour mixture to make a dough. Knead on a lightly floured surface for 7 minutes, or until smooth and elastic. Transfer to a lightly oiled bowl, cover, and let rise until doubled, about 1 hour.

2. Deflate the dough and let rest 10 minutes. Divide the dough into six pieces. You will roll the dough in three stages to give the gluten time to relax. Working one at a time, roll each piece on a lightly floured surface into a 6-inch circle. Starting with the first disk (to make sure the gluten has relaxed enough), roll each circle into a disk about 9 inches in diameter; let rest for 10 minutes, then roll out into disks about 12–14 inches in diameter.

3. Heat an inverted wok over a gas flame and oil lightly using an oiled paper towel held with tongs. Drape each disk over the rolling pin and transfer to the hot wok. Do not worry if the dough does not lay flat; let it cook before trying to straighten out any folds. Cook for 30 seconds. Turn with tongs and cook another 30 seconds; turn and cook another 15–20 seconds on the first side. Wrap in towels and keep warm while cooking the remaining breads.

⚘ 134. BRAN BREAD ⚘

Galen thought bread made from unbolted flour (flour from which the bran had not been sifted out) lacked nutritional value and was useful in treating constipation.[17] Unbolted flour was the cheapest and might have been typical for poor Romans epitomized by Baucis and Philomen or Similus. Because very poor and urban Romans often lacked ovens, this recipe has been devised as a skillet bread that can be cooked over a fire or brazier. The yogurt tenderizes the dense bread.

3/4 teaspoon instant yeast
3/4 cup water
1/4 cup yogurt
1 tablespoon olive oil, plus more for oiling the griddle
1 teaspoon salt
2 1/2 cups stone-ground whole wheat flour, plus additional for
   kneading
1/2 cup bran

1. Combine the yeast, water, yogurt, oil, and salt in a bowl. Slowly stir in 1 1/2 cups flour and 1/2 cup bran; stir for 2 minutes. Cover and let rest for 30 minutes.

2. Stir in as much of the remaining flour as needed to make a dough. Knead on a lightly floured surface for 10 minutes, or until smooth

Artist's rendering of the grain mills and ovens at a Pompeiian bakery, buried by the eruption of the volcano Vesuvius in 79 C.E. From Joseph Dommers Vehling, Cooking and Dining in Imperial Rome.

and elastic. Transfer to a bowl, cover, and let rise until doubled, about 1 hour.

3. Divide the dough into four pieces and pat each into 5-inch circles. Let rest 10 minutes and then stretch into 8-inch circles, pulling from the center of the dough outward. Preheat a griddle pan over medium heat and brush lightly with oil. Dust each loaf with additional flour and cook each bread, one at a time, in the pan, turning once or twice. Total cooking time will depend on the thickness of the bread but should be 6–7 minutes.

⚶ 135. BARLEY TISANE WITH VEGETABLES (APICIUS 4.4.2) ⚶

Soak chickpeas, lentils and peas. Crush barley and boil with the dried vegetables. When it has boiled long enough add sufficient oil and chop the following greens: leeks, coriander, dill, fennel, beets, mallows, and tender cabbage. Put all these finely chopped greens into the saucepan. Boil cabbage, pound a generous quantity of fennel seed, oregano, silphium, and lovage, and after pounding, blend with liquamen. *Pour this over the dried vegetables and stir. Put chopped cabbage leaves on top.[18]*

A tisane is an infusion usually thought to be healthful, such as this early barley water recipe. This nutritious gruel was standard fare for many Romans on the middle and lower economic rungs. The affluent also ate such gruels, as evidenced by this recipe from Apicius that specifies the luxurious silphium as an ingredient. This type of dish both had perceived medical benefits and reinforced the connection to the garden that urban sophisticates desired.

1/2 cup chickpeas, soaked overnight in water to cover
1/4 cup brown lentils
1/4 cup dried split peas
1 cup barley flour
1/2 cup olive oil, or more, to taste (or Liburnian Oil, Recipe 189)
1 leek, dark green part removed, cleaned and finely chopped
2 tablespoons chopped cilantro
1 tablespoon chopped dill
1/4 cup finely chopped fresh fennel (with fronds, if possible)
1/2 cup chopped beet greens (reserve beets for Boiled Beets with
    Vinaigrette, Recipe 182)
4 leaves chard, stems removed, chopped
1/4 head cabbage, cored and finely chopped
1/2 tablespoon crushed fennel seed
2 teaspoons dried oregano
3/4 teaspoon asafetida
1 teaspoon crushed celery seed
Fish sauce to taste
4 cabbage leaves, finely chopped

1. Combine the chickpeas, lentils, split peas, and barley flour in a large pot. Add water to cover by 3 inches. Bring to a boil and cook for about 45 minutes to 1 hour, stirring periodically, or until the chickpeas are tender and the barley flour has thickened the gruel. You may need to add additional water to keep a thick but soupy porridge.

2. In a separate pot, place the olive oil, leek, cilantro, dill, fresh fennel, beet greens, chard, and 1/4 head of chopped cabbage. Cook over low heat until the vegetables soften. Stir in the chopped fennel seed, oregano, asafetida, and celery seed.

3. Add the vegetable mix to the porridge. Season with fish sauce to taste and additional olive oil, if desired. Garnish with the remaining cabbage leaves.

ᛘ 136. PUNIC PORRIDGE (CATO 85) ᛘ

Soak a pound of groats in water until it is quite soft. Pour it in a clean bowl, add 3 pounds of fresh cheese, 1/2 pound of honey, and 1 egg, and mix the whole thoroughly; turn into a new pot.[19]

Pliny calls a similar dish *alica* and describes slaves pounding emmer grains in a wooden mortar to remove the hulls and then pounding the hulled grain into *alica* of different sizes. He also noted regional variations, praising those from Campania and dismissing those from Egypt as "of a very inferior quality, not worth our notice."[20] This recipe uses semolina as the closest practical substitute for emmer.

1 cup coarsely ground semolina
2 cups cottage cheese
1/2 cup honey
1 egg, whisked

Soak the semolina overnight in water to cover by 2 inches. Drain. Preheat the oven to 350°F. Combine the semolina, cottage cheese, honey, and egg, stirring thoroughly. Turn into a 1-quart baking dish and bake until set, about 30–40 minutes.

ᛘ 137. WHEAT PAP (CATO 86) ᛘ

Pour 1/2 pound of clean wheat into a clean bowl, wash well, remove the husk thoroughly, and clean well. Pour into a pot with pure water and boil. When done, add milk slowly, until it makes a thick cream.[21]

Cato seems to be calling for whole grains that will release starch in the cooking process to help make a thick porridge. Galen disapproved of the practice of "country people" cooking wheat flour in milk because it caused "blockages."[22]

3/4 cup *grano* (hulled wheat berries with bran removed, available in Italian markets)
3 cups water
1/2 cup rich milk or half-and-half

Combine the *grano* and water in a saucepan. Bring to a boil and simmer until thoroughly cooked and very soft, about 1 hour or more, adding more water if necessary. The *grano* should be on the verge of disintegrating. Drain any excess water and add the milk or half-and-half, simmering until absorbed.

℣ 138. MUST CAKES (CATO 121) ℣

Two gallons of bread-wheat flour to be moistened with must; add to this anise, cumin, 2 lb. lard, 1 lb. cheese, and grate in the bark of a bay twig; when you have shaped them, put bay leaves under them while you cook them.[23]

Must is freshly pressed grape juice; it is filled with wild yeasts. Commercial grape juice is pasteurized, killing the yeast. Instant yeast is added in this recipe to simulate the yeasts in must; it will leaven the cakes just a bit but is not designed to created a fully risen bread. The cinnamon substitutes for the bay bark. With a little artistic imagination or a cookie cutter, this recipe could make about eight biscuit piglets to emulate Trimalchio's Feast, as in *The Satyricon.*

2 cups all-purpose flour
2 teaspoons instant yeast
1/4 cup grated Parmesan cheese
2 tablespoons crushed anise seed
1 1/2 teaspoons ground cumin
1/4 teaspoon ground cinnamon
4 tablespoons lard
1/2 cup white grape juice
Fresh or dried bay leaves

1. Mix together the flour, yeast, cheese, and spices. Grate the lard into small flakes and toss with the flour mixture. Stir in the grape juice until the dough is moist but not sticky. Let rest in a greased, covered bowl for 20 minutes.
2. Preheat the oven to 425°F. Place the dough on a board and gently flatten into a square. Cut the dough into 16 pieces (or shape into eight piglets). Place 16 bay leaves on a baking sheet and top each leaf with a biscuit. Place in the preheated oven and bake for 25–30 minutes, or until lightly browned on top.

℣ 139. OATMEAL WITH SWEET WINE (ORIBASIUS 1:14:1) ℣

The physician Oribasius viewed oats as animal fodder and not a grain to be used to make bread unless famine diminished the stores of wheat. Oats lack the gluten needed to make leavened bread, which may explain

Oribasius's claim that oat bread is famine food. One could, however, make porridge from oats, flavored with sweet or honeyed wine.

1 cup steel-cut oats
2 cups water
Honey, raisin wine, or *defrutum* (Recipe 142) to taste

Combine the oats and water in a saucepan. Bring to a boil and simmer until the water is absorbed. Season to taste.

PANTRY STAPLES

Many of the recipes from Apicius and other sources assume a pantry filled with prepared ingredients that are added in much the way that contemporary Americans might add chicken stock, Tabasco, or soy sauce. Recipes for these essential ingredients are given here, to be incorporated as needed in preparing other recipes. These staples can be stored at room temperature, as would have been done in Roman times.

⚕ 140. AMULUM *(CATO 87)* ⚕

Clean bread wheat thoroughly, then place in a trough and add water twice a day. On the tenth day drain and dry thoroughly and mix well in a clean trough and allow the product to form. Place this in a new linen cloth, and strain the liquor into a new baking dish or mixing bowl. Repeat the whole process and make more starch. Place the baking dish in the sun and allow to dry.[24]

Romans thickened sauces with the dried starch leached from wheat, similar to modern cornstarch. Cato's instruction to clean the bread wheat thoroughly suggests using *grano*, hulled and lightly pearled wheat grains that give off starch when soaked for several days. Pliny warned *amulum* makers to strain the liquid when the wheat was "quite soft but before it turns sour."[25] You can try following Cato's directions, drying the starchy liquid in a cool oven (maintaining a temperature of about 175°F) if the weather is too cool or damp. Commercial cornstarch works on the same absorption principle to thicken sauces and is true to the spirit of the ancient recipes, albeit anachronistic.

Garum and *Liquamen*

Apicius used the term *liquamen* to identify fish sauce in most of the recipes; indeed, the term *garum* appears only when recipes call for the standard pantry ingredients *oxygarum* and *oenogarum*. By contrast, gastronomic literature and bureaucratic records (including the emperor Diocletian's Price Edict of 301 C.E., which set maximum prices for a variety of goods) seemed to use the terms interchangeably, creating considerable confusion. A plausible explanation for these two terms is that during the course of the Roman empire, *garum* became identified with a new product.

Both the Greeks and the Romans made a fish sauce from small whole fish and pieces of cleaned fish, fermented with salt into an amber-tinted liquor that was used predominantly in the kitchen as an ingredient in sauces. The Greeks called it *garos;* early Romans Latinized the name to *garum.* At some point Romans began making a new type of fish sauce, related to but different from *garos.* Made with fresh fish entrails from certain types of fish, blood, and salt, this fermented sauce was darker, stronger, and more pungent than *garos* and was used as an elite table condiment as well as a cooking ingredient for certain sauces. The confusion arose when elites, who spent little time in the kitchen and encountered finished sauces only at the table, started calling any sauce based on fermented fish *garum.* Cooks, however, needed to distinguish the milder liquid made in the tradition of the Greek *garos* that was still used as an ingredient in Roman cookery. By the time when most of Apicius had been compiled in the late empire, cooks and knowledgeable gourmets had adopted the name *liquamen* to identify traditional *garos* in recipes.[26] A modern analogue is tomato ketchup (*garum*) versus tomato purée (*liquamen*). Ketchup appears on the table, where it is added at each diner's discretion, or occasionally is used as an ingredient in recipes. Tomato purée is exclusively an ingredient and never reaches the table independently. Only cooks and gourmets care enough about this difference to pay close attention to the language.

Both *garum* and *liquamen* could be purchased throughout the Roman empire. There were minor differences in regional techniques and considerable commercial pride in a good product. An amphora from a factory in Pompeii identified the manufacturer by name and boasted that it contained "best strained *liquamen.*"

℣ 141. GARUM *(GEOPONICA)* ℣

If you wish to use the garum at once—i.e., not to expose it to the sun, but boil it—make it in the following manner: Take brine . . . [of proper strength and put] the fish into the brine in a new earthenware pot, add oregano, put it on a good fire until it boils—i.e., until it begins to reduce. Some people also add defrutum. Let it cool and strain it two or three times, until it is clear. Seal and store away.[27]

This important recipe comes from a tenth-century Byzantine agricultural treatise, the *Geoponica,* which is believed to be based on lost Greek and Latin sources. The standard *garum* recipe, which takes months to prepare, is omitted, but the chemistry is simple: small whole fish (the entrails and blood were essential in creating the best quality) were heavily salted (about seven parts fish guts to one part salt by weight) and then exposed to the hot sun for two to three months. The salt extracts moisture from the fish while inhibiting harmful bacteria. The liquid ferments, resulting in a amber-colored briny extract, virtually identical to modern Southeast Asian fish sauces such as *nam pla* and *nuoc mam*.

This ersatz *garum* recipe allows the cook to assemble a quick version of the basic sauce. Because the brine is not fermented, it will lack some of the complex flavor of true *liquamen*. Cato gives a recipe for brine of "proper strength" for preserving foods, that is, a salt and water mixture dense enough to float an egg, which is about four parts water to one part salt by volume.[28] These proportions have been used to make this quick version.

6 cups water
1 1/2 cups kosher salt
2 pounds fresh anchovies or sardines, ungutted and chopped into
    coarse chunks
5 sprigs oregano
1 1/2 cups *defrutum* (Recipe 142)

1. Combine all of the ingredients in a large pot. Bring to a boil and cook for 30 minutes, or until the liquid reduces by half.
2. Line a strainer with a double layer of moistened cheesecloth. Place over a clean bowl and strain the liquid, pressing down on the fish to extract all the juices. Discard the fish and the used cheesecloth.
3. Reline the strainer with fresh moistened cheesecloth and strain the liquid again, repeating if necessary to remove any little bits of fish. Combine with the *defrutum*.

𝄢 142. DEFRUTUM 𝄢

The Romans had a full pantry of grape syrups, all based on freshly pressed grape juice, that could be added to dishes or turned into flavorful sauces or beverage bases. Ancient writers did not always agree on the definitions of these different grape reductions. According to Palladius, an agricultural writer of the fifth century C.E., *defrutum* was unfermented grape juice, also known as must, boiled down to a syrupy consistency; *sapa* was juice reduced by two-thirds, while *caroenum* was reduced by merely one third. Columella, a first-century C.E. agricultural writer, and Pliny gave different proportions and also said fruit flavorings, especially figs and quince, were necessary in *defrutum*.[29] These reductions were a way of preserving freshly pressed grape juice, as boiling killed the naturally occurring yeasts and prevented fermentation into wine or vinegar. Contemporary cooks can please their own palates in deciding how much to reduce the juice, keeping in mind that the more it is boiled down, the longer its shelf life.

Another question is how sweet *defrutum* was. Commercial grape juice is very sweet, possibly too sweet to approximate ancient must. Verjuice is the juice of underripe grapes and is pleasantly tart, but less so than vinegar. Adding just a bit of verjuice, if available, might yield something closer to the ancient product. An alternative technique that requires several days is suggested for those with the time to produce *defrutum* in a manner closer to the Roman technique.

2 cups white grape juice
1/2 cup verjuice (optional)
2 dried figs

Combine the juice, verjuice, if using, and dried figs and bring to a boil. Simmer gently until reduced to the desired consistency, but at least by three-quarters. Strain out the figs and reserve the thickened liquid until needed.

Alternative: Crush or chop 3 pounds of grapes in a food processor. Line a colander with cheesecloth and place it over a bowl. Transfer the grape mass to the colander and let the juice drip out for 3 days, pressing down on the mass from time to time to extract the juice. Cover the mass with cheesecloth to keep out insects. Once the juice has oozed out, reduce the juice with the figs and reserve.

ॐ 143. OXYGARUM *(APICIUS 1.20.2)* ॐ

1 oz. pepper, 1 oz. each parsley, caraway, lovage. Pound, bind with honey. When needed, add liquamen and vinegar.[30]

The term *oxygarum* is a Latin borrowing from the Greek *oxygaron*; the *oxy* preface derives from the Greek word for vinegar, *oxos*, rather than the Latin, *acetum*. This recipe thus has Greek roots and perhaps explains the suffix *garum* rather than *liquamen*. The flavor of the dried herbs and spices infused the honey, which was diluted to the desired intensity with vinegar and *liquamen* when ready to use.

1 tablespoon black peppercorns
1 tablespoon caraway seeds
1 tablespoon dried parsley
1 tablespoon celery seed
2 tablespoons honey

Place the peppercorns, caraway, parsley, and celery seed in a mortar. Pound with the pestle to crush. Transfer to a small bowl and stir in the honey. When needed in a recipe, add fish sauce and vinegar to taste.

ψ *144.* OENOGARUM ψ

Oeno indicates a preparation involving wine. Wine connoisseurs are oenophiles. Apicius contains many recipes that list *oenogarum* as an ingredient, although the book has no underlying recipe to suggest proportions of wine to *garum.* Pepper was added to all *oenogarum,* and the sauces might be thickened with *amulum.*[31]

2 cups red wine
1/2 teaspoon cracked black pepper
1 tablespoon cornstarch
1/3 cup commercial fish sauce or homemade *garum* (Recipe 141)

Combine the wine and pepper and reduce by two-thirds. Add the cornstarch to the fish sauce and stir into the boiling wine, cooking for 1 minute to thicken. Reserve until needed.

ψ *145.* OXYPORUM *(APICIUS 1.18)* ψ

Oxyporum was as much health food and medicine as a seasoning blend, used to correct the perceived excessive moisture in lettuces, to aid digestion, and to prevent flatulence.

2 oz. of cumin, 1 oz. of ginger, 1 oz. of fresh rue, 6 scruples of cooking soda, 12 scruples of juicy dates, 1 oz. of pepper, 9 oz. of honey. The cumin may be either Aethiopian, Syrian, or Lybian. Moisten it with vinegar, dry and then pound. Then bind everything with honey. When needed, use with vinegar and liquamen.[32]

1 tablespoon cumin seeds
1/4 cup vinegar
1/2 tablespoon peppercorns
1/2 teaspoon ground ginger
1 tablespoon fresh rue or 1/4 teaspoon ground bay leaf or dried
   rosemary
3 dried dates, soaked in hot water if needed to soften
1/4 cup honey

1. In a small saucepan, combine the cumin with 1/4 cup vinegar. Boil to evaporate.
2. Grind the cumin and peppercorns into a powder; add the ginger and the rue, bay leaf, or rosemary.
3. Purée the dates by pounding in a mortar with pestle; add the ground spices and honey. Reserve as a pantry item. When ready to use the *oxyporum,* thin with vinegar and fish sauce to taste.

⚕ 146. AROMATIC SALTS (APICIUS 1.13) ⚕

Aromatic salts are for the digestion, and to move the bowels. They prevent all diseases and the plague, and all colds. Moreover, they are mild, beyond all expectation. Take 1 lb. dried common salt, 2 lb. dried sal ammoniac, 3 oz. white pepper, 2 oz. ginger, 1 1/2 oz. cumin, 1 1/2 oz. thyme, 1 1/2 oz. celery seed (if you do not want to take celery seed take 3 oz. parsley instead), 3 oz. oregano, 1 1/2 oz. arugula seed, 3 oz. black pepper, 1 oz. saffron, 2 oz. hyssop from Crete, 2 oz. aromatic leaves, 2 oz. parsley, 2 oz. dill.[33]

This is one of the few recipes in Apicius explicitly to offer medical advice and likely was cribbed from an earlier source. It could have been added to any food by health-conscious cooks or diners. Feel free to incorporate this seasoning in any recipe. The Roman pound equaled 12 ounces, which explains the ratios of salt to spices. White peppercorns are simply fully ripened black peppercorns that have had the dark outer coating removed; the black peppercorns are underripe berries.

2 tablespoons ground white pepper
1 tablespoon plus 1 teaspoon ground ginger
1 tablespoon ground cumin
1 tablespoon dried thyme
1 tablespoon ground celery seed
2 tablespoons dried oregano
2 tablespoons ground black pepper
1 tablespoon powdered saffron
1 tablespoon plus 1 teaspoon ground dried hyssop leaves (available in
   some health food stores; otherwise omit)
1 tablespoon dried rosemary
1 tablespoon dried parsley
1 tablespoon dried dill
1/2 cup kosher salt

Combine all the ingredients except the salt in a mortar and grind to a fine powder with a pestle. Stir into the salt. Reserve and add to dishes as desired.

DAIRY

⚕ 147. HOMEMADE FRESH CHEESE (APICIUS 7.13.9) ⚕

Apicius recommended flavoring cottage cheese either with honey and *liquamen* or with olive oil, coriander, and salt. He did not, however, offer a recipe for making fresh cheese, but the technique for curdling with acid was long known. The yield is surprisingly small: two quarts of cow milk will make no more than two cups of curds (milk solids). The leftover whey can be used in making *Silignites* (Recipe 131).

2 quarts milk, any kind
1 cup white wine vinegar
Salt, ground coriander, and extra virgin olive oil to taste

1. Bring the milk to a boil in a 3-quart saucepan, watching carefully that it does not boil over. Turn off the heat and pour in the vinegar. Stir to combine. The milk should begin to separate into curds and whey within a few minutes; if it does not, gently simmer the milk and add additional vinegar by the tablespoon until the milk curdles.
2. Line a colander with several layers of damp cheesecloth. Spoon the curds into the cheesecloth and let drain for 1 hour at room temperature or overnight in the refrigerator. Gently shake the curds in the colander from time to time to extract more whey.
3. Transfer the curds to a bowl and stir in the salt, ground coriander, and olive oil.
4. As a variation, omit the salt, coriander, and oil and season to taste with Aromatic Salts (Recipe 146), Liburnian Oil (Recipe 189), or *Oxyporum* (Recipe 145).

〽 148. MORETUM *(PSUEDO-VIRGIL)* 〽

Moretum, like its cognate *moretaria*, indicates food prepared in a mortar; several sauces in Apicius are called *moretaria*. This recipe comes from a poem that had been traditionally attributed to the first-century B.C.E. poet Virgil, although scholars now doubt the authorship and call it the work of the so-called Pseudo-Virgil. The poem describes the peasant Similus grinding prodigious amounts of garlic, salty hard cheese, oil, vinegar, and herbs together into a pungent and pale green mass. The herbs came from his garden; he sold the most desirable produce—cabbage, beets, and asparagus—at public markets, keeping the less favored garlic and herbs for himself. The paste accompanied bread, as the reference to the goddess Ceres made plain; an earlier excerpt indicates that the bread was cooked under a *testum*.

Lest Ceres unaccompanied is unpleasing to the palate, he gets ready some accompanying foodstuffs. No sides of bacon, butchered and hardened with salt weighed down his meat racks by the hearth, but a cheese, pieced through its middle of its orb with a string made of broom and an old bunch of dill were hanging there; therefore the resourceful hero toils at another resource for himself [from the adjoining garden]. . . .

[He drops four bulbs of garlic] into the hollow circle of stone. On them he sprinkles grains of salt, the cheese, hardened by the shriveling salt is added, he heaps on top the aforementioned herbs [collected in the garden: rue, celery, and cilantro]. . . . His hand goes round and round; gradually each ingredient loses its own characteristics and there is one color out of many, not all green, because the hard lumps of cheese resist . . . Often a keen waft is launched at the man's open nostrils, and he damns his breakfast with his face turned away. . . . [H]e drizzles on drops of Pallas' olive oil, pours over it a dash of strong vinegar, and . . . at last scrapes round the whole mortar with two fingers and pulls the contents into a single ball.[34]

2 heads of garlic, separated into cloves and papery skins removed
1 tablespoon coarse or kosher salt
3/4 pound aged pecorino, grated
Leaves from 3 stalks of celery
1/2 bunch cilantro
Leaves from 3 sprigs of oregano (to substitute for rue)
3 tablespoons extra virgin olive oil, or more as needed
2 teaspoons white wine vinegar

Place the garlic and salt in a mortar and mash with a pestle. Add the cheese, celery leaves, cilantro, and oregano and continue pounding to purée. Slowly drizzle in the oil until a thick paste is formed. Add the vinegar, pounding to incorporate. Remove the *moretum* and shape into a ball. Eat with a coarse bread.

⑂ 149. BAKED GOAT CHEESE (ORIBASIUS 4.3.6) ⑂

The physician Oribasius considered cheese very bad for one's health; among the cheeses, he considered baked fresh goat cheese the least harmful. Health-conscious diners might add Aromatic Salts, Recipe 146, out of dietary caution.

1 11-ounce log fresh goat cheese
Aromatic Salts (Recipe 146) to taste
Olive oil to taste

Preheat the oven to 400°F. Slice the goat cheese into medallions 1 inch thick and place in a baking dish. Sprinkle with salt and oil. Bake for 15 minutes or until softened. Serve with bread.

⑂ 150. LIBUM (SAVORY CHEESECAKE) (CATO 75) ⑂

Bray 2 pounds of cheese thoroughly in a mortar; when it is thoroughly macerated, add 1 pound of wheat flour, or, if you wish the cake to be more dainty, 1/2 pound of fine flour and mix thoroughly with the cheese. Add 1 egg, and work the whole well. Pat out a loaf, place on leaves, and bake slowly on a warm hearth under a crock.[35]

The recipe could use either a sweet-tasting, fresh cheese, such as farmer's or ricotta, or, to emphasize the savory quality, a tangy and salty feta. The original Roman technique baked *sub testu*, but the *libum* can be baked in an oven.

2 3/4 cups densely packed drained farmer's, ricotta, or moist feta
   cheese
1 1/4 cups all-purpose flour
1 egg, lightly beaten
Fresh fig or grapes leaves

1. If using a cloche, place in a cold oven. Preheat to 350°F.
2. If using feta, mash the cheese into small curds using a mortar and pestle or large spoon. (You can use the drained farmer's or ricotta cheese without mashing.) Place in a bowl and stir in the flour and egg.
3. Place the leaves in a low-sided pie pan. Pat the cheese mixture into a cakelike shape on top of the leaves. Place the cloche over the cake and return to the oven. (Or bake without a cloche; cover the cake with foil if it begins to brown too much.)
4. Bake for 45 minutes, or until the cake has set through. Cool before cutting.

⚕ 151. SAVILLUM (SWEETENED CHEESECAKE) (CATO 84) ⚕

Take 1/2 pound of flour, 2 1/2 pounds of cheese, and mix together as for the libum; add 1/4 pound honey and 1 egg. Grease an earthenware dish with oil. When you have mixed thoroughly, pour into a dish and cover with a crock. See that you bake the center thoroughly, for it is deepest there. When it is done, remove the dish, cover with honey, sprinkle with poppy-seed, place back under the crock for a while, then remove from the fire. Serve in the dish, with a spoon.[36]

This cake follows the same procedure as for *libum* but is wetter and must be baked in a deep pie dish or springform cake pan, either under a dome or uncovered. The cooking time is longer, about 1 hour and 40 minutes. When the cake is firm, poke some deep holes into it with a skewer and pour on additional honey, sprinkle with the poppyseeds, and return to the oven for about 10 minutes. Note the unusual instruction to serve with a spoon, indicating the cheesecake's delicate texture.

Combine:

3 1/2 cups drained, densely packed farmer's or ricotta cheese
3/8 cup honey
1 egg, lightly beaten
1 1/4 cups all-purpose flour

Finish with:

3/4 cup honey
2 tablespoons poppyseeds

MEATS AND POULTRY

The favorite meat of the Romans was pork, both fresh and cured. The hams of Gaul were particularly prized.

℣ 152. BRAISED PORK SHOULDER WITH BARLEY AND FIGS (APICIUS 7.10) ℣

A fresh ham is cooked with 2 lb. of barley and 25 dried figs. When done, skin, glaze the surface with a fire shovel full of glowing coals, spread honey over it, or, what's better: put it in the oven covered with honey. When it has a nice color, put in a sauce pan raisin wine, pepper, a bunch of rue and pure wine to taste. When this is done, pour half of it over the ham and in the other half soak special must cakes. . . .[37]

Fresh ham refers to specific cuts of pork from either the shoulder or the leg, not a cured or smoked meat. The pork recipe was hastily written for an experienced cook (there is no liquid listed in the instructions for simmering the meat, but simmering is the logical technique, given the instruction to cook with barley and dried figs and the subsequent instructions to brown the meat) and assumes that the cook will have the judgment to add appropriate seasonings. The inclusion of alternative ways to brown the cooked meat indicates that the cook should rely on his culinary instincts.

The large quantity of barley in this recipe from Apicius's *Gourmet* book shows the importance of grains for all social classes.

12 ounces pearl barley
12 dried figs, quartered
1 stalk celery, finely diced
1/4 cup fish sauce
1 cup white wine
1 3-pound pork shoulder roast
1 cup honey
1 recipe Must Cakes (Recipe 138)

1. Rinse the barley for 2 minutes under warm running water to remove excess starch. Combine the barley, figs, celery, fish sauce, wine, and pork in a large pot with a lid. Add water to come up halfway on the pork. Bring to a boil, then cover and reduce the heat to a gentle simmer, checking throughout the cooking that the liquid maintains a gentle simmer. Add more water if the barley absorbs too much. Cook for 2 hours, turning the pork halfway through, or until the pork is tender.

2. Preheat a broiler. Remove the cooked pork from the pot and place on a roasting pan. Brush generously with the honey and broil for about 3 minutes to brown, watching that the honey does not burn. Cut into bite-sized pieces.

3. Drain the excess liquid from the pot and spread the barley pilaf on a large serving platter. Split the must cakes in half and ring them around the outside of the platter. Top the barley with the pork and serve with Pepper Sauce (Recipe 153).

♆ 153. PEPPER SAUCE ♆

1 cup white or red wine
1 cup raisin wine
2 sprigs rosemary
1 tablespoon black peppercorns or long pepper, coarsely cracked in a
    mortar

Place the wine, raisin wine, rosemary, and cracked peppercorns in a saucepan. Bring to a boil and reduce by three-quarters. Remove the rosemary and pour over the Braised Pork Shoulder (Recipe 152) and Must Cakes (Recipe 138).

♆ 154. SUCKLING PIG À LA VITELLIUS (APICIUS 8.7.7) ♆

Garnish the pig like wild boar, sprinkle with salt, roast in the oven. In a mortar put pepper, lovage, moisten with liquamen, wine and raisin wine to taste, put this in a saucepan, adding very little oil, heat; baste the roasting pig with this in a manner so that the aroma will penetrate the skin.[38]

Suckling pig and wild boar were favorites at Saturnalia or for any festive meal. The wild boar in Trimalchio's Feast was garnished with a freedman's cap to remind the guests of Trimalchio's slave origins; a baby's knit hat would work well. To complete Trimalchio's display, fashion piglets from must cake dough and arrange as if nursing from the sow.

1 suckling pig, 12–15 pounds, cleaned and gutted
Salt, as needed
3 tablespoons black peppercorns

1 tablespoon lovage or celery seed

1/4 cup fish sauce

1/2 cup red wine

1 cup raisin wine

2 tablespoons olive oil

1. Preheat the oven to 350°F.

2. Cover the ears and tail of the pig with aluminum foil or a wet cloth to prevent burning in the oven. Using a knife, make shallow slits on the back of the pig. Salt generously and place in a roasting pan in the oven.

3. Pound the peppercorns with the lovage or celery seed. Combine with the fish sauce, red and raisin wines, and oil. Brush this mixture on the back of the pig several times while it is roasting; the slits should absorb some of the liquid into the flesh. Use any pan drippings to continue basting the pig.

4. Roast the pig for about 15 minutes per pound, or until a meat thermometer inserted into the thigh registers 165°F. Let cool slightly before garnishing.

☙ 155. SOW'S UDDER (APICIUS 7.2.1) ☙

One of the poet Martial's invitations to dinner promised "sow's udder wet from tunny's [tuna's] brine," indicating a pork belly braised in good-quality fish sauce. This is another recipe from Apicius's *Gourmet* chapter. Pork belly (albeit without the paps) is currently enjoying a renewed popularity among some of America's best chefs; it is the same cut of meat that bacon is made from but is unsalted and unsmoked, making a very rich dish.

Sow's udder or belly with the paps on it is prepared in this manner: Boil the belly, tie it together with reeds, sprinkle with salt, and place on the oven or start roasting on the gridiron. Crush pepper, lovage with liquamen, wine, adding raisin wine to taste, thicken with amulum and pour over the roast.[39]

1 pound pork belly

3/4 cup *oenogarum* (Recipe 144)

1 teaspoon crushed black peppercorns or long pepper

3/4 teaspoon lovage or celery seed

2 tablespoons raisin wine

2 teaspoons cornstarch

3/4 teaspoon salt

1. Place the pork belly in a pan and cover with water by 1 inch. Bring to a boil, reduce the heat, and simmer gently for 90 minutes. Drain and dry.

2. Place the *oenogarum* in a saucepan with the peppercorns, lovage or celery seeds, and raisin wine. Bring to a boil. Dissolve the cornstarch in 1 1/2 tablespoons cold water and stir into the *oenogarum*. Boil to thicken, about 2 minutes. Reserve.

3. Preheat a grill pan. Sprinkle the pork belly with the salt and grill over medium heat, turning once, about 5 minutes per side. Slice into bite-sized pieces. Reheat the sauce and pour over the pork belly.

♈ 156. HAM (CATO 126) ♈

After buying legs of pork cut off the trotters [hooves]. 1/2 peck ground Roman salt per ham. Spread the salt in the base of a vat or jar, then place a ham with the skin facing downward. Cover completely with salt. Then place another above it and cover completely with salt. Be careful not to let meat touch meat. . . . After standing in salt for five days, take all hams out with the salt. Put those that were above below, and so rearrange and replace. After a total of 12 days take out hams, clean off the salt, and hang in the fresh air 2 days. On the third day clean off with a sponge, rub all over with oil, hang in smoke for 2 days. On the third day take down, rub all over with a mixture of oil and vinegar, and hang in the meat store. Neither moths nor worms will attack it.[40]

Farm wives have cured hams at home for centuries, slaughtering the pigs and salting and smoking the meat in the rafters over large fireplaces. Salting meats, particularly pork, was an autumn activity; it solved the problem of keeping animals over the winter, when feed was limited in temperate Europe, and preserved large quantities of meat for use throughout the winter.

Only in the last century has commercial production supplanted the home-cured ham, although artisanally produced hams command a hefty price from gourmets. One must be careful in the curing process to draw out enough moisture to limit bacterial growth. Unless you are absolutely confident that you can provide a cool, dry environment, the technique is better left to professionals.

Modern cookbooks follow a procedure similar to Cato's; the one difference is that most recommend incorporating herbs and spices, much like the Aromatic Salts (Recipe 146), and add saltpeter (potassium nitrate), which maintains the pink color of the meat and further inhibits bacterial growth.

1 pork leg, thighbone removed but knucklebone intact
1 3-pound box kosher salt
3 batches Aromatic Salts (Recipe 146)

1. Beat the ham with a clean mallet to extract any blood or juices. Tie the ham by the knucklebone and hang over a pan in a cool, dry, dark place for 3 days to drain further. Wipe the ham twice a day with a clean cloth to blot any liquid.

2. Sterilize an earthenware crock large enough to hold the ham by rinsing with boiling water and let it air-dry thoroughly. Mix the salts and pour a layer about 2 inches thick on the bottom. Pack the space left by the thighbone with the salt and rub all surfaces thoroughly. Place the ham skin side down in the crock and cover with the remaining salt. If any part of the meat is exposed, add more salt. Cover with a clean cloth, add a 10-pound weight, and let the ham rest for 12 days in a cool (no more than 50°F), dry place. Remove the ham and brush off all the salt; juices will have accumulated in the bottom of the crock. Pat the ham dry.

3. Set up the smoker according to the manufacturer's instructions and cold-smoke (no more that 120°F) for 40 hours. (The Romans would have hung the meat in a fireplace chimney at a good distance from the fire.) The ham will develop a burnished brown exterior. Remove, wrap in cheesecloth, and store in a cool, dry larder.

4. To use, cut off the desired amount of meat and boil to remove the excess salt.

♆ 157. BOILED SALT MEAT (APICIUS 1.8) ♆

Apicius recommended boiling salted meats twice: first in milk, and then in water. There is a good reason for recommending the initial boil in milk: milk's lactic acid tenderizes the meat, which has been toughened by contact with the salt. The taste of excess salt can be removed simply by boiling in water, but the texture will not be quite as pleasant.

Apicius's recipe has been slightly modified to make this dish suitable for the poor peasants Baucis and Philemon of Ovid's *Metamorphoses*. They ate a bit of salted meat with cabbage, but boiling the meat in milk was a technique too profligate for people at subsistence level. Any milk they had likely would have been consumed directly or preserved as cheese or yogurt.

1-pound slab (whole, not sliced) bacon

Bring a large pot of water to a boil and submerge the bacon. Reduce heat to a simmer and cook for 20 minutes. Drain, cut into bite-sized chunks, and serve with Cabbage, Another Way (Recipe 180).

♆ 158. GARLIC AND SAGE CONFIT OF PORK WITH MUSTARD ♆

An archaeological find from a fifth-century Frankish tomb in the northern reaches of the Roman empire contained food offerings, including pork that had been preserved in fat. Confit is a term applied to meat dishes that are preserved in fat: after some of the meat's moisture is removed by salting, the meat is simmered in fat and then stored in fat, which cuts off oxygen and prevents spoilage. Serve with Mustard (Recipe 193).

2 pounds pork shoulder, cut into 1 1/2-inch cubes
1/4 cup kosher salt
2 tablespoons cracked black pepper
2 pounds lard
Cloves from one head of garlic, peeled
8 sage leaves

1. Season the pork with the salt and pepper. Let rest on a rack set in a tray overnight in the refrigerator. The pork should give off some moisture.
2. The next day, wipe the excess salt and moisture off the pork. Melt the lard in a large pan. Add the pork, garlic, and sage. Simmer very gently, about 2 hours, turning the cubes until the pork is tender. Transfer the pork to a glass or ceramic container and pour over the lard with the garlic and sage to completely submerge the pork. Let solidify and store in a cool place, such as a cellar or in the refrigerator.
3. To serve, remove the cubes from the fat and wipe off the excess. Sauté the cubes to warm through and serve with Mustard (Recipe 193).

♆ 159. STEWED BEEF TIDBITS (APICIUS 8.5.2) ♆

Romans ate relatively little beef. Galen considered it difficult to digest. Apicius had only four recipes for beef or veal, one of which paired beef with either onions or quinces, plus a quickly made sauce of *liquamen*, pepper, *laser* (an alternative Latin name for *silphium*), and oil. In *Satyricon*, even Trimalchio's guests were disappointed when beef was served to represent the zodiac sign of the bull Taurus as part of the "crude" repast.

Quinces are a fruit in the pome family, related to apples and pears. Quinces cannot be eaten raw, but if they are available, cut them in half, remove the stem and core, and cut them into wedges to use in place of the leeks. The asafetida substitutes for the original recipe's *laser*.

3 tablespoons olive oil
1 1/2 pounds beef stewing meat, trimmed of excess fat and cut into
    1 1/2-inch cubes
3 tablespoons fish sauce
1 teaspoon asafetida
Freshly ground black pepper to taste

♆ 161. DUCK WITH TURNIPS (APICIUS 6.2.3)

Wash and dress the bird and parboil it in water with salt and dill. Next prepare turnips and cook them in water, which is to be squeezed out. Take them out of the pot and wash them again and put into a saucepan the duck with oil, liquamen, a bunch of leeks and coriander, the turnips cut into small pieces. Put these on top of the duck to finish cooking. When half done, to give it color add defrutum. The sauce is prepared separately: pepper, cumin, coriander, laser root moistened with vinegar and diluted with its own cooking-liquor. Bring this to a boiling point, thicken with amulum and add to the turnips. Sprinkle with pepper and serve.[42]

Lacking a good substitute for laser root, the recipe uses the duck cooking liquid in place of the laser root cooking liquid to make the sauce.

1 butterflied duck, excess fat and backbone removed, breastbone
   cracked to flatten the duck
1/4 cup kosher salt
1 cup coarsely chopped fresh dill
2 pounds turnips
1 leek, cleaned and chopped
2 tablespoons coriander seeds, lightly crushed
1/4 cup fish sauce, diluted with 1 cup water
1 cup *defrutum*

For the sauce:

1 teaspoon coarsely ground black pepper
1 teaspoon ground cumin
2 teaspoons ground coriander
1/2 teaspoon asafetida
The reserved duck cooking liquid
5 tablespoons red wine vinegar, or more to taste
1 1/2 tablespoons cornstarch
Freshly ground pepper for garnish

1. Preheat the oven to 350°F. Prick the duck breast with a knife and place the duck in a pot large enough to completely submerge the duck. Cover with water, add the salt and dill, and bring to a boil. Reduce the heat to low and simmer for 15 minutes to render some of the fat. Remove the duck and reserve the cooking water.
2. Meanwhile, peel the turnips and slice into 1/2-inch rounds. Simmer the turnips in the duck cooking water for 2 minutes. Drain, pat dry, and reserve. Discard the water.
3. Place the leek and coriander in the bottom of a baking dish large enough to hold the flattened duck. Place the duck breast side down on top and add the diluted fish sauce. Cover and bake for 45 minutes.

1 1/2 cups water

4 leeks, dark green parts trimmed off, split in half, washed, and sliced crosswise into 1-inch pieces, or 2 trimmed quinces

Preheat a sauté pan over high heat and add the oil. Brown the beef tho oughly in the oil. Sprinkle the meat with the fish sauce, asafetida, peppe and water. Cover the pan, reduce the heat to very low, and stew for 1 hou Add the leeks or quince and continue stewing another 30 minutes, or un the meat is tender. Check periodically and add more water if the beef seen in danger of burning. When finished, the cooking liquid should be reduc to a sauce that coats the beef.

♆ 160. ROAST KIDNEYS (APICIUS 7.8) ♆

Split them [kidneys] in two parts so that they are spread out. Sprinkle the opening with crushed pepper and nuts, finely chopped coriander and crushed fennel seed. . . . Tie together, wrap in caul, brown in oil and liquamen, and then roast in the oven or broil on the gridiron.[41]

Caul is a lacy, fatty membrane that lines the abdominal cavity of p and sheep; it is available from good butchers or by special order. If caul unavailable, you can wrap the kidneys in a piece of bacon or pancetta (ι smoked Italian bacon).

6 kidneys, lamb or veal, soaked overnight in cold water in the refrigerator

1/2 teaspoon black peppercorns

2 tablespoons pine nuts

2 teaspoons minced cilantro

1/4 teaspoon crushed fennel seed

1/2 pound caul fat

2 tablespoons olive oil

1 tablespoon fish sauce

1. Butterfly the kidneys by splitting them nearly in half lengthwis down the larger curving side. They should remain attached alon the shorter side and open up like a book.
2. Grind together the peppercorns, pine nuts, cilantro, and fennel seed Divide this stuffing among the kidneys.
3. Close the kidneys and wrap in sheets of caul fat cut large enough t enclose the kidneys.
4. Preheat a sauté pan. Add the olive oil and fish sauce and cook th kidneys about 3–4 minutes per side; the kidneys should remai slightly pink inside. Serve hot.

4. Turn the duck breast side up, add the turnips to the pan, and pour the *defrutum* over the duck. Continue baking, covered, for another 45 minutes. Remove the duck and turnips to a carving board and let rest while you prepare the sauce. Strain the cooking liquid and reserve. Spoon off any excess fat that rises to the surface.

5. Combine the pepper, cumin, coriander, and asafetida in a small saucepan. Add the defatted cooking liquid and bring to a boil. Combine the vinegar and cornstarch and stir into the boiling sauce. Cook 2 minutes to thicken. Return the reserved turnips to the sauce to heat through.

6. Carve the duck into portions that can be taken with the fingers and transfer to a serving platter. Pour over the sauce with the turnips, sprinkle with ground pepper, and serve.

♇ 162. ROASTED HARE OR RABBIT WITH SPICED SAUCE (APICIUS 8.8.11) ♇

This is another Apicius recipe that assumes the cook knows how to prepare the rabbit and needs instruction only to prepare the accompanying sauce, which is made from the rabbit's liver, puréed and combined with onions, pepper, rue, raisin wine, *defrutum*, oil, and *liquamen*. The puréed liver helps to thicken the sauce, which also included *amulum*.

To emulate the Pegasus that formed a centerpiece of Trimalchio's Feast, present the rabbit whole with wings fashioned from feathers and attached to its shoulders. Otherwise the rabbit should be carved into bite-sized pieces.

1 rabbit, cleaned and liver reserved in the refrigerator
2 tablespoons olive oil
3 tablespoons minced onion
1 tablespoon fish sauce
1/2 cup *defrutum*
1/2 cup raisin wine
1/2 teaspoon black pepper, ground
1/4 teaspoon dried rosemary, ground
2 teaspoons cornstarch
2 tablespoons cold water

1. Preheat the oven to 325°F. Place the rabbit in a roasting pan and roast until it reaches an internal temperature of 165°F, about 1 1/4 hours. Remove to a serving platter and attach wings, if desired, or carve into serving pieces.

2. Meanwhile, in a saucepan, gently heat the oil and sweat the onion until soft. Add the fish sauce, *defrutum*, raisin wine, pepper, and

rosemary. Bring to a boil and reduce the liquid by half. Finely mince the liver and add to the sauce, stirring constantly. Stir the cornstarch into the water, add to the sauce, and cook for 2 minutes to finish thickening. Serve as a dipping sauce on the side.

☗ 163. FOR HIGH BIRDS OF ANY KIND (APICIUS 6.5.6) ☗

For birds of all kinds that have a goatish smell: pepper, lovage, thyme, dry mint, sage, dates, honey, vinegar, wine, liquamen, oil, defrutum, mustard. The birds will be more luscious and nutritious, and the fat preserved, if you envelop them in a dough of flour and oil and bake them.[43]

Wild game birds traditionally are hung to tenderize them; what this means is that bacteria begin to decompose the flesh, often with distinctive high aromas. Revered by many gourmets, hung meats are often marinated to neutralize goatish smells. Wild birds are much leaner than most farm-raised game birds, so the ancient desire to keep in the natural fat is understandable. If you do not have access to wild duck or farm-raised squab, which are naturally lean, remove all visible fat from domestic duck.

For the marinade:

1/2 teaspoon freshly ground pepper
1/4 teaspoon celery seeds
1/4 teaspoon dried thyme
1/8 teaspoon dried mint
1/8 teaspoon dried sage
2 dates, finely minced
2 tablespoons honey
1 1/2 tablespoons vinegar
5 tablespoons *oenogarum* (Recipe 144)
2 tablespoons olive oil
2 tablespoons *defrutum* (Recipe 142)
1 tablespoon mustard powder

For the crust:

6 cups all-purpose flour
1 3/4 cups water, or as needed
1/4 cup flavorless oil
1 duck or 4 squab

1. Combine all of the marinade ingredients and smear the inside and out of the birds with this mixture. Let marinate for 1 hour.
2. Meanwhile, prepare the crust by mixing the flour, water, and oil to form a dough. Let the dough rest for 30 minutes. Preheat the oven to 425°F.

3. Roll out the pastry into one rectangle large enough to encase the duck, or four smaller squares, if using squab. Place the birds in the center and wrap in the pastry, pressing to conform the dough to the bird's shape. Place the birds on a baking sheet and roast in the oven until an instant read thermometer inserted through the pastry into the thigh registers 160°F. Start testing farmed duck after 1 1/2 hours; wild duck after 1 hour, 10 minutes; or squab after 30 minutes.

4. Crack the pastry shell off and discard, reserving any juices that accumulate. Cut the birds into serving pieces and pour the juices over them.

𝕿 164. KID OR LAMB SPICED RAW (APICIUS 8.6.8) 𝕿

Rub with oil and pepper, sprinkle outside generously with pure salt mixed with [ground] coriander seed. Put in the oven, roast, and serve.[44]

This recipe shows that Roman food could be simply and brilliantly seasoned. Preheat the oven to 400°F and follow Apicius's instructions. A bone-in leg of lamb will roast to medium rare in about 18–20 minutes per pound.

𝕿 165. DAINTY DISHES OF KID OR LAMB (APICIUS 8.6.1) 𝕿

Cook with pepper and liquamen. Serve accompanied by chopped fresh beans with liquamen, pepper, and laser, or with a sauce of bread pieces and a little oil.[45]

2 pounds goat or lamb stewing meat, cut into 1 1/2-inch pieces
1/2 cup fish sauce, diluted with 1 1/2 cups water
1 teaspoon freshly ground black pepper

Combine all of the ingredients in a pan. Bring to a boil, cover, and reduce the heat to a simmer. Cook gently for about 90 minutes, or until the meat is tender, checking periodically to make sure the pan has not boiled dry; add water if needed. When done, boil to reduce the cooking liquid to a coating sauce and serve with Green Beans (Recipe 186) and White Sauce (Recipe 196).

𝕿 166. BOILED CHICKEN WITH COLD DILL SAUCE (APICIUS 6.9.1) 𝕿

This recipe is for a sauce made separately from the boiled chicken, making it useful for dressing leftovers. The sauce, based on dried dill, mint, and mustard, contained vinegar, *defrutum*, and fig wine. The ancients made wine from many fruits in addition to grapes, although grape wines were most usual. Some modern producers flavor balsamic vinegar with figs; this would be a good substitute for both the vinegar and the wine.

1 3 1/2-pound chicken
2 tablespoons salt
1 tablespoon ground dill weed
1 teaspoon ground dried mint
1/4 teaspoon asafetida
3 tablespoons vinegar, preferably fig balsamic
1 tablespoon fish sauce
2 teaspoons ground mustard
2 tablespoons *defrutum* (Recipe 142)
3/4 cup olive oil

1. Place the chicken in a large pot and cover with water by 2 inches. Add the salt. Bring to a boil, reduce heat to a simmer, and cook for about 1 hour, or until a meat thermometer inserted into the thigh registers 165°F. Remove from the pan and, when cool enough to handle, remove the flesh from the bones and tear into bite-sized pieces.
2. Place all the remaining ingredients except the oil into a bowl and whisk to combine. Slowly trickle in the oil, whisking constantly, to create a thick sauce. Toss the chicken with the sauce and serve.

⚓ 167. ROASTED DORMICE (APICIUS 8.9) ⚓

Dormouse is stuffed with a forcemeat of pork and small pieces of dormouse meat trimmings, all pounded with pepper, nuts, laser, liquamen. Put the dormouse thus stuffed in an earthen casserole, roast it in the oven.[46]

Dormice are arboreal mammals, similar to squirrel. Squirrel is available in a few areas of the United States and is the best substitute; if unavailable in your area, use quail, which will be about the right size. The honey and poppyseed garnish is borrowed from Trimalchio's Feast.

1/4 pound ground pork
1/2 teaspoon ground black pepper
4 teaspoons pine nuts
1/2 teaspoon asafetida
3 tablespoons fish sauce
4 squirrels, cleaned and ribcage removed, or 4 semiboneless quail (ribcage removed)
1/3 cup honey
1 tablespoon poppyseeds

1. Preheat the oven to 350°F. Combine the pork, pepper, pine nuts, asafetida, and 1 tablespoon fish sauce to make a stuffing. Stuff the chest cavity of whatever critter you are using.
2. Place the stuffed "dormice" in an earthenware baking dish and roast in the oven until a meat thermometer inserted into the stuffing registers 170°F, about 35–45 minutes.
3. Combine the honey, the remaining 2 tablespoons fish sauce, and the poppyseeds. Pour over the "dormice" and serve.

The polymath Varro (116–28 B.C.E.) reported that dormice were fattened for the table by confining them day and night in specially constructed containers holding acorns, walnuts, and chestnuts.[47]

---

⑦ 168. GRILLED SAUSAGES (APICIUS 2.5.2) ⑦

Make a mixture of boiled spelt grits and coarsely minced meat that has been pounded with pepper, liquamen and pine-kernels. Stuff a sausage skin and boil. Then grill with salt and serve with mustard, or serve boiled cut up on a round dish.[48]

1/4 cup whole spelt or wheat berries
1/3 cup pine nuts, coarsely chopped
1/2 pound ground pork
1/2 pound ground lamb
3 tablespoons fish sauce
Black pepper to taste
Sausage casings (optional), soaked in cold water
Aromatic Salts to taste (Recipe 146)
Mustard (Recipe 193)
Pomegranate fruitlets and black grapes (optional)

1. Put the spelt or wheat berries into a saucepan, cover with water by 2 inches, and bring to a boil. Reduce the heat to a simmer and cook until tender, about 45 minutes. Drain and pat dry thoroughly. Place the cooked grain in a food processor and pulse to chop finely. Reserve.
2. Mix the pine nuts, pork, and lamb with the chopped grain. Add the fish sauce and pepper. Cook a small bit in a frying pan to test for seasoning. Adjust as necessary; it should be very flavorful. If you do not have sausage casings, form patties and sauté them until cooked through, then skip to step 4.
3. If you have casings, stuff them with a sausage stuffer or by using a pastry bag fitted with a large plain tip to force the meat into the casing. Do not stuff the sausage too tightly, or they will burst in the

cooking. Twist the casings tightly to form links about 2 inches long. Put the sausages into a large pan and slowly bring to a simmer. Cook until the sausages feel firm, about 7–8 minutes. Drain. When ready to serve, heat a grill pan and grill the sausages to warm.

4. Sprinkle the cooked meat with aromatic salt and serve with mustard. To imitate the elaborate appetizers, or *gustatio*, from Trimalchio's Feast, cut grapes in half and arrange flat side down on a plate. Scatter with pomegranate fruitlets and place the sausages on top.

𝔜 169. SACRIFICE TO THE HEALTH OF OXEN (CATO 83) 𝔜

To Mars [god of war] and Sivanus [god of forest pastures], in the forest, in the daytime, dedicate the following per head of oxen: 3 lb. emmer, 4 1/2 lb. fat, 4 1/2 lb. lean meat, 3 pints wine. You place it all together in one jug; the wine may also be placed in one jug. They may be offered by a slave or a free person. When they have been offered, they should be consumed, at once, on the spot. No woman must be present or see the rite.[49]

Follow Cato's instructions for this particular sacrifice precisely, as one does not tinker with religion.

FISH AND SEAFOOD

Any of the fish and seafood recipes from the Greek chapter would be appropriate on the Roman table as well.

𝔜 170. DRESSING FOR OYSTERS (APICIUS 9.6) 𝔜

The original recipe lacks preparation instructions and merely lists ingredients, including egg yolk, for the dressing. Romans ate eggs both raw and cooked, so this could be a formula for a sauce like mayonnaise to dress oysters. You may simply flavor a commercially prepared mayonnaise with pepper, celery seed (for lovage), and *liquamen*, the key flavorings from Apicius's recipe, or you may make mayonnaise following the instructions below, cooking the egg yolk to minimize the risk of bacterial contamination from raw egg yolks.

1 egg yolk
2 tablespoons vinegar
1 tablespoon wine
2 teaspoons fish sauce
1/2 cup olive oil
1/2 teaspoon ground celery seed
Freshly ground black pepper to taste
1 dozen oysters, opened in the shells and kept refrigerated, covered with a clean, damp towel

1. Put 2 inches of water in the bottom of a double boiler and bring to a simmer; in the top, combine the egg yolk, vinegar, wine, and fish sauce and whisk the egg yolk mixture constantly until it slowly thickens and is very hot to the touch, about 4 minutes.

2. Remove from the heat and let cool to room temperature. Slowly whisk in the oil, drop by drop at first, until you see the oil being uniformly incorporated; the remaining oil can be added very slowly in a thin stream, whisking constantly. Stir in the celery seed and pepper. Serve a dab of mayonnaise with each of the oysters. You will have extra mayonnaise that can be used to dress any raw or boiled vegetables.

⚓ 171. BOILED MACKEREL WITH RUE SAUCE (APICIUS 10.3.1) ⚓

The poet Martial promised fish garnished with hard-cooked eggs in one of his dinner invitations, so after cooking the fish, it should be garnished with eggs and dressed. Apicius blended typical Roman spices and herbs—pepper, cumin, lovage, and fresh rue (here, a bit of fresh rosemary will provide the necessary bitter bite of rue)—with vinegar, oil, honey, and *liquamen* to make a thickened sauce that Apicius recommended for boiled mackerel.

5 cups water
1 double recipe *oxygarum* (Recipe 143)
1 mackerel, about 1 1/2 pounds, cleaned, scaled, and gutted
3 eggs
1 tablespoon peppercorns
1/4 teaspoon celery seed
1/2 teaspoon cumin seed
1 teaspoon fresh rosemary leaves, minced
2 tablespoons chopped onion
2 tablespoons honey
1/4 cup vinegar
1 tablespoon fish sauce
1 tablespoon olive oil
1/2 tablespoon cornstarch dissolved in 2 tablespoons water

1. Bring the water and *oxygarum* to a boil in a pan and add the mackerel. (If the mackerel is not covered by the liquid, add more water.) Reduce the heat to a gentle simmer and poach the mackerel until cooked through, about 10–12 minutes. Remove from the cooking liquid, pat dry, peel off the skin, and place on a serving dish.

2. Meanwhile, put the eggs in a pan and cover with water by 1 inch. Bring to a boil, cover, and remove from the heat. Let the eggs rest for

13 minutes, then drain and place in cold water. Crack the shells gently to facilitate peeling. When cool, peel and slice into thin disks.

3. Pound the peppercorns, celery, and cumin seeds in a mortar with a pestle. Transfer to a small saucepan and add the rosemary, onion, honey, vinegar, fish sauce, and olive oil. Bring to a boil and add the dissolved cornstarch. Boil for 1 minute more.

4. Lay the egg slices in an overlapping row on top of the mackerel to resemble fish scales. Pour the sauce over and serve.

♆ 172. BLACK SEA PICKLED FISH (ORIBASIUS, 4.1.40) ♆

The physician Oribasius, who lived in Pergamum (Bergama in modern-day Turkey), wrote that pickled tuna from Gades and corvi from the Black Sea were the best. The corvi is believed to be related to the North American bluefish, an oily fish that takes well to pickling, as does tuna.

3 tablespoons olive oil
3/4 pound tuna or bluefish fillet, cut into 1-inch strips
2 tablespoons fish sauce
1/2 cup vinegar
1/2 cup white wine
1 onion, peeled and thinly sliced
1 bay leaf
1 teaspoon whole peppercorns

1. Heat the olive oil in a frying pan over medium heat. Gently sauté the fish until just cooked through. Drain and place in a shallow dish in one layer.

2. Combine the fish sauce, vinegar, wine, onion, bay leaf, and peppercorns in a saucepan. Bring to a boil and remove from the heat. Pour over the fish. Store in the refrigerator until ready to eat as part of an appetizer course, or *gustatio*.

EGG DISHES

♆ 173. PINE NUT SAUCE FOR SOFT-BOILED EGGS (APICIUS 7.19.3) ♆

Apicius included three recipes for boiled or fried eggs in his *Gourmet* book, pairing a pine nut pesto seasoned with pepper and lovage and thinned with *liquamen*, vinegar, and honey. Cook the eggs according to the next recipe from the physician Oribasius.

2 tablespoons pine nuts, soaked in water overnight and drained
1 teaspoon cracked black peppercorns

1/4 teaspoon celery seed

2 teaspoons vinegar, or as needed

1 tablespoon honey, or as needed

2 teaspoons fish sauce, or as needed

Combine the pine nuts, pepper, and celery seed in a mortar and pound to a fine texture. Stir in vinegar, honey, and fish sauce, adjusting the liquids to suit your palate. Reserve.

⚘ 174. SOFT-BOILED EGGS IN VINEGAR (ORIBASIUS 4.11.14) ⚘

One should boil eggs in water whilst stirring them without pause; for when stirred they do not congeal or thicken; they are better boiled in vinegar; for then they stay still more moist.

This recipe reads oddly; it makes sense only if the eggs are warmed in the shell rather than truly boiled. The constant jostling in the shell will minimize coagulation, although given enough time, the eggs will firm up. The instruction that eggs are moister boiled in vinegar may refer to the fact that if an eggshell contains a crack, the egg can leach out and solidify. If the egg is cooked in water containing vinegar, the vinegar will coagulate the escaping egg faster, sealing most of the egg in the shell.

1 quart water plus 1 cup vinegar

4 eggs at room temperature

Bring the water and vinegar to a boil in a saucepan. Add the eggs and reduce the heat to a simmer. Cook, stirring gently, until the eggs are cooked to your preferred degree of doneness, about 4 minutes for runny yolks (perhaps what Oribasius was striving for), 7 minutes for soft yolks, and up to 12 minutes for solid eggs. Crack open the shell and serve with the pine nut sauce (Recipe 173).

⚘ 175. ASPARAGUS PATINAE TWO WAYS: SOUFFLÉ AND FRITTATA (APICIUS 4.2.6) ⚘

There are more than 30 recipes in Apicius for *patinae*, dishes that often contain eggs. Most instruct the cook to "break" or to "mix" the eggs; one in particular, however, uses the Latin *dissolvo*, which can be translated to mean to separate, to disunite, or to dissolve. While this may simply be another expression for mixing the whole eggs into other ingredients, it could indicate separating the yolks from the whites. Sixth-century Byzantine recipes instructed cooks to beat egg whites to make a lightened dish in the nature of a soufflé, so perhaps earlier cooks following Apicius's recipes also

knew how to make soufflés. This ambiguous recipe could be a simple asparagus purée, an asparagus frittata, or an asparagus soufflé. Two egg versions
are offered, but you could create a third by omitting the eggs entirely. The
recipe is unusual in specifying leaf coriander (cilantro) rather than coriander
seed.

*Throw some trimmed asparagus into a mortar, crush them, add wine and
strain. Crush pepper, lovage, fresh coriander, savory, onions, wine, liquamen
and oil. Transfer to a low greased dish and, if you want, add some separated/
dissolved [dissolvo] eggs over a fire to bind. Season with finely ground pepper
and serve.*[50]

1 bunch asparagus, trimmed
1/2 cup white wine
1/4 cup finely chopped onion
1/8 teaspoon celery seed
1/4 teaspoon coarsely cracked black pepper
1/4 cup loosely packed cilantro leaves
1 teaspoon dried oregano
1 tablespoon fish sauce

1 tablespoon olive oil, plus oil for the dish

1. Preheat the oven to 400°F. Oil the inside of a 1-quart gratin dish
   lightly.
2. If the asparagus are thick, peel the stalks. Coarsely chop them and
   pound them in a large mortar to purée. Combine the asparagus with
   the wine and force through a fine strainer. Reserve.
3. Combine the onion, celery seed, pepper, cilantro, and oregano in a
   mortar and pound to purée. Add the fish sauce, oil, and the asparagus purée and reserve.

Asparagus Soufflé

Stir three lightly beaten egg yolks into the asparagus mixture, blending
thoroughly. In a clean and dry bowl, whip six egg whites until they hold a
firm, but not hard, peak. Fold the whites into the asparagus mixture. Gently
spoon the mixture into the gratin dish and bake for approximately 20–25
minutes, or until the soufflé is just set.

Asparagus Frittata

Beat six whole eggs. Combine with the asparagus mixture and pour into
a gratin dish. Place in the oven, reduce the heat to 300°F, and bake for approximately 35–40 minutes, or until the frittata is just set.

176. PATINA *OF ANCHOVY WITHOUT ANCHOVY* *(APICIUS 4.2.12)*

Take fillets of grilled or boiled fish and mince enough to fill a pan of the size you wish. Pound pepper and add a little rue, add sufficient liquamen, break eggs and stir in, add a little oil, and mix everything in the pan with the fish so that it forms a smooth mixture. On top of this you place jellyfish, taking care that they do not mix with the eggs. Cook in the steam so that the jellyfish cannot combine with the eggs, and when they are dry sprinkle with ground pepper and serve. At table, no one will know what he is eating.[51]

This recipe illustrates the delight Roman cooks took in creating complicated dishes that would stump gourmets as to their exact ingredients. Egg whites will substitute for the jellyfish.

2 pounds white fish fillets, any type
1/2 teaspoon ground pepper
1 generous pinch dried rosemary
2 1/2 tablespoons fish sauce
3 tablespoons olive oil
4 whole eggs, beaten
2 egg whites
Freshly ground pepper, for garnish

1. Place the fish fillets in a pan and cover with cold water. Bring to a boil, turn off the heat, and let cook in the residual heat for 8 minutes, or until cooked through. Drain the fish and mince with a knife to a paste. Reserve.
2. Combine the pepper, rosemary, fish sauce, oil, and whole eggs. Add the fish paste, stirring thoroughly. Pour into a glass pie pan. Create a steamer by putting 2 inches of water in the bottom of a deep pan with a tight-fitting lid. Place several inverted custard cups or ramekins on the bottom and balance the pie pan on the inverted cups. Bring to a boil, cover, and let the egg mixture steam until set, about 20 minutes.
3. Remove the lid, pour the remaining egg whites on the top, cover, and steam until the egg whites set. Sprinkle with pepper and serve from the pie pan.

VEGETABLES AND PULSES

In describing the importance of vegetable gardens in his *Natural History*, Pliny reminded his contemporaries that even the kings who ruled in the earliest history of Rome cultivated their own gardens with their own hands. He also claimed that the lower classes got their daily food from their gardens, emphasizing the imagery of all Romans as civilized farmers.[52]

Book three of Apicius was devoted to vegetables, with 21 chapters covering different types and showing the importance of vegetable cookery.

⚚ 177. FRIED PARSNIPS (APICIUS 3.21.1) ⚚

All of the recipes in chapter 21 of Apicius's Book 3 could be applied either to carrots or to parsnips, which are close botanical relatives. Ancient carrots might be red, yellow, purple, or white, but not the ubiquitous orange of most modern carrot cultivars, which was developed by Dutch botanists in the seventeenth century. Unless you have access to appropriately colored carrots, use parsnips to be true to the Roman original. Apicius dressed the fried vegetable simply with *oenogarum*.

Olive oil, as needed
3 parsnips, peeled and cut into 1/4-inch rounds
1/4 cup *oenogarum* (Recipe 144)

Place 2 inches of oil in a deep saucepan and bring to 325°F. Working in batches, lower the parsnips with a slotted spoon into the hot oil and fry until they begin to take on a little color, about 45 seconds. Drain on paper towels. Toss with the *oenogarum*.

⚚ 178. DRESSED CHICORY (APICIUS 3.18.1) ⚚

Endive, chicory, and escarole are all part of the genus *cichorium*, and given that Apicius's recipe uses a generic name for the plant, there is some confusion about which plant he is referring to. The Romans cultivated both escarole and chicory and gathered young, wild endive; the endive became unpleasantly bitter if gathered fully mature. Modern Belgian endive has been bred for sweetness and is too mild for this recipe.

All chicories were usually cooked to reduce their bitterness, although bitter flavors were typical of Roman greens, including lettuces. When harvested fresh in season, chicories were cooked simply with oil, chopped onion, and *liquamen*; for out-of-season winter dining, pickled chicories were dressed with honey.

3 tablespoons olive oil
1 finely minced shallot
1/2 head escarole or curly chicory, washed, dried, and torn into bite-
    sized pieces
Fish sauce to taste

Heat the oil in a deep skillet and add the shallot, stirring to soften slightly. Add the escarole or curly chicory. Cook to wilt slightly. Season with fish sauce to taste and serve at room temperature.

⚕ 179. RAW CABBAGE SALAD (CATO 156) ⚕

Cato promised that by eating raw cabbage dressed with vinegar before dining, you could eat and drink with abandon at a party, without feeling too full or getting drunk.

1/2 of a small head green cabbage, core removed and leaves julienned
    (about 4 cups)
6 tablespoons white wine vinegar
Aromatic Salts (Recipe 146) to taste (optional)

Combine all the ingredients and toss thoroughly. Allow to sit for 30 minutes before eating.

> *The produce of a prosperous farm: leafy cabbages, leeks, lettuces, beets, fat thrushes, hare, suckling pig.*
>
> Martial, *Epigrams*, 3.47

⚕ 180. CABBAGE, ANOTHER WAY (APICIUS 3.9.2) ⚕

Cut the stalks in half and boil them. The leaves are mashed and seasoned with coriander, onion, cumin, pepper, passum and caroenum and a little oil.[53]

1 head cabbage, cut in half
5 tablespoons olive oil
1/2 cup minced onion
1 1/2 tablespoons ground coriander
2 teaspoons ground cumin
Salt and pepper to taste
1/4 cup raisin wine, or to taste

1. Bring a pot of water large enough to hold the cabbage to a boil. Add the cabbage and cook until the leaves are tender. Remove from the pot, drain, and cut out the tough cores. Squeeze the leaves dry and chop finely. Reserve the cabbage in a bowl.
2. Heat 3 tablespoons of olive oil in a skillet and sweat the onion until tender. Add the coriander, cumin, salt, and pepper. Add the seasoned onions to the cabbage. Stir in the wine and remaining oil.

⚕ 181. LETTUCE SALAD (APICIUS 3.18.2) ⚕

In Apicius's recipe, lettuces were dressed with *oxyporum*, vinegar, and *liquamen*; the combination was thought to make lettuce more digestible. In addition to questions of digestibility, Roman lettuces changed over time both in flavor and in the position they assumed at the meal. Like their Egyptian and Greek predecessors, Roman lettuces were bitter and contained certain compounds, primarily lactuacin, that had a mildly narcotic effect, inducing sleep after the meal. Selective breeding by the Romans reduced the amount of lactuacin, changing the flavor, and also reduced the soporific effect. This narcotic quality had been put to good use by early Romans, who served lettuce at the end of the meal as part of the dessert course. Once the lettuces were no longer sleep inducing, lettuce moved to the gustatio, or appetizer course.

One of the poet Martial's invitations to dinner promised a lettuce salad without the "salacious herb" arugula; arugula was believed to be an aphrodisiac and often was eaten with the soporific lettuce for "balance"; serving only one would inflame or smother passions, so Martial's lettuce salad promised a staid evening.

1 head romaine, cleaned and torn into bite-sized pieces
3 tablespoons *oxyporum* (Recipe 145)
Vinegar and fish sauce to taste

Combine all the ingredients in a bowl and toss thoroughly.

⚚ 182. BOILED BEETS WITH VINAIGRETTE (APICIUS 3.11.2) ⚚

Apicius's recipe called for cooking beets with mustard seed and pickling them in vinegar with a little oil. In a similar vein, Columella, in *Re Rustica*, recommended cooking turnips in a mixture of vinegar and mustard water.[54]

4 large beets, greens removed
2 tablespoons salt
2 tablespoons whole mustard seeds
1 cup red wine vinegar, plus additional for dressing
Olive oil to taste (or Liburnian Oil, Recipe 189)

1. Place the beets in a pot with the salt, mustard seeds, and 1 cup vinegar, adding water to cover. Bring to a boil and cook until tender, about 45 minutes to 1 hour, depending on size. Drain.
2. When the beets are cool enough to handle, slip off their skins and slice them into disks 1/4 inch thick. Toss with olive oil and additional vinegar to taste.

⚚ 183. BOILED CARDOONS (APICIUS 3.19.1) ⚚

Cardoons are ancestors of artichokes, an edible thistle. Botanists disagree about when the artichoke emerged, with some dating it to the late Middle Ages, while others claim it was part of Greco-Roman gardens. Cardoons are difficult to find, so this version uses artichokes, which are simply boiled and eaten with a dipping sauce of fish sauce, oil, and chopped egg.

2 artichokes
3 tablespoons fish sauce
1/2 cup extra virgin olive oil
1 hard-boiled egg, peeled and finely chopped

1. Cut off the top 2 inches of the artichokes and snap off the bottom stem. Remove the outer leaves until you reach the pale and tender leaves. Using scissors, snip off any remaining thorns at the top of the leaves.
2. Boil the artichokes in heavily salted water until tender. The time will depend on the size and age of the artichokes but can take up to 40 minutes; a knife should easily pierce the thick heart. Remove and drain.
3. Combine the remaining ingredients for a dipping sauce.
4. Eat by pulling off the leaves and dipping the wider end nearest the base into the sauce and scraping the flesh off between your front teeth. When you have eaten all the leaves, scrape out the feathery core and eat the tender heart with the sauce.

☙ 184. APRICOT STEW (APICIUS 4.5.4) ☙

Take small apricots, clean, stone, and plunge into cold water, then arrange in a shallow pan. Pound pepper, dried mint, moisten with liquamen, add honey, passum, wine, and vinegar. Pour in the pan over the apricots, add a little oil, and cook over a low fire. When it is boiling, thicken with amulum. Sprinkle with pepper and serve.[55]

Apicius specifies this recipe as a first course.

6 fresh apricots, halved and stones removed
Freshly ground black pepper to taste
1/2 teaspoon dried mint
3 tablespoons fish sauce
2 tablespoons honey
1/4 cup raisin wine
1/4 cup white wine
1 tablespoon olive oil
1/4 cup vinegar
1 tablespoon cornstarch

Place the apricots in a sauté pan. Add the pepper, mint, fish sauce, honey, both wines, and oil. Simmer until the apricots are tender, about 10–15 minutes. Combine the vinegar with the cornstarch and pour into the boiling sauce. Cook until thickened.

⚚ 185. BRAISED MUSHROOMS (APICIUS 7.15.4) ⚚

Mushrooms occupied a peculiar niche in Roman cookery. Recognized as potentially poisonous, most were subsistence fare for the poor, and physicians recommend antidotes of vinegar and salt for poisonous mushrooms.[56] Several varieties, however, including the *boletus,* or porcini, were highly praised. Special pans, called *boletaria,* were invented for cooking them, and Pliny sniped in *Natural History* that mushrooms were the only "food that the voluptuaries would cook for themselves, using amber-handled knives and silver dishes."[57] Apicius's recipe, from the *Gourmet* book, called for cooking mushrooms with slightly reduced wine and a bunch of cilantro, which was removed before serving.

2 cups white wine, reduced by half
6 sprigs cilantro
4 ounces white button or cremini mushrooms, wiped clean and
   sliced thinly
Salt to taste (optional)

Place the reduced wine, cilantro, and sliced mushrooms in a sauté pan. Bring to a boil and cook until the mushrooms are tender and have absorbed some of the wine. Remove the cilantro, sprinkle with salt if desired, and serve.

⚚ 186. GREEN BEANS (APICIUS 5.6.1) ⚚

Apicius's recipe for Dainty Dishes of Kid or Lamb (Recipe 165) specifies fresh beans as an accompaniment. In this recipe, Apicius cooked green beans in *liquamen,* oil, chopped leeks, cumin, and cilantro. The beans are not the long, thin string beans of American tables which were unknown in the ancient world, but would be a member of the *Vicia* genus, such as a broad bean that, when fresh, could be cooked in the pod. String beans were unknown in the ancient world. This recipe, with its inexpensive ingredients, might have been the "workman's" beans promised by the poet Martial in one of his dinner invitations to accompany a "kid snatched from the jaws of a savage wolf." The combination of kid and beans in both Martial and Apicius suggests that this was a common pairing in the ancient world.

3 tablespoons olive oil
1 leek, dark green leaves cut off, cleaned and chopped
3/4 teaspoon ground cumin

1/2 pound Italian Romano beans, or other broad bean with an
   edible pod
1/4 cup fish sauce diluted with 1/2 cup water
2 tablespoons chopped cilantro

Heat the olive oil in a large sauté pan. Add the chopped leek and cumin. Cook over medium heat until the leek is tender, about 4 minutes. Add the beans and diluted fish sauce. Cook, uncovered, for about 7 minutes, or until the beans are tender and the liquid reduces to coat the beans. Stir in the cilantro and serve.

ψ 187. LENTILS WITH CHESTNUT PURÉE (APICIUS 5.2.2) ψ

Take a new saucepan, place therein the chestnuts carefully cleaned, add water and a little soda and place on the fire to be cooked. This done, crush in the mortar pepper, cumin, coriander seed, mint, rue, laser root and flea-bane moistened with vinegar, honey, and liquamen; add vinegar to taste and pour this over the cooked chestnuts, add oil and allow to boil. When done, crush it in the mortar. Taste to see if something is missing and if so, put it in, and at last add green oil.[58]

This is further proof that Apicius was written for experienced cooks: the recipe omits any discussion of the lentils, an important ingredient, as it deals exclusively with preparing the chestnuts. An experienced cook could fill in the gaps. Fleabane is a European herb with a slightly soapy and bitter taste; rosemary will substitute for the rue and fleabane.

1 cup brown lentils
1 cup canned or jarred peeled chestnuts
1/2 teaspoon each black pepper, cumin seed, coriander, dried mint,
   dried rosemary, and asafetida, pounded together
1 tablespoon vinegar
6 tablespoons extra virgin olive oil or Liburnian Oil (Recipe 189)
Fish sauce to taste
Honey to taste

1. Place the lentils in a saucepan and cover with water by 2 inches. Bring to a boil and cook until tender, about 30 minutes. Drain and reserve.
2. Meanwhile, place the cooked chestnuts in a saucepan. Add the pounded spices, herbs, and vinegar. Add half the oil and warm gently. Season with fish sauce and honey to taste. Pour the seasoned chestnuts over the lentils, stirring to combine. Garnish with the remaining olive oil.

⚕ 188. PERGAMUM CHICKPEAS (GALEN) ⚕

The physician Galen described several simple chickpea preparations, noting that in his native Pergamum, people ate them sprinkled with finely grated dried cheese.[59]

2 cups dried chickpeas, covered by 4 inches cold water and soaked
  overnight
3/4 cup finely grated Parmesan
Salt and pepper to taste (or Aromatic Salts, Recipe 146)

1. Drain the soaked chickpeas and place them in a saucepan. Cover with fresh water by 3 inches and bring to a boil. Reduce the heat to a simmer and cook until tender, approximately 45 minutes to 1 hour.
2. When the chickpeas are tender, drain thoroughly and coat with the grated cheese. Add salt and pepper to taste and serve warm.

CONDIMENTS AND SAUCES

⚕ 189. LIBURNIAN OIL (APICIUS 1.4) ⚕

To Spanish oil add helenium and cyprus root and bay leaves, all this pounded and sifted until reduced to a very fine powder, and dried and powdered salt. Mix these ingredients for three days or longer. After this allow the mixture to rest for some time, and everybody will believe it is Liburnian oil.[60]

Flavored oils are an old tradition, as well as the cook's trick to try to pass off less expensive ingredients as luxurious ones. Spain provided much inexpensive olive oil to Roman Italy, so Spanish oil may have been viewed by gourmets as a common, uninteresting ingredient. Liburnia was a province conquered by the Romans along the Adriatic Sea that is now part of Croatia. This recipe suggests that Liburnia produced olive oils esteemed by connoisseurs, and it attempts to disguise the insipid Spanish oil by infusing ingredients to imitate the admired flavor of Liburnian oils. *Helenium* is elecampane, an herb related to fleabane. The dried rosemary introduces some of the bitterness of these unusual herbs.

2 bay leaves
1 tablespoon dried rosemary
1 tablespoon sea or kosher salt
2 cups olive oil

Grind the bay leaves and rosemary with the salt in a mortar to a powder. Add to the oil and let infuse for 1 week. Strain out the powder and use to dress pulses, beans, or vegetables.

⚘ 190. OLIVE CONFECTION (CATO 119) ⚘

Remove the stones from green, ripe and mottled olives and season as follows: chop the flesh and add oil, vinegar, coriander, cumin, fennel, rue, and mint. Cover with oil in an earthen dish and serve. [61]

Recipes like this could be found on the tables of Romans of all economic classes, from the poor peasants Baucis and Philomen in Ovid's *Metamorphoses* to the rich Trimalchio in the *Satyricon*.

1 cup mixed olives, pitted
2 tablespoons olive oil, or more
2 teaspoons vinegar
3/4 teaspoon coriander seed
1/2 teaspoon cumin seed
1/2 teaspoon fennel seed
1/2 teaspoon dried rosemary
1/2 teaspoon dried mint

Finely chop the olives. Transfer to a bowl and stir in the oil and vinegar. Crush the herbs and spices in a mortar with a pestle and season the olives to taste, adding more oil as necessary to create a dipping relish for bread.

⚘ 191. POUNDED OLIVE RELISH (COLUMELLA 12.49.5) ⚘

[Pausean olive] is especially suitable for the preparation of preserves which are served at the more sumptuous repasts; for, when required, it is taken out of the jar and, after being crushed, blends with any other seasoning you like. Most people, however, cut up finely leeks and rue with young parsley and mint and mix them with crushed olives; then they add a little peppered vinegar and a very little honey or mead and sprinkle them with a little green olive-oil and then cover them with a bunch of green parsley.

According to Columella, Pausean olives have a "whitish" color, indicating a particular variety of olives likely picked underripe.

1 cup green olives, pitted and finely chopped
1 tablespoon finely chopped raw leek
1 teaspoon minced fresh rosemary leaves
4 sprigs parsley, chopped
8 mint leaves, chopped
1 1/2 tablespoons vinegar
Coarsely ground black pepper to taste
2 teaspoons honey
2 tablespoons olive oil
Whole parsley sprigs for garnish

Combine all the ingredients and garnish with the whole parsley.

⚓ 192. PRESERVED CITRON (ORIBASIUS 1.64:1.3)

The physician Oribasius, living part of his life in Pergamum near the west coast of Turkey, was familiar with the citron, the first citrus fruit to reach the Near East and Mediterranean from Central Asia. He observed its tripartite structure—outer rind; white, spongy pith; and acidic fruit—and recounted that people often soaked parts of it in vinegar before eating it. The recipe may be a predecessor to the preserved lemons found in North African, Near Eastern, and Central Asian cookery. Lemon will substitute in this recipe for its botanical cousin, the citron.

2 lemons
White vinegar, as needed
1 tablespoon salt

Cut the lemons into quarters and place in a clean glass container. Sprinkle with the salt. Pour the vinegar over the quarters, making sure they are fully submerged. Set aside for 3 weeks, or until the pith softens. Use minced bits in small quantities as a piquant seasoning for any of the dishes in this chapter.

⚓ 193. MUSTARD (COLUMELLA 12.57.2) ⚓

Columella's instructions for preparing the mustard seeds are quite lengthy and involve soaking, grinding, and treating them with nitre to eliminate any bitterness. Nitre is the preserving agent potassium nitrate; some evidence suggests it is carcinogenic, so that step has been omitted. Once the seeds are treated, they are ground with almonds or pine nuts, and vinegar is added to help tame the bite of mustard seeds. Columella bragged that the mustard, properly made, had an "exquisite brilliance."

3 tablespoons mustard seeds
1 tablespoon pine nuts
1 tablespoon almonds
1/2 cup wine vinegar

Finely grind the mustard seeds and nuts with a mortar and pestle to a powdery texture. Stir in the vinegar and let sit to thicken.

⚓ 194. A SUBSTITUTE FOR SALT FISH (APICIUS 9.13.3) ⚓

Pound as much cumin as you can pick up with five fingers, half the quantity of pepper, and one peeled clove of garlic. Pour on liquamen, add a few drops of oil. This is excellent for a sick stomach, and facilitates digestion.[62]

The unusual use of garlic and imprecise measurements, in contrast to the ounce weights given in *Oxygarum* (Recipe 143), *Oxyporum* (Recipe 145), and Aromatic Salts (Recipe 146), suggest that this recipe started as a folk remedy. Use as an intense condiment, like Tabasco or Worcestershire sauce, for meats, vegetables, or grains, or take a small spoonful as a digestive.

1 tablespoon cumin seeds
1/2 tablespoon peppercorns
1 clove garlic, peeled
2 tablespoons fish sauce
Olive oil, as needed

Pound the cumin, peppercorns, and garlic in a mortar and pestle. Transfer to a bowl and stir in the fish sauce and oil to make a paste.

⚕ 195. ALEXANDRIAN SAUCE (APICIUS 10.1.7) ⚕

Apicius recommended this sauce for fish. The sweet and sour flavors of the raisins, wine, and raisin wine, combined with the typically Roman black pepper, lovage, fish sauce, and oil, work especially well with tuna, swordfish, sardines, or any other oily fish.

1/2 teaspoon cracked black peppercorns
3/4 teaspoon celery seeds, pounded
3 tablespoons golden raisins
1/3 cup red or white wine
3 tablespoons raisin wine
2 teaspoons fish sauce
2 tablespoons olive oil
1 teaspoon cornstarch dissolved in 1 tablespoon water
1 tablespoon chopped cilantro

Combine the peppercorns, celery seeds, raisins, wine, raisin wine, fish sauce, and olive oil in a saucepan. Bring to a boil, reduce the heat to a simmer, and cook for 2 minutes. Add the cornstarch-water solution and boil for 1–2 minutes to thicken. Stir in the chopped cilantro and serve.

⚕ 196. WHITE SAUCE (APICIUS 7.6.4) ⚕

This unusual recipe from Apicius's *Gourmet* book was thickened by leftover bread; it also, unusually, called for spiced wine in the list of ingredients, which could be made by infusing wine with a bit of saffron, honey, and pepper. Other ingredients included pepper, *liquamen*, plain wine, rue, onion, and pine kernels. Apicius specified this as a sauce for meats.

2 tablespoons fish sauce
3/4 cup white wine
1 pinch saffron

1/4 teaspoon ground black pepper
1 tablespoon honey
1/2 teaspoon dried rosemary
1 tablespoon finely chopped onion
1 tablespoon pine nuts, finely ground in a mortar and pestle
1 tablespoon coarse bread crumbs
2 tablespoons olive oil

Combine all the ingredients in a saucepan. Bring to a boil and simmer until the bread crumbs soften and thicken the sauce and the taste of raw alcohol is cooked out, about 10 minutes. Force the sauce through a fine sieve to smooth out the texture.

PASTRIES AND SWEETS

☥ 197. FIG BONBONS (COLUMELLA 12.15.3–4) ☥

Some people . . . heap [partially dried figs] in basins of earthenware or stone; then, after washing their feet, they tread them as they do meal and mix them with toasted sesame and Egyptian anise and the seed of fennel and cumin. When they have trodden these thoroughly and mixed in the whole mass of crushed figs, they wrap up balls of the mixture of moderate size in fig-leaves . . . and let them dry.

The success of this recipe depends on the figs still having enough moisture to be malleable. If the dried figs seem too leathery, poach them very briefly in boiling water to soften slightly.

1 pound dried figs
1/4 cup sesame seeds, toasted in a 325°F oven for 5 minutes
2 tablespoons fennel seed
2 teaspoons cumin seed

Combine all the ingredients in a food processor. Process to form a sticky, chunky purée. Take walnut-sized bits and roll them into rounds.

> *Africans and Spaniards had a unique custom of arranging figs in the shape of flowers or stars and leaving them to dry in the sun. They were then stored as fanciful winter confections.*[63]

☥ 198. CHEESE FRITTERS WITH HONEY AND POPPYSEEDS (CATO 79) ☥

Cato gave a recipe for deep-fried cheese balls rolled in honey and poppyseeds in his *De Agricultura*. Although Roman recipes do not distinguish among different types of honeys, writers such as Pliny distinguished among honeys based on their place of origin. From the cook's perspective, the flavor of honey varies depending on whether the honey is harvested from bees pollinating lavender, thyme, chestnut, or other blossoms. The darker the honey, such as the chestnut and buckwheat varieties, generally the more aggressive the flavor. For many purposes, the more delicate herb varieties will yield more pleasing tastes.

1 1/2 cups ricotta cheese, drained of excess moisture
1 1/2–2 cups semolina flour, or all-purpose flour, as needed
2 cups pure olive oil or grapeseed oil
1 cup honey
1/2 cup poppyseeds

1. Combine the ricotta with enough flour to obtain a mass that will hold its shape. The amount of flour needed will depend on the moisture content of the ricotta and the type of flour used.
2. Place the oil in a deep saucepan and heat to 360°F, measured by a deep-fat thermometer. Shape the cheese into small balls and carefully lower into the hot fat, cooking until golden brown and turning to brown all sides. When golden, drain briefly on paper towels, dip in the honey, and roll in poppyseeds. Serve warm.

199. HONEY-FRIED DATES (APICIUS 7.13.1)

Apicius's interesting recipe stuffed sweet dates with nuts and black pepper, sprinkled them with salt, and rolled them in hot honey. The combination of sweet, salty, and spicy flavors is delicious.

15 whole walnuts
Freshly ground black pepper to taste
15 dates, pitted
Coarse sea salt to taste
1 1/2 cups honey

1. Coarsely chop the walnuts and season with pepper. Stuff each date with a bit of the walnut mixture. Sprinkle with sea salt.
2. Heat the honey in a saucepan. Add the stuffed dates and simmer gently for 10 minutes. Serve warm in the honey syrup, sprinkled with additional salt and pepper if desired.

200. FRIED PASTRY WITH HONEY AND PEPPER (APICIUS 7.13.6)

Take best wheat flour and cook it in hot water so it forms a very hard paste, then spread it on a plate. When cold, cut up for sweets, and fry in best oil. Lift out, pour honey over, sprinkle with pepper, and serve. This is better if you take milk instead of water.[64]

3/4 cup milk
2 cups all-purpose flour
2 cups olive oil, or more as needed for frying
Honey and black pepper, as needed

1. Combine the milk and flour in a saucepan and bring to a boil. Reduce the heat and cook to make a thick paste.
2. Spread the paste on a baking sheet to cool. When cold, cut the paste into strips about 2 inches wide by 3 inches long.
3. Heat the oil to 360°F measures by a deep-fat thermometer. Working with 2 or 3 strips of dough at a time, fry the dough until golden brown. Drain on paper towels. When all the dough is fried, drizzle with honey and black pepper.

201. SWEET WINE CAKES STEEPED IN MILK (APICIUS 7.13.2)

Remove the crust from the best African sweet-wine cakes and steep them in milk. When they are saturated, put them in the oven—not for too long so they do not dry out. Take them out hot, pour honey over, prick them to let them absorb the honey. Sprinkle with pepper and serve.[65]

1 recipe Must Cakes (Recipe 138), split in half
1 1/2 cups milk
1/2 cup honey
Freshly ground black pepper to taste

1. Preheat the oven to 350°F. Place the must cakes, cut side down, in a baking pan and pour the milk over. Turn the cakes over several times to absorb the milk. Discard any milk that is not absorbed.
2. Bake the cakes for 20 minutes. Remove from the oven, prick with a skewer, and pour the honey over to soak into the cakes. Sprinkle generously with black pepper.

202. PRESERVED BLACKBERRIES (APICIUS 1.12.6)

Apicius's recipe for preserving blackberries in thickened grape juice specified a glass vessel to hold the fruit; glass was becoming more common in Rome with the invention in the first century B.C.E. of glassblowing, which made glass fabrication much faster and cheaper.

3 pints blackberries
Defrutum (Recipe 142), as needed

1. Rinse a 1-quart glass canning jar with boiling water. Let air-dry (do not use a cloth; it may have bacteria and contaminate the fruit). Place half the blackberries in the jar.
2. Place the remaining blackberries in a fine sieve and mash to extract the juice. Combine the juice with *defrutum* and pour over the berries in the jar, topping off with additional *defrutum* as needed to cover the berries.

⚚ 203. PEARS IN BOILED MUST (VARRO 1.49) ⚚

Anician pears keep best when put down in boiled must.

Anician pears were harvested late in the season, guaranteeing ripeness. Storing the pears in boiled-down grape juice or *defrutum* (Recipe 142) would extend the shelf life by cutting off oxygen and introducing additional sugar into the pears, which acts as a preservative. You can make whatever quantity you desire. If your pears are ripe, simply peel them, place them in a clean container, and submerge them in a syrupy *defrutum.* Store them in a cool, dark place, such as a cellar. If the pears are hard, peel them, place them in a saucepan with thinner *defrutum*, and boil gently until the pears are tender and the *defrutum* is reduced. Store submerged in the *defrutum.*

BEVERAGES

Roman vineyards were busy supplying grapes that found multiple uses in the kitchen and at the table. Grapes could appear fresh on the table, be dried into raisins for snacking or cooking, or be pressed into juice, also called must. The must could be fermented into wine or, if the fermentation went too far, turned into vinegar. Must also formed the basis of widely used pantry ingredients such as *defrutum* (Recipe 142).

One of the challenges Romans faced was wine's tendency to sour into vinegar as a result of secondary fermentation; although Romans mastered glassblowing, they did not store wine in glass bottles but rather kept it in barrels or, more often, clay amphorae, which were not airtight. Depending upon the quality of the clay, the effective storage life of wine could be limited before it turned to vinegar. Wine quality was a concern for well-to-do Romans. Cato cautioned in section 25 of *De Agricultura* that estate owners should make sure to use only fully ripe grapes in making wine; anything less could harm the estate's reputation.

⚚ 204. HOUSEHOLD WINE (CATO 104) ⚚

Put 10 quadrantals must in a vat and add 2 quadrantals sharp vinegar, 2 quadrantals grape syrup, 50 quadrantals pure water. Mix with a stick 3 times a day for 5 consecutive days. Add 64 pints old sea water, put the lid on the vat and seal after 10 days. This wine will last you till the solstice. If any remains after the solstice, it will make a very sharp and very good vinegar.[66]

This highly diluted wine is meant for the household, that is, the workers and slaves who ran the great country estates of wealthy Romans, not the elegant tables of the owners. The drink was cheap to make, with a low alcohol content. A quadrantal was a unit of measure slightly less than seven gallons (and slightly more than 55 pints). Thus, the original recipe makes over 400 gallons of household wine, with the seawater comprising less than 10 percent of the blend.

    2 tablespoons kosher salt
    16 cups water
    1 cup *defrutum* (Recipe 142), boiled to reduce by half
    1 bottle (750 milliliters) red or white wine
    5/8 cup vinegar

Heat the salt in the water in a 6-quart pot until the salt is dissolved. Turn off the heat and add the remaining ingredients. If time permits, cover with cheesecloth and let rest for 5 days, stirring it several times each day. Otherwise, it can be used immediately.

⚕ 205. POSCA ⚕

Like the household wine, *posca* was heavily diluted, but the underlying flavor was vinegary. Considered quite refreshing, similar to lemonade, *posca* might be infused with herbs and was served to soldiers in the Roman army. The "vinegar-soaked sponge" offered to Jesus at the crucifixion was likely a sponge soaked with *posca*. Although references abound to the drink, there do not seem to be any surviving recipes.

    1 1/2 cups vinegar
    1/2 cup honey
    1 tablespoon crushed coriander seed
    4 cups water

Combine all the ingredients in a saucepan. Bring to a boil to dissolve the honey. Remove from the heat and let cool to room temperature. Strain out the coriander seeds through a cheesecloth-lined sieve and serve.

⚕ 206. CONDITUM PARADOXUM
(HONEY-SPICED WINE), (APICIUS 1.1.1) ⚕

Honey-infused wines, generically called *mulsum*, were served as aperitifs at Roman dinner parties. The recipe is one of a very few in Apicius to give precise quantities for the ingredients, suggesting that it originated as a medicine.

The cooking and skimming of the honey is unnecessary with modern refined honeys. If you cannot find dates with pits, the recipe works well without the pits. Mastic is a resin from the bark of *pistacia lentiscus*, a shrub found only in the eastern Mediterranean. It is still used in some Greek and Turkish pastries and as a breath freshener.

Artist's rendering of a wine strainer, used to remove spices infused into drinks such as conditum paradoxum. From Joseph Dommers Vehling, Cooking and Dining in Imperial Rome.

15 lb. of honey are put into a bronze jar which already contains two pints of wine, so that you boil down the wine as you cook the honey. This is to be heated over a slow fire of dry wood, stirring with a stick while it cooks; if it begins to boil over it is stopped with a splash of wine; in any case it will simmer down when the heat is taken away, and when cooled, re-ignited. This must be repeated a second and a third time; then the mixture is finally removed from the brazier and, on the following day, skimmed. Next 4 oz. of pepper, 3 scruples of pounded mastic, 1 dram each of bay leaf and saffron, 5 roasted date-stones, and the dates themselves softened in wine to a smooth puree. When all this is ready, pour on 18 pints of smooth wine. If the finished product is bitter, coal will correct it.[67]

1 bottle white wine
1 cup honey
1 teaspoon freshly ground black pepper
1 small bay leaf
1/4 teaspoon crushed mastic
1 pinch saffron
2 dates, with pits if possible

1. Place all but 1/2 cup wine in a saucepan and add the honey. Stir and heat just enough to dissolve the honey. Add the pepper, bay leaf, mastic, and saffron. Remove from the heat.

2. Remove the pits from the dates if unpitted. Place the date pits in a small sauté pan and gently toast them over a low flame until lightly

colored. Add to the wine mixture. (This step can be omitted if the dates are pitted.)

3. Soften the date flesh in the remaining 1/2 cup of white wine. Puree in a blender or by pounding in a mortar. Add to the wine mixture. Stir to combine and let infuse for several hours or, ideally, overnight. Strain and serve at room temperature or chilled.

According to Pliny, Roman matrons were not allowed to drink wine in the ancient days of Rome's founding: Romulus was reported to have acquitted one Egnatius Maetennus of murder after clubbing his wife to death for drinking wine from a vat.[68]

♆ 207. HYDROMEL (COLUMELLA 12.12) ♆

Hydromel is a beverage made from water and honey and left to ferment in the sun. In this recipe, the brew is further preserved by light smoking, reminiscent of some whiskeys. Some anthropologists believe that primitive hydromel, made from honey, which is sweeter than grapes, was the first fermented beverage discovered by ancient humans. Because the greater sugar levels were easier to ferment, hydromel may have been more easily mastered than wine or beer making.

> *There is more than one way of making honey-water . . . Others, who have not taken the trouble to let rain water become stale, take fresh water and boil it down to a quarter of its volume; when it has cooled, if they wish to make rather sweet honey-water, they mix a sextarius of honey with two sextarii of water, or if they wish to make it rather harsh, they add a dodrans of honey to a sextarius of water, and, having made it in these proportions, pour it into a flagon. When the flagon has been placed in the sun for forty days, . . . they store it in a loft which receives smoke from below.*

The ancients could have used elastic animal bladders to seal off containers while the honey was fermenting. Use an airlock, available at winemaking supply stores, or a balloon to seal off the container and allow expansion of the gases given off by the fermenting honey.[69]

1 cups honey, preferably raw
4 cups water

1. Combine the honey and water in a broad pan and stir to dissolve the honey. Cover with a towel to keep out dust. Repeat the stirring several times a day for three or four days, or until the mixture is

bubbling. The time will depend on the warmth of the room and the number and quality of ambient yeasts.

2. Transfer the mixture to a large, clean glass vessel with a relatively narrow neck. Place an airlock or a large balloon over the neck of the vessel to block the entrance of additional yeasts that would cause the mixture to ferment into vinegar. Let the mixture age for several weeks, until the bubbling slows down.

 SUGGESTED MENUS

The lavish menus for the wealthier classes were common, as the wealthier regularly hosted many people at dinner parties. No one was expected to sample everything, but the host tried to impress guests with a vast array of dishes to choose from. Leftovers would enhance the next day's breakfast or lunch and also fed the household staff.

1. MESOPOTAMIA

Early-Morning Breakfast for a Temple Priest

Spelt Bread (Recipe 2)
Mun-du (Recipe 6)
Mustard Cheese (Recipe 12)
Grilled Fresh Fish (Recipe 18)
Fruit and Nut Platter (Recipe 36)
Milk, Wine, and Sumerian Beer (Recipe 38)

Breakfast for a Shepherd or Field Worker

Whole Wheat Flat Bread (Recipe 1) or *Pappasu* (Recipe 5)
Yogurt Soup (Recipe 13) or Flavored Yogurt (Recipe 26)
Leftovers from the previous night's dinner
Milk and Sumerian Beer (Recipe 38)

Late-Morning Breakfast for a Temple Priest

Twice-Cooked Fried Biscuits (Recipe 9)
Date Cakes (Recipe 32)
Lamb Tartar (Recipe 17)
Applesauce (Recipe 30)
Wine and Sumerian Beer (Recipe 38)

Early Dinner for a Temple Priest

Scallion Bread (Recipe 3)
Sasqu (Recipe 7)
Grilled Fresh Fish (Recipe 18)
Roasted Lamb or Kid (Recipe 15)
Braised and Roasted Duck with Leeks, Mint,
    and Vinegar (Recipe 16)
Eggplant Purée (Recipe 22)
Cucumber Salad (Recipe 23)
Mustard Cheese (Recipe 12)
Palace Cake (Recipe 33)
Dried Fruit Compote (recipe 35)
Apple Juice, Wine, and Sumerian Beer (Recipe 38)

Late Dinner for a Temple Priest

Whole Wheat Flat Bread (Recipe 1) dipped in
    Za'tar (Recipe 29)
Tender Cake Biscuits (Recipe 8)
Elamite Pottage (Recipe 14)
Garden Turnips Pottage (Recipe 20)
Flavored Yogurt (Recipe 26)
Mersu (Recipe 31)

Fancy Dinner for a Shepherd or Field Worker

Grilled Fresh Fish (Recipe 18)
Cress Pesto (Recipe 25)
Roasted Lamb or Kid (Recipe 15)
Roasted Onions (Recipe 19)
Dried Apples (Recipe 34)
Yogurt Cooler (Recipe 37)
Sumerian Beer (Recipe 38)

Plain Dinner for a Shepherd or Field Worker

Yogurt Soup (Recipe 13) or Pea Soup (Recipe 21)
Beet Salad (Recipe 24)
Garden Turnips Pottage (Recipe 20)
Fresh Fruit
Sumerian Beer (Recipe 38)

Dinner in Times of Famine

Ezekiel's Multigrain Flat Bread (Recipe 4)
Yogurt (Recipe 11)
Roasted Onions (Recipe 19) (or eat them raw)
Dried Apples (Recipe 34)

2. ANCIENT EGYPT

Breakfast for Pharaoh's Family

Emmer Bread with Figs (Recipe 42)
Raw Onion Relish (Recipe 68)
Pan-Fried Kidneys (Recipe 56)
Pickled Mullet (Recipe 58)
Sweet Melon Salad (Recipe 64)
Wine, Pomegranate Shandy (Recipe 74),
    and *Bousa* (Recipe 73)

Breakfast or Dinner for a Predynastic Laborer

Matzoh (Recipe 40)
Barley and Fish Soup (Recipe 47)
Bousa (Recipe 73)

Breakfast for a Worker Building the Pyramids

Emmer Bread with Figs (Recipe 42)
Raw Onion Relish (Recipe 68)
Dukkah (Recipe 65)
Dried Spiced Beef (Recipe 50)
Bousa (Recipe 73)

Dinner for Pharaoh's Family

Ta (Recipe 43)
Freek Pilaf (Recipe 44)
Foie Gras with Figs (Recipe 55)
Grilled Quail (Recipe 52)
Grilled Fish with Dill (Recipe 57)
Yogurt and Tahini Sauce (Recipe 69)
Chickpea Dip (Recipe 67)
Lotus Root Salad (Recipe 60)
Tiger Nut Cakes (Recipe 71)
Stewed Figs (Recipe 72)
Wine and *Bousa* (Recipe 73)

Dinner 1 for a Worker Building the Pyramids

Kamut Porridge (Recipe 46)
Lentil Salad (Recipe 61)
Chopped Salad (Recipe 62)
Chickpea Dip (Recipe 67)
Grilled Pork Chops with Scallions (Recipe 51)
Bousa (Recipe 73)

Dinner 2 for a Worker Building the Pyramids

Barley Meal Porridge (Recipe 39)
Shat Bread (Recipe 41)
Egyptian Cassoulet (Recipe 53)
Braised Mohluhkia (Recipe 59)
Dried Dates
Bousa (Recipe 73)

Dinner for a Merchant Traveling on Pharaoh's Behalf

Kush Bread (Recipe 45)
Batarekh (Recipe 66)
Dukkah (Recipe 65)
Dried Spiced Beef (Recipe 50)
Carob Cake (Recipe 70)
Wine and *Bousa* (Recipe 73)

3. ANCIENT GREECE

Breakfast for Everyone

Barley Porridge with Sesame (Recipe 75), *Amolgaia* (Recipe 76), or
  Folded Wheat Bread (Recipe 79)
Fresh Cheese with Olive Oil and Herbs (Recipe 85) or Curds and
  Honey (Recipe 86)
Pea Porridge with Salt Fish (Recipe 95)
Fresh or Dried Fruits
Athenian Wine (Recipe 129) or *Oxykraton* (Recipe 130)

Dinner for Peasants

Maza (Recipe 77)
Wise Lentil Soup (Recipe 112)
Spit-Roasted Hare (Recipe 101)
Mushrooms with Thyme (Recipe 115)
Olives in Brine (Recipe 116)
Poor Person's Dessert Table (Recipe 123)
Oxykraton (Recipe 130)

Dinner for Homeric Heroes

Maza (Recipe 77)
Acorn or Chestnut Cakes (Recipe 84)
Pita Bread (Recipe 80)
Fresh Cheese with Olive Oil and Herbs (Recipe 85)
Flavored Olives in Brine (Recipe 117)
Odysseus's Sacrificial Lamb (Recipe 103)
Kykeon (Recipe 128) and Athenian Wine (Recipe 129)

Dinner for Spartans

Pita Bread (Recipe 80)
Maza (Recipe 77)
Crazy Radish Hors d'Oeuvres (Recipe 104)
Green Herb Salad (Recipe 106)
Boiled Mixed Dinner (Recipe 100)
Mustard Greens (Recipe 110)
Dried Fava Beans (Recipe 113)

Poor Person's Dessert Table (Recipe 123)
Oxykraton (Recipe 130)

Dinner for Wealthy Athenians

Pita Bread (Recipe 80)
Griddle Cakes Stuffed with Cheese (Recipe 78)
Dice Bread (Recipe 82)
Barley Porridge with Sesame (Recipe 75)
Sliced Egg Hors d'Oeuvres (Recipe 96)
Grilled Asparagus (Recipe 107)
Marinated Beets (Recipe 108)
Pepper-Fried Scallops (Recipe 88)
Honey-Glazed Shrimp (Recipe 89)
Salt-Baked Sea Bass (Recipe 91)
Quail Baked in Flaky Pastry with Pomegranate
    Molasses (Recipe 99)
Spit-Roasted Hare (Recipe 101)
Silphium Sauce (Recipe 119)
Cheesecake (Recipe 124)
Brazier Bread (Recipe 125)
Athenian Wine (Recipe 129)

Dinner for Wealthy Sicilians

Pita Bread (Recipe 80)
Barley Porridge with Sesame (Recipe 75)
Cheese Pizza (Recipe 83)
Pickled Turnips in Mustard (Recipe 114)
Cheese-Stuffed Mackerel (Recipe 92)
Roasted Tuna (Recipe 90)
Pungent Brine Sauce (Recipe 122)
Baked Swordfish with Pounded Sauce (Recipe 94)
Capon in Vinegar-Oil Sauce (Recipe 98)

Snacking at the Marketplace

Fried Whitebait (Recipe 93)
Fruits and Nuts

Feast of Amphidromia

Pita Bread (Recipe 80)
Cappadocian Salt-Rising Bread (Recipe 81)
Toasted Gallipoli Cheese (Recipe 87)
Stuffed Vine Leaves (Recipe 105)
Flavored Olives in Brine (Recipe 117)
Chicken in the Pot (Recipe 97)
Grilled Lamb or Mutton Chops with Cabbage (Recipe 102)
Spiced Sauce (Recipe 118)
Walnut and Flaxseed Confection (Recipe 127)
Undiluted Wine

4. ANCIENT ROME

Breakfast for Poor Peasants and Slaves

Bran Bread (Recipe 134)
Moretum (Recipe 148)
Household Wine (Recipe 204) or *Posca* (Recipe 205)

Breakfast for Affluent City Dwellers

Water Bread (Recipe 133), *Silignites* (Recipe 131), or Wheat Pap
   (Recipe 137)
Homemade Fresh Cheese (Recipe 147) or *Libum* (Recipe 150)
Olive Confection (Recipe 190)
Fig Bonbons (Recipe 197)
Leftovers from previous night's dinner
Posca (Recipe 205) or diluted wine

Breakfast in Times of Famine

Oatmeal with Sweet Wine (Recipe 139)

Lunch for City Dwellers

Ham (Recipe 156) or Boiled Salt Meat (Recipe 157)
Water Bread (Recipe 133) or Cracker Bread (Recipe 132)
Pergamum Chickpeas (Recipe 188)
Leftovers from previous night's dinner

Dinner for Poor Peasants and Slaves

Punic Porridge (recipe 136) or Bran Bread (Recipe 134)
Pounded Olive Relish (Recipe 191)
Boiled Salt Meat (Recipe 157) and Cabbage, Another Way
   (Recipe 180), or
Barley Tisane with Vegetables (Recipe 135, minus the silphium)
Fresh or Dried Fruits and Nuts
Household Wine (Recipe 204)

Dinner for Middle-Class City Dwellers

Water Bread (Recipe 133)
Baked Goat Cheese (Recipe 149)
Olive Confection (Recipe 190)
Soft-Boiled Eggs in Vinegar with Pine Nut Sauce
   (Recipes 173 and 174)
Lettuce Salad (Recipe 181)
Boiled Mackerel with Rue Sauce (Recipe 171)
Dainty Dishes of Kid or Lamb (Recipe 165)
Green Beans (Recipe 186)
Boiled Beets with Vinaigrette (Recipe 182)
Sweet Wine Cakes Steeped in Milk (Recipe 201)
Wine and *Conditum Paradoxum* (Recipe 206)

Dinner for Rich City Dwellers

Silignites (Recipe 131)
Raw Cabbage Salad (Recipe 179)
Dressing for Oysters (Recipe 170)
Black Sea Pickled Fish (Recipe 172)
Olive Confection (Recipe 190) and Pounded Olive
   Relish (Recipe 191)
Asparagus *Patina* (Recipe 175)
Boiled Cardoons (Recipe 183)
Dressed Chicory (Recipe 178)
Apricot Stew (Recipe 184)
Patina of Anchovy without Anchovy (Recipe 176)
Roasted Dormice (Recipe 167)
Grilled Sausages (Recipe 168) with Mustard (Recipe 193)

Braised Pork Shoulder with Barley and Figs (Recipe 152), Pepper
    Sauce (Recipe 153), and Must Cakes (Recipe 138); or Sow's Udder
    (Recipe 155) with Must Cakes (Recipe 138)
Stewed Beef Tidbits (Recipe 159)
Roasted Hare or Rabbit with Spiced Sauce (Recipe 162)
Preserved Blackberries (Recipe 202)
Pears in Boiled Must (Recipe 203)
Fried Pastry with Honey and Pepper (Recipe 200)
Honey-Fried Dates (Recipe 199)
Savillum (Recipe 151)
Wine and *Conditum Paradoxum* (Recipe 206)

Saturnalian Feast

Silignites (Recipe 131)
Must Cakes (Recipe 138)
Suckling Pig à la Vitellius (Recipe 154)
Grilled Sausages (Recipe 168)
Oysters (Recipe 170)
Fig Bonbons (Recipe 197)
Cheese Fritters with Honey and Poppyseeds (Recipe 198)
Honey-Fried Dates (Recipe 199)
Conditum Paradoxum (Recipe 206)
Hydromel (Recipe 207)

MAIL ORDER SOURCES

Arrowhead Mills
800 434 7246
www.arrowheadmills.com
A good assortment of flours, grains, and legumes

Big Tree Farms
212 937 3514
www.bigtreebali.com
farm@bigtreebali.com
Source for long pepper

Faraway Foods
www.farawayfoods.com/shopping.html
Source for farro, as well as more common ingredients

Kalustyan Orient Export Trading Corp.
212 685 3451
www.kalustyans.com
sales@kalustyans.com
Extensive assortment of flours, grains, spices, legumes, fish sauces,
nuts, and oils needed for most recipes; the Web site shows only
a small fraction of the inventory, so contact them directly with
specific needs

Parthenon Foods

877 301 5522

http://parthenonfoods.com/index.php

Good selection of foods, including mohluhkia

Thai Supermarket Online

888 618 8424

http://importfood.com

Excellent assortment of good-quality fish sauces to use as *siqqu* or *garum/liquamen*; its three brands of "gourmet" fish sauces are well worth the price and will make a noticeable difference in your cooking

Tigernuts Traders, S.L.

http://www.tigernuts.com/products3.html

info@tigernuts.com

A Spanish company that sells tiger nuts and tiger nut flour; one of the few online sources for this product

Williams-Sonoma

877 812 6235

http://ww5.williams-sonoma.com

SAF instant yeast and clay bakers, as well as general kitchen equipment

Zingermans.com LLC

888 636 8162

www.zingermans.com

toni@zingermans.com

The importer of *colatura*, an Italian-produced fish sauce believed to be the direct descendent of *garum*; the product is expensive but has a slightly different flavor than Asian fish sauces

 NOTES

INTRODUCTION

1. Oswyn Murray, "Life and Society in Classical Greece," in *Greece and the Hellenistic World*, ed. John Boardman, Jasper Griffin, and Oswyn Murray (New York: Oxford University Press, 1991).
2. Apicius, *De Re Coquinaria*, critical edition with introduction, notes, and translation of the Latin Recipe Text *Apicius* by Sally Grainger and Christopher Grocock (Totnes, Devon, UK: Prospect Books, 2006).
3. Athenaeus, *Deipnosophists* (The Philosophers at Dinner), 7 volumes, trans. C. B. Gulick (London: W. Heinemann and Cambridge, MA: Harvard University Press, 1927–1941, 111f.
4. Athenaeus 113a, 114e–115c.
5. Daniel Zohary and Maria Hopf, *The Domestication of Plants in the Old World*, 3rd ed. (New York: Oxford University Press, 2001), 42–51.
6. Galen, "Wheats," in *On Food and Diet*, trans. Mark Grant (New York: Routledge, 2000).

1. MESOPOTAMIA

1. Jean Bottéro, *Everyday Life in Ancient Mesopotamia*, trans. Antonia Nevill (Baltimore: Johns Hopkins University, 2001), 61–62.
2. Edmund I. Gordon, *Sumerian Proverbs: Glimpses of Everyday Life in Ancient Mesopotamia* (Philadelphia: University of Pennsylvania Museum, 1959), 1:142.

3. Jean Bottéro, *The Oldest Cuisine in the World*, trans. Teresa Lavender Fagan (Chicago: University of Chicago Press, 2004), see especially 107–17.

4. D.J. Wiseman, "A New Stela of Assur-nasir-pal II," *Iraq* 14 (1952): 24–44.

5. Bottéro, *Oldest Cuisine*, 76.

6. Bottéro, *Oldest Cuisine*, 112.

7. Gordon, *Sumerian Proverbs*, 1:50.

8. Bottéro, *Oldest Cuisine*, 101.

9. Gordon, 1:190–91.

10. Bottéro, *Oldest Cuisine*, 28.

11. Bottéro, *Oldest Cuisine*, 43.

12. Gordon, 1:59.

13. Bottéro, *Oldest Cuisine*, 30–31.

14. Bottéro, *Oldest Cuisine*, 16.

15. Gordon, 1:125.

16. Henri Limet, "The Cuisine of Ancient Sumer," *Biblical Archaeologist* 50 (1987):132–47, at 137.

17. Bottéro, *Oldest Cuisine*, 29.

18. Bottéro, *Oldest Cuisine*, 59.

19. Bottéro, *Oldest Cuisine*, 20.

20. Limet, 134.

21. Limet, 137.

22. Bottéro, *Oldest Cuisine*, 113.

23. Bottéro, *Oldest Cuisine*, 101.

24. Limet, 145.

25. Gordon, 2:123.

26. Solomon H. Katz and Mary M. Voigt, "Bread and Beer: The Early Use of Cereals in the Human Diet," *Expedition* 28, no. 2 (1986): 23–34.

27. Solomon H. Katz and Fritz Maytag, "Brewing an Ancient Beer," *Archaeology* 44, no. 4 (1991): 24–33.

2. ANCIENT EGYPT

1. John F. Nunn, *Ancient Egyptian Medicine* (Norman: University of Oklahoma Press, 1996), 18–20.

2. Morris Bierbrier, *The Tomb-Builders of the Pharaohs* (London: British Museum Publications, 1982), 41.

3. William J. Darby, Paul Ghalioungui, and Louis Grivetti, *Food: The Gift of Osiris*, 2 vols. (London: Academic Press, 1977), 55.

4. Adolf Erman, "The Instruction of Ptahhotep," in *The Literature of the Ancient Egyptians* trans. Aylward M. Blackman (London: Methuen, 1927), 57 (language modernized).

5. Mary Anne Murray, "Cereal Production and Processing," in *Ancient Egyptian Materials and Technology,* ed. Paul T. Nicholson and Ian Shaw (Cambridge, UK: Cambridge University Press, 2000), 505–36.

6. Godon Sacks, "Kamut: A New Old Grain," *Gastronomica* 5 (Fall 2005): 95–98.

7. David Roberts, "After 4,500 Years, Rediscovering Egypt's Bread-Baking Technology." *National Geographic Magazine,* 187 (Jan 1995), 32–35.

8. Anon., *The Book of the Dead: The Papyrus of Ani in the British Museum,* transliteration, translation, and introduction by E. A. Wallis Budge (1895; repr., New York: Dover, 1967).

9. Athenaeus, *Deipnosophists* (The Philosophers at Dinner), 7 vols., trans. C.B. Gulick (London: W. Heinemann and Cambridge, MA: Harvard University Press, 1927–41), 158d.

10. Delwen Samuel, "Brewing and Baking," in *Ancient Egyptian Materials and Technology,* ed. Paul T. Nicholson and Ian Shaw (Cambridge, UK: Cambridge University Press, 2000), 537–76.

3. ANCIENT GREECE

1. Athenaeus, *Deipnosophists* (The Philosophers at Dinner), 7 vols., trans. C.B. Gulick (London: W. Heinemann and Cambridge, MA: Harvard University Press, 1927–1941), 276e–f.

2. Athenaeus 126e–f.

3. Aristophanes, *Works,* ed. and trans. by Jeffrey Henderson (Cambridge, MA: Harvard University Press, 1998), *Frogs,* 505–18.

4. Aristophanes, *Acharnians,* 770–74; 1003–07.

5. Plato, *Collected Dialogues,* ed. Edith Hamilton and Huntington Cairns (Princeton, NJ: Princeton University Press, 1971), *Republic* I: 332; II: 372–73.

6. Plato *Gorgias* 464c–465d.

7. Athenaeus 346a.

8. Anon., *The Epigrams of Homer,* in Hesiod, *The Homeric Hymns and Homerica,* trans. H.G. Evelyn-White (London: W. Heinemann and Cambridge, MA: Harvard University Press, 1936), *Homeric Epigrams* XV.

9. Athenaeus 115a.

10. Athenaeus 110c.

11. Athenaues 147e.

12. Athenaeus 110c.

13. Athenaeus 113.

14. Hippocrates, *Works,* 8 vols., trans. W.H.S. Jones (Cambridge, MA: Harvard University Press, 1923), *Regimen,* II: xlii.

15. Athenaeus 114a.

16. Aristophanes, *Acharnians,* 1125–27.

17. Xenophon, *Works*, 7 vols., trans. Carleton W. Brownson (London: W. Heinemann and Cambridge, MA: Harvard University Press, 1914–25), *Anabasis* 5.4.29; Plato *Republic*, 2:372c.

18. Plato, *Republic*, 2:372c.

19. Xenophon, *Memorabilia*, 3.14; James Davidson, "Opsophagia: Revolutionary Eating at Athens," in *Food in Antiquity*, ed. John Wilkins, David Harvey, and Mike Dobson (Exeter, United Kingdom: University of Exeter, 1995).

20. Athenaeus 658a.

21. Athenaeus 138f–139c.

22. Athenaeus 370d.

23. Athenaeus 276–77c.

24. Athenaeus 90f.

25. Philoxenus, *Banquet*, trans. and commentaries by Andrew Dalby, in *Petits Propos Culinaires*, 26 (July 1987): 28–36.

26. Archestratus, *The Life of Luxury*, trans. and commentary by John Wilkins and Shaun Hill (Totnes, Devon, UK: Prospect Books, 1994), Fr. 45.

27. Archestratus, *Hedupatheia* (The Life of Luxury), trans. and commentary by S. Douglas Olson and Alexander Sens (Oxford. UK: Oxford University Press, 2000), Fr. 32.

28. Athenaeus 285d.

29. Archestratus (Wilkins and Hill), Fr. 23.

30. Athenaeus 119e.

31. Athenaeus 60a.

32. Athenaeus. 340f–341a.

33. Anon., *Regimen*, 2.56.8, in Hippocrates, *Works*, 8 vols., trans. W.H.S. Jones (Cambridge, MA: Harvard University Press, 1923).

34. Athenaeus 384f.

35. Athenaeus 94c.

36. Archestratus (Wilkins and Hill), Fr. 57.

37. Archestratus Fr 58.

38. Athenaeus 370d.

39. Homer, *Odyssey*, trans. Robert Fagles (New York: Viking, 1996), 3:510–20.

40. Massimo, Montanari, "Food Systems and Models of Civilization," in *Food: A Culinary History*, ed. Jean-Louis Flandrin and Massimo Montanari (New York: Columbia University Press, 1999), 69–78.

41. Athenaeus 277c.

42. Athenaeus 131d.

43. Athenaeus 140a.

44. Athenaeus 62 d–e.

45. Athenaeus 120d.

46. Athenaeus 68d.

47. Athenaeus 156a–160b.

48. Athenaeus 158a.

49. Athenaeus 54f.

50. Athenaeus 407f.

51. Athenaeus 133c.

52. Athenaeus 60d.

53. Athenaeus 61d–e.

54. Archestratus Fr. 7; Athenaeus 133a.

55. Aristophanes, *Frogs*, 980–88.

56. Attributed to Hippocrates, *Regimen*, II, lvi, 78–79.

57. Athenaeus 173d.

58. Theophrastus, Study of Plants 9.1.7, trans. Andrew Dalby, "Silphium and Asafoetida," in *Spicing Up the Palate: Studies of Flavourings Ancient and Modern*, 1992 Proceedings of the Oxford Symposium on Food and Cookery, ed. Harlan Walker (Totnes, Devon, UK: Prospect Books, 1993), 67–72.

59. Athenaeus 100e–f; Philoxenus, *Banquet*.

60. Archestratus Fr. 57 (Olson & Sens).

61. As translated in John Wilkins and Shaun Hill, "The Flavours of Ancient Greece," in *Spicing Up the Palate: Studies of Flavourings Ancient and Modern*, 1992 Proceedings of the Oxford Symposium on Food and Cookery, ed. Harlan Walker (Totnes, Devon, UK: Prospect Books, 1993), 275–79.

62. Athenaeus 101d.

63. Athenaeus 101d.

64. Athenaeus 109d.

65. Galen, "On the Properties of Foods," in *On Food and Diet*, trans. Mark Grant (London: Routledge, 2000), 1:3.

66. Athenaeus 111a.

67. Athenaeus 492e.

68. Homer, *Iliad*, trans. Robert Fagles (New York: Viking, 1990), 6:754–58.

69. Hesiod, *Work and Days*, 731–32.

4. Ancient Rome

1. Cato, *De Agricultura* (On Farming), trans. and commentary by Andrew Dalby (Totnes, Devon, UK: Prospect Books, 1998), §2.

2. Pliny the Elder, *Naturalis Historiae* (Natural History), trans. William Rackham and W.H.S. Jones (London and Cambridge, MA: Harvard University Press, 1938–1963, 9.79.30; 9.167–72.

3. Cato, §§ 56, 57, 58.

4. Ovid, *Works*, trans. Frank Justus Miller and rev. G.P. Goold, 2d ed. (London: W. Heinemann and Cambridge, MA: Harvard University Press, 1977–89), *Metamorphoses*, Book 8, 629–78.

5. Psuedo-Virgil, *Moretum,* in *Appendix Vergiliana,* trans. H. Rushton Fairclough, rev. G. P. Goold (Cambridge, MA: Harvard University Press, 1999–2000).

6. Martial, *Epigrams,* ed. and trans. D. R. Shackelton Bailey (Cambridge, MA: Harvard University Press, 1993), 10.48.

7. Plutarch, *Moralia,* trans. Frank C. Babbitt (London: W. Heinemann and Cambridge, MA: Harvard University Press, 1927–76), *Dinner Questions,* 2.9.

8. Clement of Alexandria, *Christ the Educator,* trans. Simon P. Wood (New York: Fathers of the Church, 1954), 2.1.15, 2.2.33, 2.2.35.

9. Petronius, *Satyricon,* trans. with notes and topical commentaries by Sarah Ruden (Indianapolis, IN: Hackett, 2002), 22, 24, 25, 28.

10. Statius, *Silvae,* trans. J. H. Mozley (London: W. Heinemann and Cambridge, MA: Harvard University Press, 1928), *The Kalends of December,*1.6.44–50.

11. Mary Ella Milham, "In Defense of Hamburger: Apicius and Roman Cooking," *Vergilius* 12 (1966):46.

12. Oribasius, *Dieting for an Emperor: Books 1 and 4 of the Medical Compilations,* trans. and commentary Mark Grant (Leiden: Brill, 1997), 4:2:2–4.

13. Pliny, *Natural History,* ed. John Bostock and H. T. Riley (London: H. G. Bohn, 1855–57), 18.27.

14. Galen, "Wheats," in *On Food and Diet,* trans. Mark Grant (London: Routledge, 2000).

15. Cato, *De Agricultura* (On Farming), trans. William Davis Hooper and revised by Harrison Boyd Ash (Cambridge, MA: Harvard University Press), 1935.

16. Pliny (Bostock and Riley).

17. Galen, "Wheats."

18. Apicius, *De Re Coquinaria,* critical translation of *The Art of Cookery* by Barbara Flower and Elisabeth Rosenbaum (London: Harrap, 1958).

19. Cato (Hooper).

20. Pliny (Bostock and Riley), 18.29.109–14.

21. Cato (Hooper).

22. Galen, "Refined Bread," in *On Food and Diet.*

23. Cato (Dalby).

24. Cato (Dalby).

25. Pliny (Rackham), 18.17.77.

26. Sally Grainger, "Towards an Authentic Roman Sauce, Or Can We Truly Know What Liquamen Was?" in *Authenticity,* 2005 Proceedings of the Oxford Symposium on Food and Cookery (forthcoming).

27. Apicius (Flower and Rosenbaum).

28. Cato (Dalby) § 88.

29. Columella, *De Re Rustica* (On Farming), trans. Harrison Boyd Ash (Harvard University Press, 1948–55), 12.19; Pliny, (Rackham) XIV.80.

30. Apicius (Flower and Rosenbaum).

31. Grainger, "Towards an Authentic Roman Sauce."

32. Apicius (Flower and Rosenbaum).

33. Apicius (Flower and Rosenbaum).

34. Christopher Grocock and Sally Grainger, "Moretum—a Peasant Lunch Revisited," in *The Meal*, 2001 Proceedings of the Oxford Symposium on Food and Cookery, ed. Harlan Walker (Totnes, Devon, UK: Prospect Books, 2002).

35. Cato (Hooper).

36. Cato (Hooper).

37. Apicius, *De Re Coquinaria*, ed., trans., and commentary by Joseph Dommers Vehling (Chicago: Walter M. Hill, 1936; repr., New York: Dover, 1977).

38. Apicius (Vehling).

39. Apicius (Vehling).

40. Cato (Dalby).

41. Apicius (Vehling).

42. Apicius (Vehling).

43. Apicius (Vehling).

44. Apicius (Flower & Rosenbaum).

45. Apicius (Flower and Rosenbaum).

46. Apicius (Vehling).

47. Apicius (Flower and Rosenbaum).

48. Varro, *De Re Rustica* (On Agriculture), trans. William Davis Hooper, rev. Harrison Boyd Ash (London: W. Heinemann and Cambridge, MA: Harvard University Press, 1934), 3.15.

49. Cato (Dalby).

50. Apicius (Flower and Rosenbaum).

51. Apicius (Flower and Rosenbaum).

52. Pliny, (Rackham) 19.19.

53. Apicius (Vehling).

54. Columella 12.57.

55. Apicius (Flower and Rosenbaum).

56. Celsus, *De Medicina* (On Medicine), trans. W.G. Spencer (London: W. Heinemann and Cambridge, MA: Harvard University Press, 1935–38), 5:27.

57. Pliny (Bostock and Riley), 22.47.

58. Apicius (Vehling).

59. Galen, "Chickpeas," in *On Food and Diet*.

60. Apicius (Flower and Rosenbaum).

61. Cato (Hooper).

62. Apicius (Flower and Rosenbaum).

63. Columella, 12.15.5.

64. Apicius (Flower and Rosenbaum).

65. Apicius (Flower and Rosenbaum).
66. Cato (Dalby).
67. Apicius (Flower and Rosenbaum).
68. Pliny, (Rackham) 14.13.89.
69. Sandor Ellix, Katz, *Wild Fermentation: The Flavor, Nutrition and Craft of Live-Culture Foods* (White River Junction, VT: Chelsea Green, 2003), 124–29.

BIBLIOGRAPHY

GENERAL

Adams, Judi. "Wheat as a Food." In *Encyclopedia of Food and Culture.* Vol. 3. Edited by Solomon H. Katz. New York: Charles Scribner's Sons, 2003, 535–40.

Avitsur, Shmuel. "The Way to Bread: The Example of the Land of Israel." *Tools and Tillage* 2, no. 4 (1975):228–41.

Bedigian, Dorothea, and Jack R. Harlan. "Evidence for Cultivation of Sesame in the Ancient World." *Economic Botany* 40, no. 2 (1986):137–54.

Billing, Jennifer, and Paul W Sherman. "Antimicrobial Function of Spices: Why Some Like It Hot." *Quarterly Review of Biology* 73 (March 1998):3–49.

Bober, Phyllis Bray. *Art, Culture and Cuisine: Ancient and Medieval Gastronomy.* Chicago: University of Chicago Press, 1999.

Brotherwell, Don, and Patricia Brotherwell. *Food in Antiquity.* Baltimore: Johns Hopkins University Press, 1998.

Brown, Elizabeth Burton. *Grains: An Illustrated History with Recipes.* New York: Prentice-Hall, 1977.

Butzer, Karl W. "Environmental Change in the Near East and Human Impact on the Land." In *Civilizations of the Ancient Near East,* edited by Jack M. Sasson. New York: Charles Scribner's Sons, 1995.

Cooper, John. *Eat and Be Satisfied: A Social History of Jewish Food.* Northvale, NJ: Jason Aronson, 1993.

Curtis, Robert I. *Ancient Food Technology.* Leiden: Brill, 2001.

Dalby, Andrew. *Food in the Ancient World From A to Z.* London: Routledge, 2003.

Davidson, Alan. *Mediterranean Seafood.* 3rd ed. Berkeley, CA: Ten Speed Press, 2002.

Davis, Sharon. "Wheat: Natural History." In *Encyclopedia of Food and Culture,* edited by Solomon H. Katz. Vol. 3. New York: Charles Scribner's Sons, 2003, 527–35.

Eyre, Christopher J. "The Agricultural Cycle, Farming, and Water Management in the Ancient Near East." In *Civilizations of the Ancient Near East,* edited by Jack M. Sasson. New York: Charles Scribner's Sons, 1995.

Farrell, Kenneth T. *Spices, Condiments, and Seasonings.* 2nd ed. New York: Van Nostrand-Reinhold, 1990.

Forbes, R.J. *Studies in Ancient Technology.* Vol. 3, 3rd ed. Leiden: Brill, 1993.

Grant, Michael. *Atlas of Classical History from 1700 BC to 565.* 5th ed. New York: Oxford University Press, 1994.

Harris, Marvin. *The Sacred Cow and the Abominable Pig: Riddles of Food and Culture.* New York: Simon & Schuster, 1985.

———. *Cannibals and Kings: The Origins of Cultures.* New York: Random House, 1977.

Hawkes, Jacquetta. *The First Great Civilizations: Life in Mesopotamia, the Indus Valley, and Egypt.* London: Hutchison, 1973.

Hesse, Brian. "Animal Husbandry and Human Diet." In *Civilizations of the Ancient Near East,* edited by Jack M. Sasson. New York: Charles Scribner's Sons, 1995.

Katz, Solomon H., and Mary M. Voigt. "Bread and Beer: The Early Use of Cereals in the Human Diet." *Expedition* 28, no. 2 (1986):23–34.

McGee, Harold. *On Food and Cooking.* Rev. ed. New York: Scribner, 2004.

McGovern, Patrick E. *Ancient Wine: The Search for the Origins of Viniculture.* Princeton, NJ: Princeton University Press, 2003.

Miller, Naomi F., and Wilma Wetterstrom. "The Beginnings of Agriculture." In *The Cambridge World History of Food,* edited by Kenneth F. Kiple and Kriemhild Coneè Ornelas. Cambridge, UK: Cambridge University Press, 2000.

Montanari, Massimo. "Food Systems and Models of Civilization." In *Food: A Culinary History,* edited by Jean-Louis Flandrin and Massimo Montanari. New York: Columbia University Press, 1999.

Renfrew, Jane M. "Vegetables in the Ancient Near East Diet." In *Civilizations of the Ancient Near East,* edited by Jack M. Sasson. New York: Charles Scribner's Sons, 1995.

Smith, Bruce D. *The Emergence of Agriculture.* New York: Scientific American Library, 1995.

Turner, Jack. *Spices: The History of a Temptation.* New York: Alfred A. Knopf, 2004.

Vaughan, J.G., and C.A. Geissler. *The New Oxford Book of Food Plants.* Oxford, UK: Oxford University Press, 1997.

Wilkins, John, David Harvey, and Mike Dobson, eds. *Food in Antiquity.* Exeter, UK: University of Exeter, 1995.

Younger, William. *Gods, Men, and Wine,* Cleveland, OH: The Wine and Food Society in association with World Publishing, 1966.

Zeder, Melinda. "The Role of Pigs in Near Eastern Subsistence: A View from the Southern Levant." In *Retrieving the Past: Essays on Archaeological Research and Methodology in Honor of Gus W. Van Beek.* Joe D Seger, ed. Winona Lake, IN: Cobb Institute of Archaeology, 1996.

Zohary, Daniel, and Maria Hopf. *The Domestication of Plants in the Old World.* 3rd ed. New York: Oxford University Press, 2001.

GENERAL COOKBOOKS AND COOKING TECHNIQUES

Alford, Jeffrey, and Naomi Duguid. *Flatbreads and Flavors.* New York: William Morrow, 1995.

Berenbaum, Rose Levy. *The Bread Bible.* New York: W.W. Norton, 2003.

Carroll, Ricki, and Robert Carroll. *Cheesemaking Made Easy.* Pownal, VT: Storey Communications, 1996.

Katz, Sandor Ellix. *Wild Fermentation: The Flavor, Nutrition and Craft of Live-Culture Foods.* White River Junction, VT: Chelsea Green, 2003.

Peterson, James. *Fish and Shellfish.* New York: William Morrow, 1996.

Roden, Claudia. *A Book of Middle Eastern Food.* New York: Alfred A. Knopf, 1972.

Wolfert, Paula. *The Cooking of the Eastern Mediterranean.* New York: HarperCollins, 1994.

Wood, Ed. *World Sourdoughs from Antiquity.* Berkeley, CA: Ten Speed Press, 1996.

Wood, Jacqui. *Prehistoric Cooking.* Mount Pleasant, SC: Tempus, 2001.

Wright, Clifford. *Mediterranean Vegetables.* Boston: Harvard Common Press, 2001.

MESOPOTAMIA

Bottéro, Jean. *The Oldest Cuisine in the World: Cooking in Mesopotamia.* Translated by Teresa Lavender Fagan. Chicago: University of Chicago Press, 2004.

———. *Religion in Ancient Mesopotamia.* Translated by Teresa Lavender Fagan. Chicago: University of Chicago Press, 2001.

————. *Everyday Life in Ancient Mesopotamia.* Translated by Antonia Nevill. Baltimore: Johns Hopkins University Press, 2001.

————. "The Cuisine of Ancient Mesopotamia." *Biblical Archaeologist* 48 (1985):36–47.

Civil, Miguel. "Ancient Mesopotamia." In *Encyclopedia of Food and Culture,* 2:482–87. New York: Charles Scribner's Sons, 2003.

Crawford, Harriet. *Sumer and the Sumerians.* 2nd ed. Cambridge, UK: Cambridge University Press, 2004.

Ellison, Rosemary. "Methods of Food Preparation in Mesopotamia, c. 3000–600 B.C." *Journal of the Economic and Social History of the Orient* 27 (1984):89–98.

————. "The Agriculture of Mesopotamia, c. 3000–600 B.C." *Tolls and Tillage* 4 (1982):173–84.

Gordon, Edmund I. *Sumerian Proverbs: Glimpses of Everyday Life in Ancient Mesopotamia.* Philadelphia: University of Pennsylvania Museum, 1959.

Hoffner, Harry A. Jr. *Alimenta Hethaeorum: Food Production in Hittite Asia Minor.* New Haven, CT: American Oriental Society, vol. 55 (monograph series), 1974.

Joannes, Francis. "The Social Function of Banquets in the Earliest Civilizations." In *Food: A Culinary History,* edited by Jean-Louis Flandrin and Massimo Montanari. New York: Columbia University Press, 1999.

Katz, Solomon H., and Fritz Maytag. "Brewing an Ancient Beer." *Archaeology* 44, no. 4 (1991):24–33.

Keith, Kathryn. "The Spatial Patterns of Everyday Life in Old Babylonian Neighborhoods." In *The Social Construction of Ancient Cities,* edited by Monica L. Smith. Washington, DC: Smithsonian Books, 2003.

Levey, Martin. "Food and Its Technology in Ancient Mesopotamia: The Earliest Chemical Processes and Chemicals." *Centaurus* 6 (1959):36–51.

Limet, Henri. "The Cuisine of Ancient Sumer." *Biblical Archaeologist* 50 (1987):132–47.

Mamul, Meir. "*Ze/irtu:* The Olive Tree and Its Products in Ancient Mesopotamia." In *Olive Oil in Antiquity,* edited by David Eitam and Michael Heltzer. History of the Ancient Near East Studies, Egypt Exploration Society, 7 (monograph series), 1996.

Nasrallah, Nawal. *Delights from the Garden of Eden.* Rev. ed. Self-published, First Books, 2003.

Nemet-Nejat, Karen Rhea. *Daily Life in Ancient Mesopotamia.* Westport, CT: Greenwood Press, 1998.

Oppenheim, A. Leo. *Ancient Mesopotamia: Portrait of a Dead Civilization.* Rev. ed. completed by Erica Reiner. Chicago: University of Chicago Press, 1977.

Robertson, John F. "The Social and Economic Organization of the Ancient Mesopotamian Temple." In *Civilizations of the Ancient Near East,* edited by Jack M. Sasson. New York: Charles Scribner's Sons, 1995.

Sacks, Godon. "Kamut: A New Old Grain." *Gastronomica* 5, no. 4 (Fall 2005):95–98.

Stol, Marten. "Private Life in Ancient Mesopotamia." In *Civilizations of the Ancient Near East,* edited by Jack M. Sasson. New York: Charles Scribner's Sons, 1995.

Thompson, Campell. *The Assyrian Herbal.* London: Luzac, 1924.

Van der Steen, Eveline J. *"Zukanda* and Other Delicacies: Haute Cuisine in the Days of Hammurabi."*Petits Propos Culinaires* 51 (1995):40–46.

Wiseman, D. J. "A New Stela of Aššur-nasir-pal II." *Iraq* 14 (1952):24–44.

Zeder, Melinda. "Food Provisioning in Urban Societies: A View from Northern Mesopotamia." In *The Social Construction of Ancient Cities,* edited by Monica L. Smith. Washington, DC: Smithsonian Books, 2003.

EGYPT

Ahituv, Shmuel. "Observations on Olive Oil in Ancient Egypt." In *Olive Oil in Antiquity,* edited by David Eitam and Michael Heltzer. History of the Ancient Near East Studies, Egypt Exploration Society 7 (monograph series), 1996.

Anon. *The Book of the Dead: The Papyrus of Ani in the British Museum.* Transliteration, translation, and introduction by E. A. Wallis Budge. 1895. Reprint: New York, Dover, 1967.

Bierbrier, Morris. *The Tomb-Builders of the Pharaohs.* London: British Museum Publications, 1982.

Brewer, Douglas J., Donald B. Redford, and Susan Redford. *Domestic Plants and Animals: The Egyptian Origins.* Warminster, UK: Aris & Phillips, 1994.

Brewer, Douglas J., and Renée F. Friedman. *Fish and Fishing in Ancient Egypt.* Warminster, UK: Aris & Phillips, 1989.

Butzer, Karl W. "Irrigation." In *The Oxford Encyclopedia of Ancient Egypt,* edited by Donald B. Redford. Oxford, UK: Oxford University Press, 2001.

Crawford, Dorothy J. "Food: Tradition and Change in Hellenistic Egypt." *World Archaeology* 2, no. 2 (1979):136–46.

Darby, William J., Paul Ghalioungui, and Louis Grivetti. *Food: The Gift of Osiris.* 2 vols. London: Academic Press, 1977.

Davies, Norman de Garis. *The Tomb of Rekh-mi-Rē at Thebes.* New York: Plantin Press, 1943.

Emery, W. B. *A Funerary Repast in an Egyptian Tomb of the Archaic Period.* Leiden: Nederlands Instituut Voor Het Nabije Oosten, 1962.

Erman, Adolf. *The Literature of the Ancient Egyptians,* Trans. Aylward M. Blackman. London: Methuen, 1927.

Gardiner, Alan H. "The Mansion of Life and the Master of the King's Largess." In *Journal of Egyptian Archaeology* 24 (1938):83–91.

Geller, Jeremy. "Bread and Beer in Fourth Millennium Egypt." *Food and Foodways* 5 (1993):255–67.

Harlan, Jack R. "Lettuce and the Sycamore: Sex and Romance in Ancient Egypt." *Economic Botany* 40, no. 1 (1986):4–15.

Hecker, H.M. "A Zooarchaeological Inquiry into Pork Consumption in Egypt from Prehistoric to New Kingdom Times." *Journal of the American Research Center in Egypt* 19 (1982):59–71.

Ikram, Selima. *Choice Cuts: Meat Production in Ancient Egypt.* Leuven: Uitgeverij Peeters en Departement Oosterse (Studies Orientalia Lovaniensia Analecta 69), 1995.

———. "Food for Eternity: What the Ancient Egyptians Ate and Drank" (in 2 parts). *KMT, a Modern Journal of Ancient Egypt* 5, no. 1 (Spring 1994):25–33 and 5, no. 2 (Summer 1994):53–60, 75–76.

Lesko, Leonard. *King Tut's Wine Cellar.* Berkeley, CA: B.C. Scribe, 1977.

Manniche, Lise. *An Ancient Egyptian Herbal.* Austin: University of Texas Press, 1989.

Murray, Mary Anne. "Cereal Production and Processing." In *Ancient Egyptian Materials and Technology,* edited by Paul T. Nicholson and Ian Shaw. Cambridge, UK: Cambridge University Press, 2000, 505–36.

———. "Fruits, Vegetables, Pulses, and Condiments." In *Ancient Egyptian Materials and Technology,* edited by Paul T. Nicholson and Ian Shaw. Cambridge, UK: Cambridge University Press, 2000, 609–55.

Nunn, John F. *Ancient Egyptian Medicine,* Norman: University of Oklahoma Press, 1996.

Roberts, David. "After 4,500 Years: Rediscovering Egypt's Bread-Baking Technology." *National Geographic Magazine,* 187 (Jan. 1995): 32–35.

Römer, Malte. "Landholding." In *Oxford Encyclopedia of Ancient Egypt,* edited by Donald B. Redford. Oxford, UK: Oxford University Press, 2001.

Saffirio, L. "Food and Dietary Habits in Ancient Egypt." *Journal of Human Evolution* 1 (1972):297–305.

Samuel, Delwen. "Brewing and Baking." In *Ancient Egyptian Materials and Technology,* edited by Paul T. Nicholson and Ian Shaw. Cambridge, UK: Cambridge University Press, 2000, 537–76.

———. "Brewing and Baking in Ancient Egyptian Art." In *Food in the Arts,* edited by Harlan Walker. 1998 Proceedings of the Oxford Symposium on Food and Cookery. Totnes, Devon, UK: Prospect Books, 1999, 173–81.

———. "Their Staff of Life: Initial Investigations of Ancient Egyptian Bread Baking." *Amarna Reports,* edited by Barry J. Kemp. London: Egypt Exploration Society 5:253–88, 1989.

Samuel, Delwen, and Peter Bolt. "Rediscovering Ancient Egyptian Beer." Brewer's Guardian. www.broonale.co.uk/ancient.html.

Strouhal, Eugen. *Life of the Ancient Egyptians.* Liverpool: Liverpool University Press, 1997.

Trigger, Bruce G., Barry J. Kemp, David O'Connor, and Alan B. Lloyd. *Ancient Egypt: A Social History.* Cambridge, UK: Cambridge University Press, 1983.

Wilson, Hilary. "Pot-Baked Bread in Ancient Egypt." *Discussions in Egyptology* 13 (1989):89–100.

———. *Egyptian Food and Drink.* Aylesbury, Bucks, UK: Shire, 1988.

———. "A Recipe for Offering Loaves?" *Journal of Egyptian Archaeology* 74 (1988):214–17.

Winlock, H.E. *Models of Daily Life in Ancient Egypt from the Tomb of Meket-Rē at Thebes.* Cambridge, MA: Harvard University Press for the Metropolitan Museum of Art, 1954.

Wood, Ed. "Sourdoughs: From Antiquity to Today and Tomorrow." Cultural Aspects of Foods, Oregon State University. Available http://food.oregonstate.edu/ref/culture/wood.html.

PRIMARY SOURCES FOR GREECE AND ROME

Anon. *The Epigrams of Homer.* In Hesiod, *The Homeric Hymns and Homerica.* Translated by H.G. Evelyn-White. London: W. Heinemann; Cambridge, MA: Harvard University Press, 1936.

Apicius. *De Re Coquinaria.* Critical edition with introduction, notes, and translation of the Latin Recipe Text *Apicius* by Sally Grainger and Christopher Grocock. Totnes, Devon, UK: Prospect Books, 2006 (forthcoming).

———. *De Re Coquinaria.* Critical translation of *The Art of Cookery* by Barbara Flower and Elisabeth Rosenbaum. London: Harrap, 1958.

———. *De Re Coquinaria.* Edited, translation, and commentary by Joseph Dommers Vehling. Chicago: Walter M. Hill, 1936. Reprint, New York: Dover, 1977.

Archestratus. *Hedupatheia* (The Life of Luxury). Translated and commentary by S. Douglas Olson and Alexander Sens. Oxford, UK: Oxford University Press, 2000.

———. *The Life of Luxury.* Translated and commentary by John Wilkins and Shaun Hill. Totnes, Devon, UK: Prospect Books, 1994.

Aristophanes. *Works.* Edited and translated by Jeffrey Henderson. Harvard University Press, 1998.

Athenaeus. *Deipnosophists* (The Philosophers at Dinner). 7 vols. Translated by C.B. Gulick. London: W. Heinemann and Cambridge, MA: Harvard University Press, 1927–41.

Cato. *De Agricultura* (On Farming). Translated and commentary by Andrew Dalby. Totnes, Devon, UK: Prospect Books, 1998.

———. *De Agricultura* (On Farming). Translated by William Davis Hooper and revised by Harrison Boyd Ash. Cambridge MA: Harvard University Press, 1935.

Celsus. *De Medicina* (On Medicine). Translated by W.G. Spencer. London: W. Heinemann and Cambridge, MA: Harvard University Press, 1935–38.

Clement of Alexandria. *Christ the Educator.* Translated by Simon P. Wood. New York: Fathers of the Church, 1954.

Columella. *De Re Rustica* (On Farming). Translated by Harrison Boyd Ash. Harvard University Press, 1948–55.

Galen. *On Food and Diet.* Translated by Mark Grant. London: Routledge, 2000.

Hesiod. *The Works of Hesiod and the Homeric Hymns.* Translated by Daryl Hine. Chicago: University of Chicago Press, 2005.

Hippocrates. *Works.* 8 vols. Translated by W.H.S. Jones. Cambridge, MA: Harvard University Press, 1923.

Homer. *Iliad.* Translated by Robert Fagles. New York: Viking, 1990.

———. *Odyssey.* Translated by Robert Fagles. New York: Viking, 1996.

Martial. *Epigrams.* Edited and translated by D.R. Shackelton Bailey. Cambridge, MA: Harvard University Press, 1993.

Oribasius. *Dieting for an Emperor: Books 1 and 4 of the Medical Compilations.* Translated and commentary Mark Grant. Leiden: Brill, 1997.

Ovid. *Works.* Translated by Frank Justus Miller and revised by G.P. Goold. 2nd ed. London: W. Heinemann and Cambridge, MA: Harvard University Press, 1977–89.

Petronius. *Satyricon.* Translated and commentaries by Sarah Ruden. Indianapolis, IN: Hackett, 2002.

Philoxenus. *Banquet.* Translated and commentaries by Andrew Dalby. *Petits Propos Culinaires* 26 (1987): 28–36.

Plato. *Collected Dialogues.* Edited by Edith Hamilton and Huntington Cairns. Princeton, NJ: Princeton University Press, 1971.

Pliny the Elder. *Naturalis Historiae* (Natural History). Edited and translated by John Bostock and H.T. Riley. London: H.G. Bohn, 1855–57.

———. *Naturalis Historiae* (Natural History). Translated by William Rackham and W.H.S. Jones., London and Cambridge, MA: Harvard University Press, 1938–63.

Plutarch. *Moralia.* Translated by Frank C. Babbitt. London: W. Heinemann and Cambridge, MA: Harvard University Press, 1927–76.

Psuedo-Virgil. "Moretum." In *Appendix Vergiliana,* translated by H. Rushton Fairclough, revised by G.P. Goold. Cambridge, MA: Harvard University Press, 1999–2000.

Statius. *Silvae.* Translated by J.H. Mozley. London: W. Heinemann and Cambridge, MA: Harvard University Press, 1928.

Varro. *De Re Rustica* (On Agriculture). Translated by William Davis Hooper and revised by Harrison Boyd Ash. London: W. Heinemann and Cambridge, MA: Harvard University Press, 1934.

Xenophon. *Works.* 7 vols. Translated by Carleton W. Brownson. London: W. Heinemann and Cambridge, MA: Harvard University Press, 1914–25.

Secondary Sources for Greece and Rome

Alcock, Joan P. "Flavourings in Roman Culinary Taste with Some Reference to the Province of Britain." In *Spicing Up the Palate: Studies of Flavourings Ancient and Modern*, edited by Harlan Walker. 1992 Proceedings of the Oxford Symposium on Food and Cookery. Totnes, Devon, UK: Prospect Books, 1993, 11–22.

Arndt, Alice. "Silphium." In *Spicing Up the Palate: Studies of Flavourings Ancient and Modern*, edited by Harlan Walker. 1992 Proceedings of the Oxford Symposium on Food and Cookery. Totnes, Devon, UK: Prospect Books, 1993, 28–35.

Borza, Eugene N. "The Symposium at Alexander's Court." In *Proceedings of the Third International Symposium on Ancient Macedonia*. Thessalonika: Institute for Balkan Studies 193 (1983), 45–55.

Braund, David, and Wilkins, John, eds. *Athenaeus and His World: Reading Greek Culture in the Roman Empire*. Exeter, UK: University of Exeter Press, 2000.

Brotherwell, Don R. "Foodstuffs, Cooking, and Drugs." In *Civilization of the Ancient Mediterranean: Greece and Rome*, vol. 1, edited by Michael Grant and Rachel Kitzinger. New York: Charles Scribner's Sons, 1988, 247–61.

Carcopino, Jerome. *Daily Life in Ancient Rome*. Translated by E. O. Lorimer. London: Yale University Press, 1940.

Dalby, Andrew. *Flavours of Byzantium*. Totnes, Devon, UK: Prospect Books, 2003.

———. *Empire of Pleasures: Luxury and Indulgence in the Roman World*. London: Routledge, 2000.

———. *Siren Feasts: A History of Food and Gastronomy in Greece*. London: Routledge, 1996.

———. "Silphium and Asafoetida." In *Spicing Up the Palate: Studies of Flavourings Ancient and Modern*, edited by Harlan Walker. 1992 Proceedings of the Oxford Symposium on Food and Cookery. Totnes, Devon, UK: Prospect Books, 1993, 67–72.

Dalby, Andrew, and Grainger, Sally. *The Classical Cookbook*. Los Angeles: J. Paul Getty Museum, 1996.

Donahue, John F. *The Roman Community at Table During the Principate*. Ann Arbor: University of Michigan Press, 2004.

Dupont, Florence. *Daily Life in Ancient Rome*. Translated by Christopher Woodall. Cambridge, MA: Blackwell, 1992.

Faas, Patrick. *Around the Roman Table: Food and Feasting in Ancient Rome*. New York: Palgrave Macmillan, 2003.

Frayn, Joan M. "Home-baking in Roman Italy." *Antiquity* 52 (1978): 28–33.

Garnsey, Peter. *Food and Society in Classical Antiquity.* Cambridge, UK: Cambridge University Press, 1999.

———. *Famine and Food Supply in the Graeco-Roman World.* Cambridge, UK: Cambridge University Press, 1988.

Giacosa, Ilaria Gozzini. *A Taste of Ancient Rome.* Translated by Anna Herklotz. Chicago: University of Chicago Press, 1992.

Grainger, Sally. "Towards an Authentic Roman Sauce, or Can We Truly Know What Liquamen Was?" In *Authenticity,* 2005 Richard Hosking, ed. Proceedings of the Oxford Symposium on Food and Cookery (forthcoming).

Grant, Mark. *Roman Cookery.* London: Serif, 1999.

Grocock, Christopher, and Sally Grainger. "Moretum—a Peasant Lunch Revisited." In *The Meal,* edited by Harlan Walker. 2001 Proceedings of the Oxford Symposium on Food and Cookery. Totnes, Devon, UK: Prospect Books, 2002.

Halstead, Paul, and John C. Barrett, eds. *Food, Cuisine and Society in Prehistoric Greece.* Sheffield Studies in Aegean Archaeology 5 (monograph series), Oxford, UK: Oxbow Books, 2004.

Jasny, Naum. "The Daily Bread of the Ancient Greeks and Romans." *Osiris* 9 (1951): 227–53.

Kaufman, Cathy. "Remembrance of Meals Past: Cooking by Apicius' Book." In *Food and the Memory,* edited by Harlan Walker. 2000 Proceedings of the Oxford Symposium on Food and Cookery. Totnes, Devon, UK: Prospect Books, 2001.

King, Helen. "Food as Symbol in Classical Greece." *History Today* 36 (September 1976): 35–39.

Kremezi. Aglaia. "*Paximadia* (Barley Biscuits): Food for Sailors, Travellers and Poor Islanders." In *Food on the Move,* edited by Harlan Walker. 1996 Proceedings of the Oxford Symposium on Food and Cookery. Totnes, Devon, UK: Prospect Books, 1997.

Mason, Sarah. "Acornutopia? Determining the Role of Acorns in Past Human Subsistence." In *Food in Antiquity,* edited by John Wilkins, David Harvey, and Mike Dobson. Exeter, UK: University of Exeter, 1995.

McGovern, Patrick E., "The Funerary Banquet of 'King Midas'." *Expedition* 42 (1) (2000): 21–29.

Milham, Mary Ella. "In Defense of Hamburger: Apicius and Roman Cooking." *Vergilius* 12 (1966): 46.

Miller, J. Innes. *The Spice Trade of the Roman Empire.* Oxford, UK: Clarendon Press, 1969.

Murray, Oswyn. "Life and Society in Classical Greece." In *Greece and the Hellenistic World,* edited by John Boardman, Jasper Griffin, and Oswyn Murray. Oxford, UK: Oxford University Press, 1991.

Nielsen, Inge, and Hanne Sigismund Nielsen, eds. *Meals in a Social Context.* Aarhus Studies in Mediterranean Antiquity. Aarhus, Denmark: Aarhus University Press, 1998.

Richter, Gisela M. A. *The Furniture of the Greeks, Etruscans, and Romans.* London: Phaidon, 1966.

Rickman, Geoffrey. *The Corn Supply of Ancient Rome.* Oxford: Clarendon Press, 1980.

Ricotti, Eugenia. *Dining as a Roman Emperor.* Rome: "L'Erma" di Bretschneider, 1995.

Signe, Isager, and Jens Erik Skydsgaard. *Ancient Greek Agriculture.* London: Routledge, 1992.

Smith, Andrew F. "From Garum to Ketchup: A Spicy Tale of Two Fish Sauces." In *Fish, Food from the Waters,* edited by Harlan Walker. 1997 Proceedings of the Oxford Symposium on Food and Cookery. Totnes, Devon, UK: Prospect Books, 1998.

Sparkes, Brian A. "The Greek Kitchen." *Journal of Hellenic Studies* 82 (1962):121–37.

Sparkes, Brian A., and Lucy Talcott. *The Pots and Pans of Classical Athens.* Princeton, NJ: American School of Classical Studies at Athens, 1977.

Stambaugh, John E. *The Ancient Roman City.* Baltimore: Johns Hopkins University Press, 1988.

White, K.D. "Farming and Animal Husbandry." In *Civilization of the Ancient Mediterranean: Greece and Rome,* vol. 1, edited by Michael Grant and Rachel Kitzinger. New York: Charles Scribner's Sons, 1988, 211–45.

———. "Food Requirements and Food Supplies in Classical Times in Relation to the Diet of the Various Classes." *Progress in Food and Nutrition* 4 (1976): 143–91.

Wilkins, John, and Shaun Hill. "The Flavours of Ancient Greece." In *Spicing Up the Palate: Studies of Flavourings Ancient and Modern,* edited by Harlan Walker. 1992 Proceedings of the Oxford Symposium on Food and Cookery. Totnes, Devon, UK: Prospect Books, 1993.

INDEX